Planning
Educational Facilities

Planning Educational Facilities

What Educators Need to Know

Fifth Edition

Glen I. Earthman

Published in partnership with the
Association of School Business Officials, International

ROWMAN & LITTLEFIELD
Lanham • Boulder • New York • London

Published by Rowman & Littlefield
An imprint of The Rowman & Littlefield Publishing Group, Inc.
4501 Forbes Boulevard, Suite 200, Lanham, Maryland 20706
www.rowman.com

6 Tinworth Street, London SE11 5AL, United Kingdom

British Library Cataloguing in Publication Information Available

Library of Congress Cataloging-in-Publication Data
Names: Earthman, Glen I., author.
Title: Planning educational facilities : what educators need to know / Glen I. Earthman.
Description: Fifth Edition. | Lanham : ROWMAN & LITTLEFIELD, [2019] | Previous edition: 2013. | Includes bibliographical references.
Identifiers: LCCN 2018050407 (print) | LCCN 2018052263 (ebook) | ISBN 9781475844443 (electronic) | ISBN 9781475844429 (cloth) | ISBN 9781475844436 (paper)
Subjects: LCSH: School facilities—United States—Planning. | School facilities—United States—Design and construction. | School facilities—United States—Finance. | School buildings—United States—Design and construction.
Classification: LCC LB3218.A1 (ebook) | LCC LB3218.A1 E34 2019 (print) | DDC 371.6/20973—dc23
LC record available at https://lccn.loc.gov/2018050407

Contents

List of Tables and Figures

Preface

In the last edition of this book, several movements and practices were identified as being employed in the field of school facilities that have had some influence upon the manner in which school buildings have been planned, designed, constructed, utilized, and how students are housed. These movements or practices are not new, but they have continued to expand. The first of these practices is the continued rapid expansion of charter schools in almost every state in the nation. This expansion has influenced where students are now housed for learning. The second practice is the expanding use of the public/private partnerships in completion of major capital projects, which has influenced how school systems plan, design, and construct new schools.

Traditionally, school systems have employed a planning/designing/bidding/construction program to erect new schools or to perform major renovations on existing buildings. This system has effectively served public schools for centuries in solving their housing needs. However, modifications to this system have been developed over the past few decades to speed up the delivery of school buildings. Likewise, with the development of new types of school organizations that are released from some of the rules and regulations of the public schools, the solving of the housing problem has taken a different tack. Both of these measures have had an influence upon the public school method of planning, designing, constructing, and utilizing school facilities.

The first influence has been the rapid expansion of the development of charter schools. Although charter schools have been in existence for a longer period of time than the last decade, there has been an exponential growth in the number of such institutions with that same period of time. It is estimated that there are approximately seven thousand such individual school organizations in forty-four states and the District of Columbia this year, housing approximately 3.2 million students in a variety of facilities, according to the National Alliance for Public Charter Schools.

When a group of individuals or an organization form a charter school, one of the first needs to address is to find a place to house the organization. There are a variety of ways of locating suitable buildings in which to place the students. In some instances charter schools are housed in former public schools buildings that have been either leased or sold to the charter school organization. In some localities the charter schools are located in a building that has been converted into a school function from a commercial function. In such instances the planning mode of the organization has been changed from planning for a school building into finding a building in which to house the school and students. As a result of the lack of constraint of regulations regarding the acquisition of buildings to house students, the lack of training on planning school buildings and the lack of sufficient funds to acquire a new structure has resulted in charter school students being housed in a variety of structures ranging from very good to very marginal. Research has indicated that students in marginal facilities do not do as well on achievement examinations as students in good facilities.

The other influence that has directly modified some of the planning for new schools that public school systems have done in the past is the idea of public/private partnerships. The idea that the private sector can assist the public school or any governmental agency in planning/designing/constructing facilities has been enacted into law in many states. This is a recent development in the traditional method of planning/designing/bidding/constructing facilities. The thinking behind such legislation is that the private sector can deliver a new facility quicker than the public sector and might be able to deliver the facility more economically. Additionally, the private sector would be required to initially fund the building and thereby relieve the public school from accruing debt. In some cases the school building would be leased to the school system over a period of years and eventually take title to the school.

Using a public/private partnership to acquire a new school building has a tremendous influence on the public schools and especially the activities of public school personnel in their planning. The usual method of using the public/private partnership is that the private sector responds to a Request for Proposals detailing the needs of the public school. Then the successful private firm, independent of the public school personnel, designs and constructs the school building. Input from the public school personnel may or may not be permitted after the contract is signed. If there is no opportunity for school personnel input, this effectively eliminates valuable input into the design process that public school personnel need to have. Nevertheless, this method of acquiring new school facilities has become popular with many school systems throughout the country.

In spite of this influence, the vast majority of school systems still employ the traditional method of planning, designing, bidding, and constructing new school facilities. In some states local school systems are required to go through certain procedures to secure outside professional help such as an architect or builder. The standard procurement method is prescribed for all local governmental units in these states.

Educational administrators have a unique responsibility in the planning process for a capital improvement project. They have a distinct leadership position that can help to insure a successful project. Conversely, lack of proactive leadership on the part of educational administrators can greatly hinder the successful completion of the building project. The ability to help a school staff to complete such a project depends upon the solid knowledge base of the superintendent of schools.

The responsibility of administering the planning process demands considerable leadership on the part of the educator as well as the school board. In the absence of leadership, someone will step in to fill the vacuum. Sometimes architects and other professionals outside of the school system will fill a leadership vacuum in the school system by making decisions that should be properly made by administrators and school boards. For this reason, it is very important for the educator to know the various processes involved in planning a new school or major capital project, and whose responsibility it is for administering the process.

Such a discussion can be done only by a thorough analysis of each process involved in planning schools and the responsibility attached. The content of this book relies heavily upon a description of the planning process and the role an educator has in it. This book presents, in readily understandable terms, the processes for which educators have responsibility and which they should understand and be able to administer prudently.

There is always the temptation on the part of educators to rely upon the professional judgment of another profession when there are very limited personnel resources in the public schools. There are many school systems in the country where the superintendent has little or no support from administrative staff. It is not unusual for a superintendent of a small school system to be the sole administrator, with no one other than clerical personnel on staff. This may sound alarming, but of the approximately fifteen thousand separate school systems in the United States, less than 5 percent have a student population of over ten thousand.

The majority of school systems have between five hundred and two thousand students. In these school systems, the superintendent has very limited support, if any.

Nevertheless, in such school systems, the superintendent can obtain competent assistance from an educational consultant that will provide the assistance needed to make the decisions that an educator should make. The cost of the educational consultant is small when compared to the cost of a major capital improvement project, but the results are more than worthwhile.

A superintendent should not rely solely upon the architect to do the planning and programming of any capital improvement project because this is the responsibility of the educator. Only the educator knows what the educational program of the school system currently is and will be in the future. In this way, the superintendent and staff must be able to tell the architect exactly what facilities the school needs to support the educational program and the teaching staff. The superintendent and staff must take the responsibility of expressing the needs of the school system in order to end up with the type of facility that is really needed by the students and teachers for effective and efficient teaching and learning.

The educational facility planning process should also be treated as an integral part of the overall planning process of the school system. Many authors present the planning process for a new school and for any capital improvement project as a separate event in the history of the school system, sometimes not even related to what else the school system does. Some descriptions go so far as to present the project as something done by people outside of the school system for people inside the school system. In other words, the planning for a new school in no way relates to the usual educational program planning processes that go on in the school system. Planning and constructing a school building should be part of the overall planning of the school system, not something independent of the plan.

The long-range plan thus becomes the key to all planning efforts in the school system, including capital improvement planning. From the long-range plan adopted by the school board come many other plans that are implemented by various departments and offices in the school system so that all efforts work toward completing the objectives of the overall school system plan.

This cyclical effort ensures a concentration of available resources to complete objectives and systematic work toward adopted goals of the organization. Under the umbrella of the long-range plan, all employees of the school system work to complete a specified objective, which in turn propels the organization in the pursuit of goals. Without this direct link between school facility planning and long-range planning, the latter is probably a futile effort and the former a separate event in the history of the school system.

This book takes a systematic approach to the planning of educational facilities. Each phase of the process of planning capital projects is discussed in detail sufficient for the educational administrator to understand the responsibilities required of those individuals in the schools who make decisions regarding the kinds of buildings in which students will be housed. The text also speaks to the moral responsibility of educators to make certain students are in safe and modern school facilities. Lastly, the tragic events that have taken place within the past few decades involving school students and teachers has prompted a chapter on safe school designs and practices to help school authorities plan for the safest physical environment possible.

The inextricable link between the long-range planning effort and all physical facility planning work of the school system is emphasized in this text, and can, therefore, be used as a guide to foster effective planning. As a result, the practitioner can use this book as both a guide for action in planning schools and as a staff development vehicle for personal edification. The text can also be used effectively for any college or university course in school facility planning because the book gives the potential school administrator an idea of the scope of systematic approach to planning necessary in the school system and how that can be tied into the planning effort for the school buildings.

Glen I. Earthman
Virginia Tech
March 2019

Chapter 1

Organization and Policy Planning

All organizations need some type of structure in order to function effectively and efficiently. This applies regardless of what the organization does and the size of its staff. In fact, the more complicated the task, the more structure is needed. A small business firm that sells one product needs an organizational structure just as much as a complicated one. All organizations formulate some type of structure to get the job done.

A school system is no different from any other organization in needing some type of structure. School systems are organized around the tasks to be done. In this way, those who specialize in a certain subject area or a specific administrative capacity can contribute to the total school effort.

Likewise, specialization allows individuals to become expert in a field of knowledge or a function needed by the organization. Specialization is, of course, one element of a bureaucracy, which is exactly what every school system in the United States is. This is not to deride the fact that school systems are bureaucracies, because a bureaucracy is really the only logical way to accomplish a complicated task. Sometimes a school system's bureaucracy is blamed for inefficiencies in the organization; but it is not the concept of bureaucracy that is at fault, but untrained or inept employees that cause the breakdown in efficiency. In some situations outdated or restrictive rules, regulations, or policies can be blamed for inefficient responses to the needs of individuals.

The more complex the organization, however, the more specialization is evident in the working force, hence the bigger the organization, the more it reflects the bureaucratic model. Bureaucracy allows staff to specialize. Through this type of organization, employees can become expert in one area and not have to be expert in all. This principle works especially well in the school system where people are employed to do certain highly specialized tasks that require a specified amount of specialized education.

The task of planning for school buildings is a complicated one involving a large number of highly trained individuals who possess specialized skills and knowledge (Kowalski, 2002). The head of the planning process for new school buildings, therefore, needs to be knowledgeable about all the facility planning tasks involved so that proper evaluation of the effort can be made. The administrator who heads facilities planning for a school system does not have to be an expert in all the technical fields involved in planning/designing/constructing a school, but that person should be knowledgeable about those fields and, at the same time, know what the school system expects.

There are many tasks to complete that require individuals who possess high degrees of professional and technical skills in the area of school facility planning. In addition, the demand for new school buildings and other capital improvements creates a need for sufficient staff to do the work. In other words, the larger the demand for new schools and other types of capital projects, the more personnel a school system needs to employ. Conversely, the less demand for new schools and similar work, the smaller the school facility planning staff needs to be employed. This is reflected in the organizational chart of the school system and in school board policies. All school systems must have their organization described in the school board policies. Such a description permits the entire school system staff to recognize which office is responsible for which tasks, and delineates the chain of command.

LARGE SCHOOL SYSTEM

In large school systems, the school facilities staff is rather numerous and includes many individuals with specialized knowledge and skills. This is necessary because of the demand for new schools and other capital improvements. In the United States, there are approximately fifteen thousand separate school systems. Of this number, a little over 5 percent are larger than ten thousand students.

The facilities department in a large school system usually is divided into sections that follow the division of the disciplines in the planning process. Figure 1.1 shows the organizational chart for the school facilities planning department of a large school system of perhaps one hundred thousand students or more. Normally, the top administrator is an assistant superintendent or executive director reporting directly to the superintendent of schools. This position should be high enough in the organization to be in the decision-making process of the school system. Generally, someone heading such a

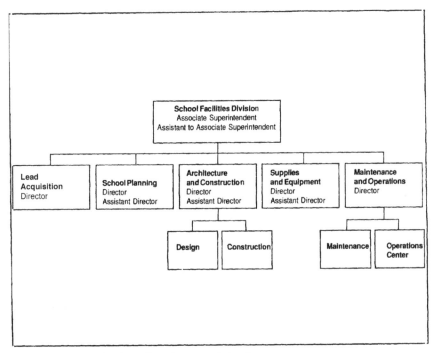

Figure 1.1.   Organization Chart for Large Schools

department would be in the superintendent's cabinet, council, or team. This committee of high ranking administrators serves as a decision-making group for the entire school system. It's crucial that the head of the school facility planning effort in this decision-making body be high enough to be answerable only to the superintendent.

The facility planning department is divided into groups or sections representing the various disciplines associated with school buildings. There is a section responsible for selecting and acquiring the site, another for programming the new school building, and yet another section, which monitors the work of the architect. These sections or subdepartments are on the director level. The heads of these sections are supported, as the case may be, by assistant directors and supervisors.

The section responsible for design and construction is subdivided into the architecture and construction groups, each headed by an assistant director. The assistant director of architecture monitors the work of the architect, while the person heading the construction group supervises and monitors the firms doing construction work. These groups are staffed with several supervisors who actually provide the monitoring service.

The maintenance and operations section is also included under the facilities department in this school system. This is a common organization arrangement in a school system of this size. In school systems larger than this example, maintenance and operations may be located in a separate section or department that may or may not report to the same head. The maintenance function is usually located in the facilities planning department because of the overlap in activities such as evaluating buildings, monitoring the design and construction, and writing specifications. All these functions, plus the planning function, are common to both new construction and many maintenance projects (Kowalski, 2002).

The final section in the organizational chart in Figure 1.1 is responsible for procuring furniture and equipment for buildings. On the surface, this may seem elementary and not demanding or needing of a separate section. However, purchasing equipment for school buildings is an exacting task that requires writing technical specifications, comparing similar pieces of equipment, conducting the bidding, evaluating bids, purchasing, warehousing, and delivering equipment to the correct site. These tasks require a great deal of knowledge about the types and kinds of equipment needed for a modern educational program to function well. In addition, the equipment requirements of a new school building represent a large sum of money that must be spent wisely.

MEDIUM-SIZED SCHOOL SYSTEMS

Medium-sized school systems usually do not have the building demands a large school system does and, as a result, do not employ many people on a regular basis to plan new schools. A medium school system is defined as one with at least two thousand, but no more than seventy-five thousand students.

The size of school systems in the United States ranges from less than fifty students to more than a million students in one school system. In spite of the fact that the median size of school systems in United States is about 2,500 students, school systems with fewer than two thousand students are normally considered small school systems, and usually do not employ even one person to guide the planning process for new buildings.

Even a medium-sized school system may employ educational consultants to augment school staff during facility planning. Typically, these systems do not have staff expertise in writing educational specifications, projecting student population growth, evaluating existing buildings, and selecting architects. Since this type of expertise is needed by school systems during facility planning, the system must employ outside consultants.

Figure 1.2 shows the organizational chart for a medium-sized school system and identifies the office and person responsible for facility planning

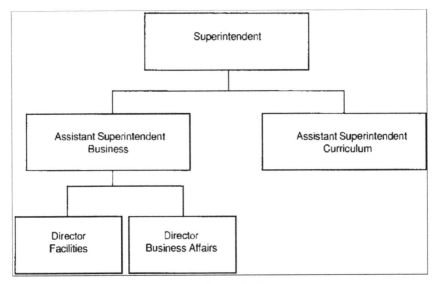

Figure 1.2. Organization Chart for Medium Schools

and maintenance. As can be seen, the office is located on the director level, not on the second level down from the superintendent. The position location does indicate, however, the relative importance of school buildings in the school system.

SMALL SCHOOL SYSTEMS

The majority of the fifteen thousand-plus separate school systems in the United States can be considered small by most indices of measurement. A little more than 5 percent of school systems have an enrollment of more than ten thousand students. This is a very small number of school systems, and yet more than 80 percent of the students in the United States are enrolled in this select group. In contrast, 20 percent of the students are enrolled in the remaining fourteen thousand-plus school systems.

The paucity of students in the remaining approximately fourteen thousand school systems presents problems for school administrators in housing students in proper facilities. The problems of housing students in these school systems range from not having enough funding authority to construct modern and efficient facilities to having to overbuild any facility in order to have a regulation building. For instance, the size of a gymnasium is the same regardless of the size of the student body; it is just as important, and necessary, to construct a regulation-sized gym for fifty students as it is for one thousand students.

Moreover, this type of overbuilding is necessary in other sections of the school building. In addition to this, the financial capacity of many of these school systems is so small it is virtually impossible to raise sufficient funds to construct needed facilities. As a result, school administrators in small school systems have unique problems to contend with and solve when considering any type of capital improvement project.

The typical staff of a small school system may consist of a superintendent of schools and one or two clerical assistants. In addition, the superintendent will have someone charged with the responsibility of the maintenance and operations of the school buildings. This person may be called a director, supervisor, or coordinator. This is typical for school systems that have as few as five hundred students. The only other administrators in the school system would be the building principals, who have the full responsibility of administering a school building. As a result, the superintendent cannot rely upon assistance from these individuals in many administrative decisions.

Planning for any type of capital improvement project in small school systems is also constrained by limited personnel resources. With virtually no other administrator available for assistance, the superintendent must look outside the school organization. The most likely type of outside assistance would be an educational consultant. An educational consultant normally has had experience in public schools and is familiar with the needs of school systems. Procuring an educational consultant is not difficult; however, finding one that will provide the type of assistance needed requires some necessary work on the part of the superintendent. A list of educational consultants can be found through most professional organizations. Organizations such as the Association of Physical Plant Administrators, the Council of Educational Facility Planners International (now Association 4Learning Environments), and the Association of School Business Officials International all have access to educational consultants.

The superintendent of schools must be able to articulate the needs of the school system in order to find consultants who have that type of expertise. Employment of a consultant is the same as for any other employee in that the credentials are examined carefully before an interview is conducted. The decision to employ an educational consultant is the responsibility of the school board, but the superintendent must do the preliminary work of identifying an expert in the field and culling out the rest based upon qualifications and finally recommending someone for the job.

Some superintendents in small school systems are fast to seek out architectural expertise whenever there is a problem with buildings. This may or may not be the best way to go in getting expertise in solving problems, even though the problems relate to housing students. The planning and programming for any type of capital improvement project is the responsibility of educators and those who have a background in education. Engaging architects to provide advice on educational matters is not in keeping with prudent administration. Employment of an architect always comes after the educators decide what they need. Superintendents in small school systems should not feel alone in seeking out assistance because oftentimes the state's Department of Education has expertise that is available to the local school system. This source should be examined before any other expertise is sought.

SCHOOL BOARD POLICIES

All organizations are governed by policies that specify areas of responsibility and authority. These policies enable people within and outside the organization to know and understand who is responsible for each task assigned in the organization. Thus, policies delineate and circumscribe the responsibilities of various people and offices throughout the organization and, at the same time, place responsibility. Policies also grant authority to a person or office to do certain tasks and jobs. This authority goes along with the responsibility for completing a task. Both authority and responsibility flow from organizational policies (BEST, 2005).

School systems are governed by school board policies. These policies are resolutions, rules, guidelines, procedures, and regulations adopted by the school board to assist and direct the governance of the system and to eliminate questions of propriety and the need to legitimize actions.

Good policies prevent people from duplicating efforts and eliminate staff confusion. For example, school board policies would allocate responsibility and authority to a certain office to select and acquire a site for a new school. For the curriculum development office to select and acquire a site would be duplicative and confusing, not only to the entire staff, but also to people outside the organization.

In addition to organizational procedures, school policies also address other phases of schoolwork. Policies should identify areas of concern for the school system and the manner in which things are to take place. For instance, the way purchases are to be made is usually covered in school board policy because this is an important task. Even tasks that may seem insignificant might be covered by school board policy.

It has often been said that school board policy evolves from problem situations. This means that when a problem arises, the school board solves the problem and creates policy to prevent it from reoccurring. There may be some grain of truth to that maxim; some policies can be traced to such situations, but, for the most part, policies are adopted following deliberation by the school board (Lunenberg, 2012).

There are many rules, regulations, and procedures imbedded in school board policies that deal directly with the process of school facility planning. As mentioned above, the general policy on purchasing and bidding governs the work of individuals in the school facility planning department. Other areas of concern for which policies may be needed include:

- site selection and acquisition
- school name selection
- site size
- school size and capacity
- design submissions and approvals
- student feeder patterns
- monitoring the design process
- involvement of the community in the planning process
- school boundaries
- awarding contracts
- costing of the capital project
- bidding process
- evaluation of existing buildings
- development of educational specifications
- capital improvement program planning
- surety and performance bond requirements
- change orders
- construction process and supervision
- utilization of school facilities
- protection and guarantees for the school division
- cooperation with governmental agencies
- occupancy and orientation of new facilities
- energy conservation measures
- architectural and engineering services
- school closing procedures
- construction records and reports
- operation of air-conditioning systems

Written policies are needed in all these areas to provide school personnel guidance on how these activities should be executed and who is responsible for doing so. Undoubtedly, there are other areas that need policies in certain school systems. Each school system must decide what additional policies are needed. Whatever policies a school system has, they should be periodically reviewed and evaluated for relevance. This is especially true in light of certain recent court decisions and local conditions. Although each school system needs to organize itself to fit local custom, because of legal requirements and size of its staff, certain elements are common among all school systems.

Organizing the school staff for planning a new school building follows certain divisions of labor to fit the disciplines represented. Additionally, there are specified tasks that have to be completed by individuals competent in the field. These individuals should be employed by the school system. Therefore, among different school systems, there is often a great deal of similarity in the staff that is responsible for planning new school buildings.

SUMMARY

The larger the school system the greater the demand for school buildings and the greater the need for enough staff to help plan the buildings. As a result, large school systems have school planning staffs that can carry out many school facility planning efforts at one time. Medium-sized school systems may have some school planning expertise to complete a capital project, but in many cases may need some outside help. Conversely, small school systems do not have a large demand for new schools and thus have little or no staff to handle that task. When a new school facility is needed in these school systems, outside assistance and consultation is normally employed. All school systems, regardless of size, need policies governing the various parts of the planning process for new schools or renovations of existing buildings.

Chapter 2

Planning Considerations

Planning activities probably consumes more of our daily time than any other function outside of those designed to maintain our body. Humans spend their lives planning things to do. The level of planning extends from the basic and simple to rather sophisticated and complex activities. Planning how to go home after work may consume no more than a few seconds of mental activity. On the other hand, planning an expedition to the moon may consume the better part of many lives; people are quite adaptable regarding the level of difficulty of the planning activity in which they engage. While working on a complicated planning task, the same individuals may be planning more simple personal activities without any loss of efficiency on the main task, otherwise known as multitasking.

Organizations function in much the same way as far as planning activities are concerned; they usually have long-term goals toward which members work. At the same time, there are many short-term planning activities going on at the same time. Not all these short-term plans contribute in the same fashion toward the organizational goals. Because an organization is composed of individuals with personal needs to be met, some short-term plans are designed solely to satisfy the individual and do not contribute to the goals of the organization. In spite of this behavior, the organization moves purposefully toward its goals (Withum, 2006).

Planning is a purposeful activity that helps achieve something. Planning can be defined as the ordering of resources and events to achieve an agreed upon objective. This definition applies equally to individuals and organizations. Without planning, nothing is accomplished, unless by accident. Organizations could not successfully pursue a goal without some sort of planning.

Plans are devised in order to accomplish certain things. Without plans, an organization could not long continue to offer the services for which it is responsible. There are several reasons for planning, most of which center around the idea of cooperative efforts on the part of individuals in the organization. Random activities, on the other hand, do not accomplish important things and do not move an organization toward some goal. Therefore, the purposes of organizational planning are the following:

- To develop and approve acceptable goals
- To allocate and use available resources efficiently
- To marshal and conserve staff cooperation and input into goal efforts

NOMENCLATURE OF PLANNING

There are several terms or descriptors used in the general field of planning. These descriptors endeavor to illustrate the characteristics of the particular kind of planning. Thus, long-range planning means planning for a period that may extend from several months to several years. Long-range must be defined by the person or persons doing the planning.

Likewise, operational planning is generally thought of as being planning activities designed to accommodate a shorter period, such as the life of the operating budget, which is normally one year. Each of the following adjectives or descriptors defines the accomplishment of the planning process, rather than expressing a different method of planning.

- long-range planning
- strategic planning
- operational planning
- tactical planning
- incidental, or problem-solving planning
- comprehensive planning
- master planning
- integrated planning

Are all these planning models the same, or is there some degree of difference between the various models? The similarities of these planning models are striking, but the differences are hard to distinguish. The actual process used in the various planning activities is the same basic process: goals are identified, resources are identified and appropriated, some action responsibility is decided upon, and perhaps a time limit might be imposed. In any event, these processes are the same regardless of the scope of the planning process.

Some of the models can be distinguished by the time frame of the planning. For instance, problem-solving planning would seem to be a very specific activity devoted to a small objective, whereas the comprehensive planning effort would seem to encompass a great deal of data and effort. Therefore, the time frame is a good peg upon which to tack a planning effort. The reason or purpose for planning also differs from one model to another. Obviously, comprehensive planning would indicate an activity that requires a wide swath of data and a long time frame.

ELEMENTS OF PLANNING

There are three elements that govern the type of planning that is done in every school system. These elements deal with the purpose of planning, the level of planning, and the time frame for planning. Each of these elements guide the type of planning that is done.

Purpose of Planning

Coupled with the confusion of planning nomenclature is the confusion of the various strands of planning that take place within the school organization as well as the many purposes of planning.

For example, school systems plan for the adoption of textbooks, which in itself is a purpose, and at the same time the school system plans for staffing the schools as well as planning curricular matters. All these purposes are a little different, but the nature of the planning is the same for all purposes.

Level of Planning

In schools there is also planning at different levels. Planning activities are carried on by every employee of the school system at every level. Teachers plan for daily activities, for the entire semester, and even for the entire academic year. On the school building level, the principal and staff plan for a variety of activities, both educational and social. A principal must plan and execute an annual plan for the school.

On the central administration level each department plans for a number of activities that may include the staff of several schools or even the entire school system. These employees also develop an annual plan as well as intermediate seminal activities and goals. Of course, the school system, mainly through the office of the superintendent, develops an annual plan to coincide with the operational budget.

In addition, there is usually a school system-wide planning activity to develop a six year plan. All these activities proceed throughout the year, many at the same time. In some cases, there is coordination between the planning at different levels; however, planning on a school building level does not necessarily coordinate with planning on the school division level. Likewise, planning done by departments and offices in the central administration should reflect school system-wide planning and the planning done on the school building level. Often times this is not the case.

Time Frame of Planning

For every planning effort, there is a time frame in which the planning takes place, but there is also the period for which the planning takes place. The questions usually deal with how far into the future the plan is to take effect. Is the planning for just today, next month, next year, or ten years hence? The distinguishing mark here is the degree of difficulty of the planning process which in turn is affected by the goal to be achieved and the amount of data needed to accomplish it.

In every planning effort this dimension is present. Some planning models are better suited for certain planning activities and are not appropriate for others. For example, a teacher would not use a strategic planning model to plan the reading activities of a group of students for the next day. Likewise, the principal would not use a problem-solving planning model to develop an annual plan for the school building. There is a certain degree of appropriateness of planning models to fit the situation.

Sometimes there is confusion concerning the planning effort that exists in the capital improvement planning for the school system because planning for a capital project is made up of many different planning processes which taken as a whole are a process in itself. For example, within the planning process for new buildings there is a separate process used for hiring an architect.

It would be senseless to go through the process of hiring an architect, unless the school division is going to need the services of an architect to design a new building or renovate an existing building. Therefore, the process of hiring an architect is embedded within the total process of planning a new building. One could go through the entire process of planning a building with the same analogy. Suffice it to say, the process of planning educational facilities is composed of many different processes. All these processes are usually housed in one department within the school division.

NEED FOR PLANNING

There are two main pistons that drive the need for school buildings. The first is the type of educational program that is to be carried on in the building.

The second main piston is that of the numbers of school children who will be housed in the school building. Sometimes, only the number of students enrolled drives the need for new buildings, and the type of educational program is either assumed or in some cases not addressed directly. This is definitely not the way to plan a school facility.

The educational program should be the first consideration when planning a new school building. Capital Improvement Planning needs to be part of the total planning effort of the school system. Sometimes this kind of planning effort is referred to as Integrated Planning. In any event, the planning of a new school building should include a reexamination of the educational program.

PLANNING TYPES

Lewis (1983) lists three types of planning processes that differ only in the time frame: problem solving, operational, and strategic. All these processes use the same methodology but they differ in the time spent in the process. There is, however, some difference in the scope of what is to be planned. Problem-solving planning covers activities that can be completed quickly or, at most, within three months. The intensity of planning activities and the focus of work is no less than in other planning processes but the time frame is shorter.

Operational planning covers activities that last up to a year. Most operational planning is tied directly into the operational budget of the school system (which is also effective for one year). Strategic planning is used for those goals and objectives that need considerable time to meet. This type of planning lasts from three to seven years. The long-range plan of a school system is directly related to strategic planning methodology.

Some authorities feel that strategic planning should be used to develop a long-range plan for a school system (Cary, 2011). Strategic planning incorporates the process of environmental scanning that the school system uses to analyze the world in which it finds itself. This environmental scanning is the assessment of forces, constraints, social movements, and similar events outside of the school system that might influence what happens inside the school system and how it might respond to these pressures and demands.

Much of what is done in the school system lends itself to long-range or strategic planning, especially activities related to housing students in school buildings. Although some of the work of the school facilities department involves short-term and operational planning efforts, most of their projects are long range. This department actively works to implement the long-range plan of the school system through the capital improvement program.

All states require local school systems to produce a long-range plan of some sort.

As a result, school systems plan for the long term because organizations cannot change, improve, or respond to community needs in a short period of time. All school systems have limited resources, and to apply these limited resources wisely to the needs of the community, planning for the long term is necessary.

Planning Steps

The actual steps in planning consist of the activities of an individual or group to accomplish some objective. It is the ordering of events and resources that produces results. Most experts agree that, no matter how difficult or simple the planning task, the steps in planning are the same. The nature of planning governs the steps needed to implement a plan. The following are steps in planning, regardless of the activity:

1. identification of who is to be involved
2. identification and agreement on the problem or goal
3. identification of the data needed
4. formulation of alternative solutions
5. identification of preferred solutions
6. implementation of solution or plan, and
7. evaluation of results

It is assumed that a constant feedback loop allows the group to go back to a previous step or even to begin again. Some authorities include an additional step: planning to plan. Some have also suggested another step: identify those who should be included in the planning process. While these two initial steps might be germane in some instances, the first step above includes all the activities that go into the identification and agreement on the problem or goal. This would include consideration of the people to be involved as well as the method of organizing the effort. Thus, those individuals who are concerned with the goal-setting activity would be involved already. The seven steps above speak well for the process and cover all activities needed to plan adequately.

The types of planning activities that occur daily within the school system vary; there are many short-term planning activities as well as many long-term ones. Indeed, much of the planning activity of the school system could be classified as long term.

Long-term planning affords the school system sufficient time to raise the needed funds for a particular project. In the area of school facility planning, it is impossible to plan, design, and construct a building in less than three to five years. Because of this, long-term planning must take place to have a new school building ready when needed. For a new school project, staff members are engaged in planning activities for several years. Therefore, if the school system needs a new building at a certain place at a certain time, long-term planning must proceed and, to complete the long-term project, many short-term planning efforts must transpire first. These short-term planning efforts go together to form the long-term plans.

STRATEGIC PLANNING

The discussion on the use of strategic planning versus the use of long-range planning is still an important topic for many writers in the field. In spite of the fact that there is a variety of planning paradigms and methods, the major distinction between strategic and long-range planning is still evident in much of the literature on the subject (Cary, 2011). Some of these discussions give the impression that educators have a choice between two types of planning. This is a misconception of the nature and purpose of planning. A common characteristic of all organizational planning modes is that their time frames and processes are defined by the needs of the organization, not necessarily by changing environmental conditions (Rollins, 2012).

The standard argument regarding the difference between the two planning modes is that long-range planning is limited in value to the planning process for educational organizations because the process is so linear and rigid and is entirely data driven. Opponents of long-range planning techniques stress the fact that long-range planning does not take into consideration the environment in which the schools operate. Further, this type of planning does not give direction to the organization.

Strategic planning, on the other hand, is characterized as being dynamic and active. By scanning the environment and the realities of life, the process produces useful strategies and tactics that will permit the organization to go in new directions. Such simplified descriptions of a very complex process do not give it proper perspective.

The most distinguishing feature of the process, however, is the interaction of the organization with the environment with resultant changes in how the organization operates. This feature incorporates extensive data gathering about the environment and a determination of how the organization can respond to service opportunities and possible threats to effectiveness. In this manner, the operation and emphasis of the organization might be modified or changed (Kaufman, Herman, and Watters, 2002).

One of the most classic examples of successful strategic planning resulting in a change of direction for the organization might be in the private sector, where, through extensive environmental scanning and analysis, a company can and does change direction. For example, when research studies indicating the dangers of smoking became public in the 1960s, tobacco companies read the writing on the wall. When the numbers of cigarette smokers dropped dramatically as a result of the research findings, they realized something had to be done to maintain profits. The organization had to change dramatically in order to remain viable.

One form of change to counteract the loss of tobacco-consuming customers was to diversify by producing other products a large number of consumers would want. Such a strategy changed the direction of the parent company, making it a more diversified or comprehensive firm. One tobacco company diversified through buying several food-producing and -distributing companies.

In this manner, the tobacco company became a conglomerate rather than a single-product firm. The direction of the company was changed as a result of external forces. Although there is no publicly documented evidence of such strategic planning and implementation, it serves as a good example of the use of strategic planning that changes the direction of an organization (Kaufman, 2006).

When public schools employ rigorous strategic planning, such dramatic change in the direction or purpose of the organization is not possible. This is mainly because public schools are a part of the government, which has a mandate that cannot be changed much beyond what the state legislature or local community desires (Guthrie, Hart, Hack, and Candoli, 2008). This kind of external oversight limits the flexibility of the public schools to dramatically change directions or expand services.

Change in direction or purposes of public schools comes much more gradually and usually through outside legislative pressure and intervention more so than through internal planning, regardless of the type of planning. This is not to say that public schools should not use strategic planning to the fullest. Quite the contrary, schools should use strategic planning, or some derivative of it, when and where appropriate. Because it is very complex, the strategic planning process requires the use of a great deal of data in order to identify and consider viable alternatives.

Strategic planning is best suited for a discrete organization. A segment or department within an organization might find it difficult to complete major planning independent of the planning of the parent organization. For instance, a teacher would not attempt strategic planning for the instructional program in the classroom. The planning the teacher does may involve others and employ some recognition of what is happening in the neighborhood of the school, all of which are elements of strategic planning, but the formal process of strategic planning is absent.

On the other hand, the principal and faculty can do some strategic planning for the annual school plan and employ many of the elements of strategic planning and management. However, even this level of strategic planning must be limited in scale because of time and budget constraints. Nevertheless, elements of strategic planning can be employed on a school building level.

Strategic planning best serves an organization that has a time frame of several years, not one or two years. In addition, the school system is the organizational entity of the community, regardless of the size of individual public schools. Strategies and decisions emanating from a strategic planning process must be allocated sufficient resources by the school board to be successful. This is not always true on the school building or classroom level. Finally, the local school system, through the school board, interfaces with the state authority that created it, mandates certain courses of study, and services the general public (Kaufman, Herman, and Watters, 2002).

Figure 2.1 illustrates a modification of the strategic planning model that would fit a school system planning effort as well as a school building unit. Many of the components of formal strategic planning are included here, and

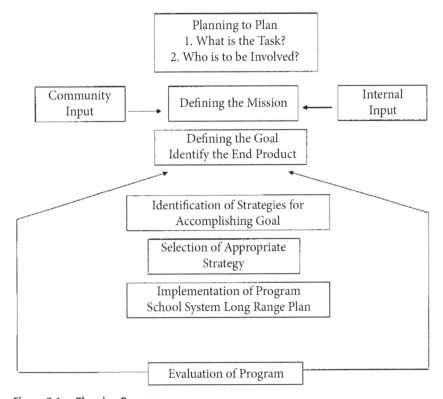

Figure 2.1. Planning Process

the planning effort results in a long-range planning document that can be used to subsequently modify the plan.

Planning for the long term is very characteristic of public schools. As stated above, a variety of different planning modes are utilized for specific purposes. Many of the day-to-day activities of the personnel within the school system are governed by short-term planning. There are, however, very specific long-term planning activities in which the school system must engage. Almost all the capital improvement projects completed by the school system are considered long-term activities. These activities span several years and involve many subplans within an overarching plan for each project.

The question then is, *How do these long-term planning activities fit into the overall planning of the school system*? If strategic planning is done by the school system, how do other planning activities fit into the scheme developed through strategic planning?

Public school systems probably do not engage in what might be called pure-type strategic planning, mostly because of the mandated nature of the schools. Public schools do not have the freedom of changing focus or direction as much as other organizations, especially private corporations. As a result, public schools practice a more moderated form of strategic planning. Nevertheless, the strategic planning efforts of the school system are just as important to the general direction of the schools as such efforts are to private firms.

There must, however, be a direct tie into the other planning activities of the schools from the strategic plan. The key for educators is to link the strategic planning activities to the more traditional planning efforts, such as the operational plan and budget, the long-range plan of the school system, and instructional planning that spans several years.

Each school system must devise a strategic planning effort that fits that locality. These plans are indigenous to each school system and must account for their individual latitude of freedom to incorporate new ideas, the expertise of school staff, and the state legislative mandates in operation.

From the strategic planning effort, a document should evolve that states quite precisely what the school system will do in the coming years. The exact terminology for this document will vary from state to state depending upon requirements of the department of education or local usage. Some of the terms used to identify these documents include: Comprehensive Educational Plan, School District Master Plan, The Six-Year Plan, Long-Range Plan, Long-Range Development Plan, Long-Range Educational Plan, Educational Development Plan, or School District Educational Plan. Regardless of the name, the contents of these documents are greatly similar.

SUMMARY

Planning is a very important characteristic of school systems. Without planning, nothing could be effectively accomplished. Planning is the ordering of events and resources to accomplish an objective. There are three main elements of planning: purpose of planning, level of planning, and time limit of planning. There are many names for specific types of planning. The adjective before the word planning indicates the type of planning used. The user of the planning activity must describe the kind of planning that is being used. Much of the planning activities of the school system are long-range in nature, however the main planning activity of the school system is operational planning, which is planning for one year. School systems employ a modified form of strategic planning because of the state mandated purpose of the school systems.

Chapter 3

Planning in Public Schools

Planning for new school buildings or for major renovations to existing facilities requires considerable effort on the part of many highly skilled professional and technical personnel, both inside and outside the school system. In some instances, the working efforts of these individuals comprise separate and distinguishable steps. These steps, however, can be thought of as separate processes that must be completed in order to accomplish the project. In spite of the fact that most individuals speak about planning a school as if it were a single process, the fact of the matter is that planning for any major capital project consists of a series of processes and is directly related to the educational planning that takes place in the organization.

If one could take an overall view of the planning process for any major capital project, it would be possible to view it as a series of separate steps or processes that comprise a whole process. Imagine, that on a certain date, the superintendent of schools and the school board have concluded that a new school or a major renovation is needed to accommodate an increasing student population or a planned major change in the educational program. The question immediately comes to mind, What are the steps that they must go through before the project becomes a reality? There are many identifiable separate steps or processes the school staff and school board must go through to complete the task and end up with a new or renovated facility.

Planning, designing, and constructing a capital project can be thought of as a rather complex process composed of many steps or processes. These processes have certain requirements that must be met. For instance, hiring an architect is one major step, but there is also a process the school board must go through before the architectural contract is signed. Moreover, the work of the architect is a different step than his or her actual employment and, again, the school board and staff have some responsibilities to make certain the design meets the needs of the school staff.

Each of the steps can be perceived as a separate process that certain actors must complete in order for the capital projects to be constructed. In the usual progression of events, the school staff and school board must complete the following steps or processes:

- organize the staff
- determine the size of the student population
- develop a set of educational specifications to define the educational program
- develop a funding package
- select and acquire a site for a new school building
- select and employ an architect
- monitor the design of the building
- advertise and bid the project
- monitor the construction phase to completion
- orient the staff to the building
- evaluate the building and planning processes

These are the usual steps a school system must normally go through to complete a new building. These steps or processes may not strictly follow the order listed above, although that is the usual progression of events. Sometimes political decisions might delay one or more of these processes and throw the entire process out of order.

Nevertheless, some of the processes can precede independent of others. For instance, school staff may develop a set of educational specifications without serious consequences long before either a school site is selected, or an architect is employed. There are, however, some processes that must precede or follow others, such as securing sufficient funds before a site is acquired or an architect is employed. Likewise, a school system would not want an architect to begin designing the facility before the necessary educational planning is completed. There is, however, a certain amount of fluidity in the order of these processes (Garcia-Diaz and MacGregor, 2008).

Staff of the school system and school board members must properly supervise and administer all these processes. Outside personnel are normally contracted to complete some of the processes above, but the overall supervision and direction rests with school personnel. In small school systems, most of the processes above are completed with the assistance of outside expertise because the school does not have the staff to complete the work. Even in these systems, there must be sufficient school personnel to properly interface with outside consultants and design professionals.

PLANNING RESPONSIBILITY

In every school system someone must be responsible for all planning efforts on an organizational level. In a small school system the responsibility might be lodged with one person, such as an administrative assistant. That person organizes school staff to produce the long-range plan. In large school systems there may be an office of research and planning that assumes the planning responsibility. In a very large system the department of planning may service the entire school system (Tompkins et al., 2002).

Regardless of who or what office is directing the planning effort, there will always be a certain amount of discord resulting from the planning efforts. The planning office or person will always be perceived as planning for others, rather than planning *with* them. This cleavage is normal, but disquieting, because planning that involves staff should truly be a cooperative affair. Unfortunately, this is not always the case, especially when staff members feel they do not have a say in how planning takes place. To forestall such feelings, the planning office or officer should actively seek ways to involve staff early in the process. The planning process should produce a plan that is acceptable to everyone and that staff members will work toward, and, at the same time, should be one that represents the needs of the school system.

The planning efforts directed toward a long-range plan never come to an end. The planning process for a long-range plan is cyclical in nature in that there is no beginning and no end. Changes in the current long-range plan take place periodically through the normal process of review and approval. When one long-range plan is adopted, work begins on modifications and changes, so the document is continually updated. In this manner, a school system always has a current long-range plan from which it is working.

Developing a long-range plan is not an easy task, especially considering the number of people involved. Considerable lead time must be allowed to complete the document early enough for review and adoption. The office or person in charge of planning must adopt a schedule and publish it widely to gain support and cooperation in getting the task completed.

LONG-RANGE PLANNING DOCUMENT

Planning is a purposeful activity designed to reach an objective. Planning of any sort is the ordering of events, resources, and individuals to achieve an objective. Planning activities within the school system assist in accomplishing certain things within the overall long-range plan. The long-range plan serves as a means for all the departments in the school system to work toward common goals. It serves as the authority for the activities of all segments of the organization for a number of years. The long-range plan, therefore, should address the goals of the school system, the recipients of the services, and the resources available (Dewar, 2002).

The requirements for the content of the long-range plan vary from state to state and from school system to school system. There are, however, some essential elements that must be included in any long-range plan. As stated above, the purpose of the document is to identify goals and apply resources to those goals; therefore, the long-range plan should contain considerable information about the school system. At a minimum, the document should address the major issues of where the organization is located, what it is doing, who it benefits, where the activities take place, and how the efforts are being financed. In other words, the following topics are included:

- the community: location, resources, constraints of the local school system
- the educational program: a description of the number and kinds of programs
- student projections: how many and what kinds of students will be enrolled in the future
- school facilities: number and kinds of teaching spaces that are available
- the needed capital projects to meet student needs
- the financial plan: sources and amounts of funds

These headings are convenient divisions of the school system's total plan. Each heading contains considerable information about what is to be done and the resources available to the school system.

The Community

The long-range plan should describe the community in which the school system is located. This description should include a listing of resources available to assist the schools in doing their job. The community description should also detail the socioeconomic problems people face and its effects upon the schools. Where the schools have tried to mount programs to assist the general population with their community problems, these programs should be identified.

The results of the environmental scanning could be presented here because the description of this scanning should be of considerable value to those working within the school system. This section should present enough information so that readers not associated with the school system gain an accurate picture of the community and its effects upon the schools.

The Educational Program

This section deals with the type of educational program offered by schools. The description must be precise so that the entire scope of the educational activities is listed. The main thrust may be the pre-kindergarten through twelfth grade program, but all the programs for which the school assumes responsibility should be described, and each program must in some way relate directly to the goals identified for the school system.

The section dealing with educational programs should contain a specific description of the programs, starting with the goals of the school system and translating them into enabling goals, and finally into objectives and behavioral objectives. Subject matter included in the various programs should be included in the description. Readers should have a detailed view of the educational program offered by the entire school system.

New educational programs and activities that are projected to be started during the life of the long-range plan should also be identified. A description should include the population to be included, the numbers of individuals or groups, and the number and kind of staff needed. In addition, the year of planning and implementation should be identified. New initiatives will require funding at some point. Identifying these programs and their impact on staffing will allow the personnel department to mount a human resource plan to procure the needed staff.

Further, information contained in this section will affect the financial plan developed to fund the long-range plan. Therefore, this section should be in great detail so that all pieces—needed staff, materials, space, and funds—will come together and be available at the appropriate time.

Student Projections

The number of students the school system will serve in the future is an important piece of information. The school system must plan for the appropriate number of students and adults the system will expect to have in the next few years. This is necessary in order to have the right kinds of educational spaces and in the right locations at the propitious time. Planning and constructing a new school building consumes many years, and a school system needs lead time to complete the task. This section of the document should show projections of how enrollment in the school system will grow or decline, in what locations, and the kinds of students that will be in attendance.

School Facilities

This section should describe the educational spaces available in the school system. To prepare this document, all the school facilities owned and operated by the system should be evaluated. The results should indicate the number of classroom spaces that can be used and how many students they can hold. The difference between the number of instructional spaces available and the number projected needed would indicate the need for new space.

If the school system is experiencing a decline in student population, surplus instructional spaces should also be identified. In this situation, decisions must be made for the disposition of the surplus by identifying different uses for these spaces. Whether there is a surplus of space, or space is needed, a plan must be devised to deal with the difference, no matter the direction.

Needed Capital Improvements

This section of the long-range plan should enumerate and identify the capital needs for the school system. Any new buildings or major renovations of existing buildings should be included. The section should also contain an estimated cost of the additional new facilities as well as the major renovations.

The Financial Plan

The final section of the planning document should deal with the financial package developed to fund the long-range plan. This funding plan should deal with both operational and capital funding. When adopted, the operational funding plan becomes the operational budget for the school system. Even though this budget is for only one year, projections of operational budgets for the future should be made so that the school board can see the future financial impact of the proposed programs. This is important because it allows the school board to anticipate financial need, assuming the educational program is implemented.

The other part of the financial plan should deal with the need for capital funds. In as much as capital funds are obtained differently than operational funds, a plan detailing how these funds are obtained must be presented. If a new school is needed, the plan should provide a way to obtain capital funds through whatever means available to the school system. Most school systems rely upon general obligation bonds to pay for new facilities. This means a bond issue will need to be floated. If state programs exist to aid local school systems in constructing a new building, the plan should include anticipated funding from this source.

Capital funds are usually under a separate budget from the operational budget, but the payback for the bonds or loans is included in the debt deduction section of the operational budget. The impact of the bond issue repayment on the operational budget should be examined. The financial analysis should also look at the existing bonded indebtedness of the school system and the effect on the system's capability to go further in debt. All these considerations should be discussed thoroughly in the financial plan section of the long-range plan.

ACTION PLANS

The long-range plan itself is never intended to be implemented directly or completely. This rather large compendium of data gives direction to the entire school system, but the actual implementation of what the long-range plan stipulated is left to more refined and precise documents. After acceptance of the long-range plan by the school board, departments, offices, and individuals within the school system must break down the long-range plan into manageable parts to complete what the overall plan contains.

The document that will actually serve as the implementation tool is called an action plan or work plan. Sections of the long-range plan are divided into discrete portions and assigned to personnel who have expertise in that certain field. These sections are then converted into work instruments with precise objectives that can be accomplished.

Each segment of the long-range plan contains work that must be done in order for the total plan to be completed. These segments have a cluster of responsibilities that will need special expertise, such as the finance plan needing individuals with expertise in many different areas of financial planning. Table 3.1 illustrates the actual department or individual that has responsibility to develop and implement an action plan. As can be seen, these responsibilities cover the entire spectrum of the functions of the school system. In small

Table 3.1. Action Plans and Responsibility

Section of Long-Range Plan	Type of Action Plan	Responsibility
1. Community Characteristics		
2. Educational Plan	Curriculum Plan	Director of Curriculum
	Instructional Plan	Director of Instruction
	Human Resources Plan	Director of Personnel
3. Student Projections	Demographic Study for SDOE Funding	Director of Research
4. Facility Needs	Capital Improvement Plan	Director of Facilities
5. Financial Plan	Budgetary Plans	Director of Finance
	Operating Budget	
	Capital Budget	

school systems, several of these functions may be incorporated under one person or office. Nevertheless, the action plan must be developed and discharged for each of these responsibilities. Regardless of the size of the school system, all these jobs need to be completed by someone.

The long-range plan of the school system permeates all segments of the organization. These segments in turn develop action plans to be implemented. The most obvious manifestation of these action plans is in the individual school building, where the principal and staff formulate and complete an annual school plan. These individual school site plans complement the school system long-range plan, yet display the necessary individualization of planning to meet the needs of the children in each school building.

The exact format of the work plans or action plans, on all levels of administration, may vary according to each locality. The plans, however, should contain several segments that enable the department, office, or individual to identify:

1. the job to be completed
2. the objectives of the job
3. measures of effectiveness
4. costs associated with attainments of the objectives
5. deadlines for completion

These plans might also contain statements relating to the further division of work and task responsibilities into smaller units, the quality of the product that is needed, and sources of assistance available. There may also be statements relating to certain limitations, handicaps, and constraints the department will have to overcome to be successful.

One important aspect of the action plans is the need for assigned resources to complete the objectives. These resources are in the form of personnel, time, and funds. Without these resources, work under the action plans cannot be accomplished. This resource allocation is in the form of department, office, school site, or individual budgets that are derived from the general operational budget of the school system.

The action plans usually have a life of one year, and new action plans are developed each year. Those tasks or objectives not completed in year one are then recast into the plan for the following year until they are either completed or changed. An objective can be declared redundant because of changing circumstances and, therefore, dropped from the plan. This would result from evaluations of the action plan and would reflect back on the changes in the long-range plan, which seeps into the document each year.

These changes can result from several influences both inside and outside the school system. Naturally, changes emanating from the state department of education, for example, could influence the long-range plan immensely. Such changes are not a negative aspect of the long-range plan but a simple recognition of the fact that the long-range plan is a living document that can change as circumstances inside and outside the school system change.

Each department, office, school building, and individual is evaluated according to the amount of work completed. This evaluation can take the form of formal reports to the superintendent and school board or informal conversational evaluations on a personal basis. Each school system must develop a system of accountability and evaluation to determine the success of those involved in this work. Successful work toward the completion of the action plan for each department, office, school, or individual is expected. Rewards of some sort should then be supplied to effective managers who complete the action plan. Conversely, remediation in some form is applied to those individuals who cannot or did not accomplish the work assigned under the action plan.

The work of the school system proceeds through the implementation of each action plan. In this manner, the long-range plan of the school system is implemented. Completion of all objectives and tasks under an action plan indicates the school system is moving successfully toward its general goals. This movement is more of a gradual accomplishment than sudden spurts of activity.

SUMMARY

The planning process for a major capital project is comprised of approximately eleven separate processes that can be independent in and of themselves yet are integral to the entire process of planning any capital project. To guide these processes, a long-range plan needs to be developed and implemented. The content of the long-range plan normally consists of the following: description of the community, description of the educational plan, student projections, facility evaluation, recommendations for capital needs, and the financial plan. These elements serve to guide the development of a comprehensive plan of action. The long-range plan can never be completed but should then lead to the development of an action plan that serves as the engine to complete the plan. The action plan contains steps that guide the educators in completing all necessary work efforts of the school system employees. Most action plans serve the school system for only one year and then a new action plan is developed that will pick up the projects not completed during the previous year.

Chapter 4

Long-Range Planning

Educational Program Development

The first part of the long-range planning effort examines the community in which the school system is located and the type of educational program delivered to the youth of that geopolitical area. This examination can take many forms and can use various types of instruments for gathering data. Data may be solicited from sources within and outside the school system.

The community in which the school system is located contains many elements that impinge upon as well as support the individual school organizations (Ohio School Facility Commission, 2008). For the long-range plan, however, the description of the community should report both assets and liabilities. The educational program developed by the school system should reflect the particular needs of the community. For example, in areas with social problems, school systems many times develop educational programs to lessen the impact of those problems on the citizens and students of the community. Essentially, the community problems influence the school system to respond to a particular problem. In this manner, the educational program of the school system is influenced by community problems. Therefore, identifying community problems is an important part of the long-range plan.

Likewise, the community has assets that various school organizations can use to augment the educational program. Examples of this include museums, zoos, transportation systems, and parks and recreation programs that the community operates. In addition, there is private sector assets that schools can and do use. Examples of this are private museums, musical and sporting organizations, social groups, and medical associations. These, too, should be described in the long-range plan.

In each community there are various social and governmental programs and services designed to assist citizens who need them. The extent of these programs and services depends upon the community itself. In some communities there are very few services, but in others the range is extensive. In many cases the school system depends upon these services and programs to assist in the development and growth of students. Many of these programs and services aid the lower-income population of the school system or those who have trouble helping themselves, but some programs serve the entire range of the school-age population in the school system.

Nevertheless, all of these activities assist the school staff in educating children who live in the school system. Because of this, precise documentation of these programs and services is important, for it will enable school system employees to become familiar with these assets and how they might assist in their work.

Because each community is unique, the community asset description is place specific. Therefore, much of the educational program is affected by the availability (or the lack) of these programs and services in the community. This is the reason an enumeration and documentation of community assets and problems should be printed in the long-range plan of the school system.

The second item to be addressed in the long-range plan is the educational program. On first thought, describing the educational program of the school system must seem like an impossible task if done properly. A simple listing of subjects on each level might be more appropriate and less time-consuming. However, the curriculum is more than the subject matter taught in the schools, and for that reason more detail and precision is needed in the description than a simple listing of courses and subject matter. This section of the plan should not only describe in detail the present educational program, but also the program that will be implemented in the next five to seven years or through the end of the long-range plan. The latter is very important because of the implication for change in the school system in the future (Clark, 2007).

Much of the educational program of the school system is now mandated on the state level. In the last twenty years each state has exercised its control over its school systems by mandating more and more courses of study and services. The number of courses or subject matter prescribed by states during this period has increased greatly. Therefore, the differences between school systems have decreased over the past two decades. This is not to say that all school systems are alike; such is not the case. Nevertheless, there are many similarities and considerable uniformity throughout the states. This means that each school system needs to describe its educational program in detail to delineate the differences. Because of the Every Student Succeeds Act (ESSA) legislation (2018), the emphasis upon subject matter mastery has increased considerably in every state. Although ESSA may be changed in the near future, its effects on public schools may last for a long time.

Each school system changes and enlarges the programs offered to its students. This is a never-ending process of improving the educational program. Each school system improves its offerings by adding services as well. While one school system may have a certain course of study or service, another may not, but will be working to acquire that course, or some other. Each of these program changes or improvements must be described in the long-range plan so resources are allocated to achieve that improvement.

As stated in the previous chapter, the long-range plan serves as a stem from which other plans of action branch and develop. These action plans may be in staff development for a new program, in human resources to secure new teachers for the changed program, in the curriculum department to develop curricular materials, or in the school facilities department to develop a capital improvement plan. Therefore, it is necessary to spell out the changes to the educational program of the school system envisioned in the immediate future.

The first task in describing the educational program is to identify the goals and purposes of the school system (Hill, 2005). They explain why the organization exists and what it does. The goals and purposes guide the organization in its task of educating the youth of the community.

Each organization has a printed document that contains generalized statements about what it purports to do and what it actually does. These statements give direction to the workers and identify what the organization does to those who are outside of it. Such statements also limit the scope of operation and focus the efforts of workers. Both purposes—internal and external—are served equally by these goal statements.

In extremely small organizations, a definition of purpose can be understood by all concerned without a purpose or goal statement. This is because everyone knows what the goal is and how to work effectively toward that goal. The more complex the organization becomes, the less likely employees will know what the goal is or how they are to work toward it unless there are written statements they can refer to occasionally. In a very complex, large organization, such as a school system, the purposes and goals need to be identified and written for the edification of everyone.

There are many ways of writing the purpose and goals of an organization. They may be expressed as a vision statement, a mission statement, a philosophy of education statement, goals, and behavioral objectives. While each has a specific meaning, many school systems use the terms interchangeably, with little distinction between them. Such indiscriminate use of these terms does not facilitate clarity.

There are precise distinctions between the terms cited above. Each describes a specific part of the organization's goals and purpose in decreasingly global aspects and scope. To lessen confusion about their use, the following section will examine these terms.

VISION STATEMENT

A vision statement declares an organization's objective in what it would like to achieve or accomplish. It guides the organization toward creating a better world. This statement is of a rather grand order and describes what the organization would like to work toward and how it can contribute. Although a vision statement may be constructed to be something like a blue-sky wish, it must conform to the area of responsibility of the organization. The vision statement cannot deal with all the problems of the world, but must confine itself to education, as in the case of the school system. A vision statement is something everyone concerned with the organization would like to see in the future. The following is an example of a vision statement developed by a local school system:

> Vision Statement—Every child can learn and every child has unique talents that our schools must identify and develop. The most important investment the Montgomery County Public Schools can make for the future is to provide for all students a viable and useful educational program based upon excellence and equity.

This statement identifies two general areas in which that organization would like to see the school system move toward, excellence and equity. Both these qualities are worthwhile and need to be included in the vision people have of a good school system. This vision statement is also global in that it addresses the future state of education.

MISSION STATEMENT

The mission statement is much different from the vision statement as well as from the philosophy, goal, or behavioral objective statements that are frequently used. Where a vision statement points the organization to the future, the mission statement explains what the nature of the organization is. Likewise, the mission statement does not address goals of the organization specifically, nor the belief system in operation in the schools, nor the goals toward which the school system is working. The mission statement may be akin to the purpose statement in that the mission of a school system also is its purpose. The purpose and the mission statements may, in fact, be the same thing, however, the term "mission statement" seems to be in favor with educators today.

The mission statement of a school system must answer the twin questions of why this organization was formed and what it is supposed to do. In essence, the mission statement cites the legal basis of the organization of the school system. In all states, the legislature has created local schools for a specific purpose—to provide an appropriate education for all youth in the community. That is, indeed, the purpose and mission of the local school system, rather than to maintain law and order, such as the local police department does, or to provide recreational services, which is the responsibility of the recreation department. However, the local school system, as represented by the school board, may also wish to express the type of educational program to be offered in the community based upon the needs of the people to be served. In that case, the mission statement must also reflect this local need.

A mission statement of a local school system is shown below. This statement alludes to the state constitution as the source of authority and power for the schools, but the statement also addresses the specific work of the school board as that body sees it. This specific mission statement should be read in conjunction with the vision statement cited above in this chapter:

Mission Statement—In accordance with the laws of the Commonwealth of Virginia, the mission of the Montgomery County Public Schools is to provide a stimulating and appropriate educational program for all students so that they will develop the knowledge and skills to achieve success and become active citizens who contribute to their communities.

This mission statement is for a local school system and addresses the responsibility of that organization. In a local school system, the responsibility is to the citizens of the geopolitical area served by the schools. This mission statement could serve almost any local school system. The mission of a local school system is to provide an appropriate education for all youth in accordance with the constitutional provisions of the state school system. Every school system should have a clear and concise mission statement, whether or not there is a vision statement. Such an expression provides everyone concerned with a clear idea of what the organization does.

PHILOSOPHY

Of course, defining what an appropriate education is must follow from the philosophical statement and the goals identified for the school system. The mission statement simply tells what the organization is and defines its purpose.

Defining what is meant by education must stem from other statements. This is where both the philosophical statement and goals carry on the mission of the organization.

Philosophy deals with belief systems and tries to explain certain phenomena, such as:

- How do individuals learn?
- What is knowledge?
- Where does knowledge come from?
- What are values?
- Where do values come from?

These are very important questions for school system employees because much of what is done is governed by the beliefs these individuals hold about these questions. What is taught in the schools is determined to a large extent by what we believe is knowledge. Likewise, how an individual believes children learn will greatly determine the methods used to teach. The values teachers try to instill in their students depend to a large measure upon what values the teachers believe important. In spite of the fact that each teacher must have answers to these questions, the school system also has an interest in these questions and should have some answers to guide the teachers and administrators when they work with students.

This does not mean that the school system should force teachers and administrators to hold common beliefs, but there should be a common statement that answers the questions above, to which all can ascribe. There should be room for individual belief systems within the overall philosophical statement of a school system.

The philosophical statement of a school system should confine itself to answering the questions of belief listed above. This statement should not address the purpose of the school system, nor the goals toward which the organization is working, but rather how individuals learn, the type of setting or environment that is conducive to learning, and the larger picture of values and where knowledge originates. These are the only areas that a philosophical statement should cover. To include other items in a philosophical statement is to miss the real meaning of the belief statement that a school system should have.

GOALS

The next level of expression of what a school system should be doing addresses goals. These statements express how an organization should direct its efforts and what the program can do for individuals. In other words, the school system will direct resources to assist individuals to become more productive or gain certain knowledge, skills, and attitudes. The goals of an organization can never be achieved, but are something toward which an organization works. For example, if educating the youth of the community is a goal of the school system, then that goal cannot be achieved until the last youngster in the community graduates and there are no more students left to be educated, a situation that is most likely never to occur.

The goal statements should reflect all previously developed statements. If a school system has developed vision, mission, and philosophical statements, then the goal statements are usually thought of as program goals. A set of goals might be:

The Goals of the Washington Public Schools are the following:

1. To develop in each student, by relevant, interesting, and diversified instruction, a command of the basic skills and the ability to think clearly, communicate effectively, and learn easily.
2. To help each student to be creative and make cultural and recreational activities a part of his/her life.
3. To give each student a clear and honest understanding of the United States, including contemporary urban problems, historical interpretation, and international relations.

These program goals reflect what the school system works toward and where it will commit its resources. The goals identify activities legally within the purview of the school system and focus on the individual student. As goals can never be fully met, they are stated in generalized terms rather than by using measurable or quantifiable terms.

Enabling goals sometimes augment the goals of a school system. These are statements that direct the organization to do certain things so that the general goals of the school system can be addressed. For example, certain services must be available before any instructional program can be activated, so an enabling goal would focus on the services. Enabling goals are assumed by certain segments of the school system to assist the instructional segment of the organization; the enabling goals move the organization toward the general goals.

Examples of enabling goals are:

- To develop an efficient, responsive, and flexible organization with the motivation, ability, and resources to meet the needs of the school system.
- To engage in every effort to attract, train, and retrain the most competent personnel.

- To provide functional physical plants, in which teachers can utilize modern teaching methods, students can effectively learn, and to which community residents will come.

As with program goals, enabling goals are never fully met but are something toward which the organization works until the goals change. For example, the third goal is something toward which the school facilities department continuously works. The goal will never be fully achieved because there will always be a continuing need to provide modern, functional buildings to house students. This particular goal drives the maintenance program to provide such housing for students. So long as there are buildings, the enabling goal will be relevant and there will be a need to have a maintenance program.

The other two enabling goals address the organization of the school system and its staffing. Both these areas are of vital concern in working toward the program goals. Without an efficient organization and staff, work efforts would be handicapped. Other enabling goals may be needed to augment the program goals. These should be developed in conjunction with the major program goals.

Behavioral Objectives

Assuming goals cannot be achieved as such, there must be some way to measure the effectiveness and efficiency of the organization in working toward its goals. To do so, the goals of the organization must be translated into statements that are measurable. These statements are termed behavioral objectives.

Behavioral objectives are written in terms of observable student behavior that can be measured by some type of instrument or observation. This means that students will be measured or examined to determine how much of a predetermined amount of knowledge has been gained after appropriate instruction. Behavioral objectives are derived from the program goal, which in turn was developed from an organization goal.

The list below is an example of the breakdown from an organization goal to a program goal, and finally into a series of observable behavioral objectives:

Develop in each student, by relevant, interesting, and diversified instruction, a command of the basic skills and the ability to think clearly, communicate effectively, and learn easily.

Program Objective 1.0:
During the XXXX–XX school year, each student will master the basic learning skills of reading at a level commensurate with his/her ability as measured by norm-referenced tests. Behavioral Objectives:

1.1. As of June XXXX, approximately eighty-six percent (86%) of students in grades K–3 will have demonstrated mastery of certain basic learning skills of reading at a level commensurate with his/her ability, as measured by the State Basic Learning Skills Testing Program.

1.2. Students in Grades K–3 who have not demonstrated mastery of certain basic learning skills of reading at a level commensurate with his/her ability will receive remedial instruction through the Chapter 1 Remedial Reading Program, State Primary Remedial Program, and regular classroom instruction.

1.3. As of June XXXX, approximately seventy percent (70%) of students in grades 4–7 will have demonstrated mastery of the basic learning skills of reading at a level commensurate with his/her ability, as measured by the State Basic Learning Skills Testing Program.

1.4. Students in Grades 4–7 who have not demonstrated mastery of certain basic learning skills of reading commensurate with his/her ability will receive remediation through regular classroom instruction and the Chapter 1 Remedial Program.

1.5. As of June XXXX, approximately eighty-nine percent (89%) of students in grade 9 will have achieved a mastery score of seventy percent (70%) or more on the State Reading Minimum Competency Testing Program.

1.6 Students unable to obtain a mastery score on the State Reading Minimum Competency Tests will receive remedial instruction through the Metra-Structured Reading Tutorial Program, individual and small-group tutoring assistance, and special service personnel, when applicable.

1.7. All students deficient in the basic learning skills of reading will be identified, diagnosed, and remedial instruction will be prescribed and provided. Student performance will be assessed on a systematic and routine basis.

1.8. Enrichment activities in reading will be provided to students identified as academically gifted in this area.

The behavioral objectives shown in this list measure how well students are performing and, in turn, indicate how effectively the school system is performing and working toward its identified goals. These objectives are for only one program. Each program of the school system should have such behavioral objectives to measure student achievement. Only through this form of measurement can the school system accumulate data regarding achievement.

The educational program can be developed from the educational goals, program objectives, and behavioral objectives. The actual description of the educational program for the long-range document, however, must be by subject area. Special programs and activities of the school system should also be included in the description of the educational program for the long-range plan.

PROGRAM DEVELOPMENT

Local school systems are required to offer all state-mandated programs and services (unless especially exempted). As state program mandates have increased rapidly in the past decade, much of the educational program offered in any school system is a result of state action. While there is no reason to believe this trend will abate, school boards do have some freedom to incorporate programs and services demanded by the local constituency. Examples of both state-mandated and locally requested programs abound in the curriculum of the public schools. Family-life education and driver education might be examples of the former, while English as a Second Language might be included because of local demand or need.

Most program options adopted by the local school board are the result of pressure from some group. Pressure may come from local, national, or state groups, or from the school staff itself.

The curriculum of the local school system is constantly changing because of these types of pressures. Through a well-developed long-range plan, curriculum changes can be orderly and anticipated well enough in advance to provide the resources necessary for full implementation. There are times and circumstances where an educational program change is required to be implemented in a short period of time, such as the National Defense Program in the 1950s, which demanded more, or at least updated, science and math course offerings in high schools during the Eisenhower administration.

NEEDS ASSESSMENT

The school board desires at times to know how the community feels about the effectiveness of the school system. In such circumstances school boards may conduct a community attitude assessment. This assessment can take many forms, but the purpose is to determine how people perceive the school (Tanner and Lackey, 2005). The results of these assessments can prompt the school board to extend or reduce an existing program, or to establish a completely new program. The results may also serve to confirm existing goals or provide data to revise others.

This is a way of finding out if the community believes there is a difference between *what the school is doing* and *what they believe could be done*. Such assessments provide the school board with valuable community input into not only the program offered, but into the goals of the school system (Hill, 2005). Many school systems conduct assessments on a regular basis and thereby accumulate data for a longitudinal study of trends.

Not only members of the community, but also the staff of the school system should have an opportunity to have strong input into the goals formulated by the school board. One of the most influential resources is the superintendent, who should have a great deal of input into the process as well as into the final product. Sometimes a school will select a particular candidate for the school superintendent because that person is believed to possess enough vision and insight to help the school system clarify new goals.

All the sources of change and goal formulation are important to the school system, and all must be incorporated into the process of educational program development. The long-range plan should reflect the needs of these sources by funding the programs detailed in the document. The long-range plan is not a static document but one that changes as needs change. The long-range plan is usually developed for a five-to-seven-year period. In spite of this length of time, the document changes to meet certain needs. Each year of the long-range plan, resources may be reallocated to meet specific identified needs.

SUMMARY

Long-range planning requires a document that spells out the philosophical foundation of the school system and then describes how that is put into practice. The long-range planning document contains a description of the vision and mission of the school system and contains the philosophical foundation upon which the vision of the school system is based. The long-range plan document also contains a description of the educational program the school system offers and breaks this down to goals and behavioral objectives. Finally, the school system should at least know how the community feels about the entire school system effort to educate its youth. This can be done through a needs assessment effort.

Chapter 5

Long-Range Planning

Student Enrollment Projections

Every school system needs to know how many students will be enrolled in the future to do any worthwhile planning. During the planning process the school system identifies and develops the educational program to be offered in the areas served by the organization. The next step is to determine the number of students that need to be educated—both now and in the future. Using this information, school buildings can be located to accommodate population increases or, in the case of declining enrollment, the student population can be housed in fewer buildings.

PURPOSE OF PROJECTIONS

In order to address the "four F's" of administration—funding, faculty, facilities, and function—the number of future students is needed. Each of these aspects of school administration centers on how many students a local school system will educate. State funding for the educational program is based on the number of students enrolled. The number of students also determines the number of faculty members.

Of course, the number of classrooms and buildings a school system uses is a result of the number of individuals enrolled. Even the function of the school system, meaning the type of program offered, is determined by the type and kind of student makeup within the school system. Not only student enrollment, but also the types of individuals that comprise the student body are important in the planning process. The extent and types of special services employed in the school system are directly related to the numbers and types of students in the serving area. Every aspect of administering schools is tied into the number of students enrolled.

For the most part, school systems cannot respond quickly to the need for programs and/or housing of students. Planning a new educational program may take the better part of a year (plus advanced notice for funding), before it can be successfully implemented. In as much as it takes from two to five years to plan, design, and construct a new school building, school systems need to project far in advance the number of students that will enroll in the school system. For these reasons, school systems need to look to future enrollments to plan the work of the organization (Tanner and Lackey, 2005).

BASIS OF PROJECTIONS

Projections of student enrollments are not glimpses into the future or precise revelations of things to come. Unless one believes in crystal ball gazing, tarot cards, dream interpretation, or some other device for seeing into the future, student enrollment projections can only be, at best, an educated guess. This is precisely what student enrollment projections are—a guess, but one based upon the most accurate available data.

In developing projections, administrators must keep in mind that they are dealing with two of the most unpredictable areas of human behavior: procreation and the ability to move from one geographical location to another. In some locales, the latter behavior is not as unpredictable as the former; nevertheless, either behavior is something demographers can only guess, based upon previous behavior.

Social and even natural phenomena affect both human behaviors in a very direct way. For instance, several decades ago an electrical blackout in New York City resulted in an increase in the birth rate approximately nine months later, and then to an increase in kindergarten enrollment five years later. As humorous as that episode may seem, similar occurrences can be documented throughout the country. The opposite reaction would be with Hurricane Katrina. The school systems in New Orleans lost student enrollment as a result of that devastating event. Some phenomena have an immediate impact, such as the cases above, while other phenomena may take longer to appear.

Economic factors may cause a gradual movement of individuals and families from one area to another, with a subsequent loss or gain of students spread over a period of time. The opening or closing of a factory in a town may be the direct cause of student loss or gain, but often the social or economic factors operating in a community are so intertwined that it is difficult to identify one cause as the main source of change in enrollment.

Demographers try to look at the entire community when developing projections. Many times the environmental scanning of the community, done during development of the long-range plan, will help identify factors in the community that may affect enrollment at a later date.

The main thing to keep in mind when developing enrollment projections or in using the results of projections, is that they must be developed based upon previous behavior of individuals. Demographers assume that, based upon previous behavior, individuals will continue to act in the same manner. Without this premise, projections of future student enrollments can be misinterpreted and misapplied.

PROJECTION ASSUMPTIONS

Student projections, like any population projections, are based upon certain beliefs about how the area will grow or decline. These beliefs are drawn from data gathered about the area studied. Based upon these data, certain assumptions or beliefs are developed. These assumptions serve to guide demographers in deciding which methodology to use in developing projections and the direction of change in current enrollment.

For instance, if a community shows definite signs of growth in certain segments, it might be safe to assume the community will continue to grow in the same manner for a period of time. All projections must be based upon some assumptions of growth or decline, otherwise, projections of any worth cannot be developed. In discussing the projections, demographers must identify these assumptions as the rationale for the manner in which projections are cast.

As long as the developed assumptions reflect the pattern of growth in a community, a greater reliability can be placed upon the projections themselves. The set of assumptions developed are not static; assumptions can become obsolete quickly if changes in the community do not continue to support them. Demographers must continually monitor the community for signs of growth or decline.

Indices such as housing starts and completions, electric and sewer connections, give the demographer an insight into the development of a community. As these indices are the same ones used originally to develop the assumptions, changes in the indices will cause the demographer to reconsider the original assumptions and change or modify them if necessary. Areas in which assumptions may be developed include the following:

- immigration/emigration rates of the local community
- employment rate and certain economic factors
- social conditions in the community

- fertility rates
- number of students attending private or charter schools
- dropout rate of the schools
- ratio of births to deaths in a community
- number of military or federal installations in a community

All these factors have a direct impact upon families and, in turn, student enrollments and their projection. Therefore, demographers must decide whether or not there will be any changes in these factors and in which direction changes will occur. Without addressing these areas, reliable projections cannot be developed.

PROJECTION DATA

Hard data is needed to forecast the approximate number of students a school system will have in the future. This data may be of the number of people in a geographical area or of a selected group of persons, such as children between certain ages in a selected area. Whether all the individuals are in an area or just a portion of it, a count must be taken upon which the projection will be based. The basic data of a set of projections provide an accurate count of the people included in the projection. This accurate count comes from a census enumeration, which is simply the actual counting of people at a certain time and place.

A basic fact of projection methodology is that future trends in community development may be derived from past development. In other words, the community will develop the same way in the future that it developed in the immediate past; past trends indicate development trends of the future, unless there is some major change, such as the opening of a new factory or other enterprise, or a major decline (Cary, 2011). This is the very heart of all types of projections, regardless of the population.

Other types of data are also used in projection methodology to provide indicators of possible growth or decline. Housing starts and completions and sewer and electric connections provide information about the development in a community. The more housing starts and completions, the more new families will be in the community and the greater the increase in student enrollment. A definite rate of growth can be developed from the data of several years of housing starts and completions. This rate of growth can be used in several methodologies to determine the population growth rate. This growth rate can also be compared to growth rates developed using a different methodology.

All of the indices of community development can be compared with the student population to determine congruence of patterns of growth, stabilization, or decline. The most influential community factors affecting immigration and emigration in the community are the availability of adequate, affordable housing and employment opportunities that draw families and individuals into a community. The absence or decline in these factors cause movement away from the community. These factors should be monitored continually by school administrators and others who develop student enrollment projections.

CENSUS ENUMERATION

Every school system is required to conduct a census enumeration of the students within its geographic area. The census may cover students from certain ages such as two to eighteen or from birth to age twenty-one. State law may stipulate school-age children only, but recent court decisions regarding the availability of educational services to special populations may mean the school system is required to count every person from birth to age twenty-one to have an accurate picture of those needing educational services.

If the school census enumeration data is to be the basis of projected enrollment, then an accurate count of those individuals from birth to adulthood should be taken. Without this data, projections can be only a partial view of the clientele to be served. With birth data and an accurate count of all preschool children in the community, the school district gets a count of all future clients of the organization and this can form the basis of future-needed services.

Many states stipulate when the census should take place. If this is the case, local leeway is eliminated. There may be some benefit to allowing local school systems to set the date of the census enumeration because of certain local factors. For instance, in some communities seasonal workers immigrate to the community for a time and then leave, greatly affecting student population. If the workers and their families are in the community during the school year, educational services must be provided to these migrant students. This cohort then becomes a significant population to account for in making projections. If there are no local circumstances that would demand a census enumeration at a certain time, a fall enumeration coinciding with the first report to the state on student enrollment would be a propitious time.

Usually the highest enrollment of the school year is in the fall, with enrollment peaking during the third month of the school term. Most school systems must report enrollment to the state by the end of the first month of the school term. Census enumeration at this time probably produces the best results, as the school system has nearly the largest enrollment of the school year. Once started, it is crucial to take the enumeration at the same time each year to ensure comparable data.

A census enumeration card can be used to gather data for the school system. This card lists all individuals living at a certain address, the ages of each person, and any disabilities school-aged children may have. This last point is important because the school system must identify disabled students early and serve these children in some cases even before they are enrolled in school. The box below shows a census enumeration form a school system could use for data gathering.

The school census is organized and conducted by an office or person in the school system. Usually, this responsibility is lodged in the office of research and planning, the pupil services office, or, in some rare instances, in the school facilities department. In small school systems this function may be housed in the office of the administrative assistant to the superintendent or pupil personnel. No matter which department conducts the census enumeration, the resources to do so must be in the operational budget of the school system for the year in which the census count will take place.

To perform the census, the school system must canvas individuals. This may be done by organizing lay people to go from door to door to gather data. A systematic visit by a representative of the school system to every residence in the geographic area served by the district is needed for an accurate count.

For a door-to-door, house-to-house count, usually the school district is divided into smaller areas based on the elementary school areas. Alternative geographic designations, such as census blocks or political wards, may be followed. The elementary school attendance areas are usually subdivided into smaller units for ease in making visits. A leader is assigned to each area and a series of workers are assigned to each subunit. Data gathered in the subunits are combined to form a total elementary attendance area count of individuals. Counts from these units form the basis of the projections for each elementary school attendance area and subsequently for secondary school attendance area projections. In large attendance areas, a subleader may be used to provide enough supervision for the complete house-to-house visit. The accuracy of the count for each area can be assured only through closely monitoring the canvasser.

Census data is eventually combined to form the total school system census count. This data is the basis of total school system projections. Most of the time the projections are started on the elementary, middle school, and high school levels, eventually combining to form the total school system projections.

Virginia Triennial School Census
May 1, 2019
WASHINGTON COUNTY SCHOOLS
Message to Washington County Residents:

The Triennial School Census is an enumeration of all individuals ages one to twenty-one, and all handicapped persons ages one to twenty-two. The Census is the basis on which the counties, cities, and towns of the Commonwealth of Virginia receive their fair share of the 1 percent state sales tax and other tax monies. All individuals ages five through nineteen, and handicapped persons ages two, three, four, twenty, and twenty-one are counted for revenue purposes. Counts of individuals ages one to four are used for educational planning by the state and locality.

The enumeration of (a) all persons between ages one and twenty-one and (b) all handicapped persons between the ages of two and twenty-two will be reported to the State Department of Education in a summary form. Names, addresses, and telephone numbers of individuals are required to be held by the Washington County School Board in a confidential file, available only to the state auditor of the Census, until destruction of the file three years later. The Washington County School Board is required to conduct this Triennial School Census in accord with Sections 22.1-281 through 22.1-286 of the Code of Virginia. Prompt return of the Census Form received at your address will help Washington County Public Schools to meet state legal requirements and to plan effectively for educational facilities and programs.

PROJECTION TIME

Population projections can be developed for different times depending on the purposes intended. General projection time periods are set for convenient and practical reasons. Many times, governments require population projections for longer periods than other organizations. It is not unusual for a government to need to project population change for twenty, or even fifty, years in the future.

School systems generally plan for much shorter periods of time. There are some practical reasons for a shortened planning time. Generally, the shorter the projection time the more accurate the projection. In most cases there is a turnover in school board members every five to ten years. In addition, the chief school administrator's tenure is sometimes shorter than the planning period of the school system. However, trends in growth for a sustained period of time enable administrators to plan for the eventuality of the population.

School population changes on a short cycle. Every six years the population of the elementary school changes completely, as does the entire population of the secondary schools. The needs of the community that the school system serves change quickly, necessitating changes in the educational program. Such forces require a shorter period for planning and implementing programs.

A five-year student enrollment projection might have served the needs of a school system many years ago. Today, school systems need to project further into the future. Some states even require the local school system to project the student enrollment for ten years, or even up to twenty years. Extending projection times will undoubtedly increase with more demands for a longer planning period. These longer projection periods will not increase the accuracy of projections. A twenty-year student enrollment projection can only provide a guide to growth trends and will not indicate the actual number of students that will be enrolled two decades hence.

The accuracy of student enrollment projections is directly related to the accuracy and currency of the data. If the data is accurate, the more current the data, the better the projections. In addition, projections must be updated each year with fresh data derived from the school system. Only in this manner can the projections approach an actual count of students.

This also means that the accuracy of the projections can be guaranteed only one year at a time. There can be a reasonable degree of accuracy in the first five years of projections, but beyond that, accuracy falls quickly.

PROJECTION METHODS

Many methods are used to project populations. The methodology is usually determined by the purpose of the projections. Projections for short periods usually do not require complicated methodologies, but the longer the period of projecting, the more complicated and involved the methodology is. Some governmental agencies and commercial organizations project populations for an extended period of time. In such cases, rather sophisticated methodologies are used, but such methodologies are not necessary for shorter periods of projections.

Both the purpose of the projection and the population involved determine the methodology, but regardless of the method, all projections must rely upon previous data and previous trends. The basic questions to be asked in generating student enrollment projections include:

- Will the enrollments increase or decrease?
- Will the increase or decrease be like increases and decreases that have oc-curred in the past?
- If the increase or decrease is not similar, in what ways will it be different?

There are limited numbers of basic methodologies used for projections, but there are large numbers of variations on these basic methods. Hoy (1947) lists the following methods of projecting school populations:

- forecasting school enrollment from total population
- forecasting by analysis
- forecasting by mathematical techniques
- forecasting by the multiple-factor method, which assumes that funda-mental relationships exist between certain economic factors and school enrollment
- forecasting by analogy

MacConnell (1957) expands these methods and identifies more than nine methods that could be used to project student populations. Some of these methodologies can be classified as variations rather than separate methods:

- forecasting by analysis
- forecasting school enrollment from total population
- prediction based wholly on past census data
- method of analogy
- multiple-factor method
- the "law of growth" principle—Pearl-Reed logistic curve
- projecting natural increase
- combined method

Other authorities have identified fewer methods. Schellenberg and Ste-phens (1987) state that two general approaches may be used in projecting populations. One general approach uses historical enrollment data as the basis of projections. Projections are made by using previous trends that are believed to apply to the future. This is basically a survival methodology. The other approach combines historical data with selected variables believed to impinge upon student enrollments. This is a form of multiple-regression analysis.

In addition to these two approaches, there are other projection methods that are not based on student historical enrollment data. These methods rely on data derived from sources other than the school base, such as the number and kinds of individuals who live in a house. These kinds of data are developed by an enumeration of the housing units of a school system, then by determining the composition of the persons living in each house. This factor becomes the basis of projecting population by applying it to each house in a certain geographical area.

Apart from the variations listed above, there are basically three ways of projecting student populations. Some are more appropriate than others in trying to project student populations:

1. Forecasting by retention or survival of the population
2. Forecasting by use of multiple-regression analysis
3. Forecasting by use of georeferenced data

Of the three approaches, the first is the most widely used and applicable for school purposes. Some school systems in countries other than the United States use the multiple-regression method to project student populations; however, few, if any, school systems in the United States use this method. Almost every state uses the survival method of projecting student populations. Although multiple-regression analysis is perhaps more accurate than the survival method, school systems and state departments of education have not used this methodology to any extent.

However, some projection methodology experts contend that the survival method is as accurate as the regression models and is simpler to use. Every state uses a form of the survival method for projecting student enrollment in succeeding years. In as much as the survival method is so universally used, both on the state and local level, it is important for the school administrator to be able to produce and interpret results using this methodology.

For school population projection purposes, the survival and georeferenced data methods are probably the most useful and widely used. There are three variations of the survival method that should be considered for use in school systems in certain circumstances. These variations all use some sort of rate of survival of a designated group or groups to produce projections or data for further analysis. These methods include: forecasting by analogy, forecasting from the total population, and forecasting by grade or age survival ratio. These methods, along with the georeferenced methods, seem to be the best methods of projecting student enrollments available to school systems.

Forecasting by Analogy

This method of projecting student populations assumes that growth characteristics between two different, but similarly situated, school systems will correspond. This method is best used in suburban settings where there are discernible rings of growth from the center of population density. Projectionists assume, based upon an analysis of community characteristics that their school system will grow in the same manner as a neighboring school system, has already grown. Thus, the rate and direction of growth of the neighboring school system can be determined and applied to the school population of the subject school system. From this application of rate and direction of growth, a set of projections can be derived. The rate of growth will be a mean of the percent of growth for each year. This mean is then applied to the present student population for each year to be projected to determine the future student population.

The direction of growth is not directly applicable to the projection of numbers of students in the future but can enable planners to do some extrapolation of where growth may take place. This is a very rudimentary exercise. Direction of growth usually follows arterial highways or other forms of transportation, such as public transportation, into and from the population center of density.

Forecasting from analogy is an easy-to-use method of projecting student population because the data is easily available from the neighboring school system. With a minimum of mathematical manipulation, the mean rate of growth per annum can be determined and applied to a known student population. This method is perhaps the easiest to perform. The accuracy of the results may be less than desired. There must be a strong assumption that the subject school system in fact will grow in the same fashion as the neighboring school system. This assumption should be based on a thorough analysis of the two school systems and the unequivocal conclusion of comparable growth.

The advantages of this method are the ease of obtaining data and the simple manipulation of the data. The disadvantage is the doubtful accuracy of the projections. Another disadvantage is that it is possible to project only on total student enrollment, not on an individual school building basis. So long as the assumption that the two systems will grow alike remains viable, the results may prove valuable. When the slightest change in growth patterns occur, the accuracy of the projections is suspect. This method of projection should probably be used as a check or backup for another type of student enrollment projection methodology.

Forecasting from Total Population Projections

This method of projection is based upon the assumption that an observable correlation between total population and school enrollment has existed in the past and will continue in future populations. From previous census data, the exact percentage of each age group of the total population can be determined. This percentage is then applied to previously prepared projections of total school system populations. Various government units, such as city or county planning commissions, prepare total population projections for geopolitical areas. However, usually these projections do not contain any breakdown according to age groupings. Projections of the total population are usually made through a survival ratio applied to previous total population counts derived from the U.S. Census. The school system uses the figure for the total population to determine what percent each age group will be in the future, assuming the percentages remain the same. The approximate number of students in each age group can thus be determined.

Here, again, this methodology is simple and easy to apply. Data is readily available from a governmental agency with no conversion necessary. The mathematical manipulation of the data is not complicated and the results are straightforward. There are, however, several disadvantages to this method.

The first disadvantage is that the age groupings of the U.S. Census are not consistent with the enrollment policies of the school systems. The census is broken down according to full age groupings. For example, individuals will be included in the age four grouping whether the child is four years old, or four years and eleven months. School systems usually enroll all individuals in kindergarten up to four and a half years. In addition, there are seventeen and a half-year-old students who are still in the high school, and in some limited instances students who are eighteen years old. The U.S. Census breakdown does not accommodate these divisions within an age grouping. Because of this, the results must be extrapolated to arrive at a sensible enrollment figure. This extrapolation exacerbates the possibility of inaccuracy of results.

The school organizational levels such as elementary, middle, and high school are not consistent with the age groupings of the Federal Census either. This causes a problem in the distribution of students. Here again, one must extrapolate the results to fit into the organizational levels.

Another difficulty is that a total population projection cannot be fit into individual school attendance areas. Demographers must develop a percentage approach for dividing the projected student population for each school building. This is done by determining the percent of the total school population that each school building enrollment makes up and then applying this factor to the projected student population. There is always a margin for error.

In some areas, the boundaries of the school system do not coincide with the county or city boundaries, so there may be more than one school system within a local governmental area. Here again, the percentage of the total population that each school system contributes to the whole must be devoted to the school population projections. The margin for error in this mathematical process may present a problem in accuracy of results.

The dates when the total population projections are done by the planning commission or other governmental agency usually do not coincide with the needs of the school system. Usually, the planning commission projects on a decade and not on a shorter term. Most school systems rely more upon short-term projections than long term, even though the school system may be required to develop ten-year projections. In addition, often the local planning commission projections are tied directly into the beginning of each decade to use the census data obtained through the federal enumeration. This exact projection date may not be helpful to a school system that is developing student projections beginning three to seven years into the decade.

Obviously, this would cause some problems in the length of time of the projections.

Table 5.1 presents a set of student enrollment projections developed by using total population projections obtained from a county planning commission. The table uses the total population count of 2019 to make the 2020–2029 projections. These were developed to confirm the direction of growth in a set of projections developed using a different methodology.

Forecasting by Cohort Survival Ratios

This projection methodology is also known as forecasting by age, class, or grade-retention rates, or grade-progression ratios. Other terms used for this methodology are percentage of survival, percentage of retention, grade persistence, forecasting by analysis, survival-ratio method, and retention-ratio projection. Regardless of the terminology, the method uses the survival of the members of a designated cohort or group as the basis of predicting the size of the cohort or group in the future (Tanner and Lackey, 2005). A cohort is simply a designation of a certain group of individuals such as the entire first-grade class or some other group. There is always a ratio between the size of a certain identified group of students one year and the size of that same group the following year. This ratio is the basis of the projections in this method. As a kindergarten class moves through the school system and eventually emerges as graduates of the twelfth grade, the composition and number of students in the class change. These changes result from students moving into the school system and joining the group or moving out of the school to decrease the group.

These annual changes represent growth or decline of population in the school system. Under the assumption that the group's size in the future will reflect the changes of similar groups in the past, predictions of the size of any

Table 5.1. School Enrollment Projections from Total Population, 2019–2029

Ages	Population	2019	2020	2021	2022	2023	2024	2025	2026	2027	2028	2029
5–9	Total	1,416	1,446	1,460	1,429	1,417	1,427	1,442	1,465	1,504	1,610	1,683
	School	1,395	1,321	1,301	1,264	1,292	1,301	1,315	1,336	1,372	1,468	1,533
10–14	Total	1,499	1,446	1,434	1,488	1,473	1,488	1,503	1,511	1,510	1,508	1,616
	School	1,468	1,439	1,413	1,434	1,450	1,465	1,480	1,488	1,487	1,484	1,591
15–19	Total	1,574	1,599	1,617	1,576	1,537	1,494	1,452	1,416	1,423	1,458	1,468
	School	721	679	672	731	676	657	639	623	626	642	646
	Spec Ed	87	95	107	73	83	83	83	83	84	87	91
	Total	**3,671**	**3,534**	**3,593**	**3,505**	**3,501**	**3,506**	**3,517**	**3,530**	**3,570**	**3,681**	**3,861**

class or group can be made. This is the basic assumption of this methodology. This is no different from the assumptions used for all other methods of projecting when existing census data are used.

The first step in building a database for cohort survival ratios is to determine the kindergarten enrollment in the future. There is always a relationship or ratio between the number of live births occurring in one year and the enrollment of kindergarten students five years later. The percentage of live births that enroll in the public school is affected by the number of individuals who enter private schools or move out of the school system boundaries.

In either case, the percentage of live births that will end up enrolling in the public schools must be determined. The live birth count can be obtained from the state or county department of vital statistics. The birth count for the prior most recent five years is obtained, and the percent of that group who enroll in the public schools is applied to that figure. This becomes the expected number of kindergarten students in the first five years of the projections.

These figures are the base data for the remaining projections. In some cases, accurate live birth count is not possible to obtain, or the projections are to be done on a school building-by-building basis, in which case the live birth count for the whole school system cannot accurately be dispersed to each school building. In these circumstances, an alternative method of deriving the kindergarten count must be used. A linear survival ratio can be developed in such cases.

The linear survival ratio is simply the difference in percentage of the number of individuals in a grade one year and the number of individuals in the same grade the following year. This is not the growth or decline of a single group of individuals but rather the change in size of groups occupying a grade from one year to the next. There is a sizable but subtle difference in the two approaches. The survival ratio of a group is more accurate than the difference in the size of a group from one year to another. Nevertheless, this approach can be used if live birth count is not available or accurate.

The survival ratios for the remainder of the grades are developed by dividing the number of students in one grade into the number of students in the next grade a year hence. Students in the first grade one year are in the second grade the next year, or at least a percentage of the original number are then in the second grade. Students who were retained in the original grade, students moving into the school system, and those moving out are accounted for through this mathematical process. The growth and decline of the group is thus accounted for as it progresses through the school system.

The ratio between a cohort in a grade and that same cohort in succeeding grades is developed for all grades, kindergarten through twelfth grade, for the number of years data is available. For example, if there were one hundred students in the kindergarten class one year and only ninety-nine students in the first grade a year later, there would be a loss of students, and that would mean that only 99 percent of the students survived. If this kind of ratio were developed for each kindergarten class for a period of five to ten years, there would be an appropriate number of ratio factors. Each of these ratio factors would be used to obtain a mean ratio between the kindergarten and first grade cohorts for the period of time.

This arithmetical average would be used to project kindergarten cohorts into the first grade for succeeding years. Similar mean ratios would be developed for each grade, using the number of students in one cohort divided into the number of students in that same cohort a year later. The number of years of student enrollment history available will determine the base years for the mean ratios. The more years included in the database, the better the results of the projections.

A mean survival ratio should be developed for each grade, kindergarten through eleven, by using the same mathematical process of dividing the number of students in one grade cohort into the number of students in the next grade cohort for the succeeding year. The mean survival ratio should then be applied to the current enrollment in each grade of the school system. The mean survival ratio is applied for each year the projections are to be developed, five or ten years. The result will be a set of student enrollment projections for kindergarten through grade twelve for a specified period of time that can be used for a variety of planning purposes throughout the school system.

Linear ratios can be developed between the size of a grade cohort one year and the size in succeeding years. These ratios can be used to develop a complete set of student projections. This is done by dividing the number of students in the particular grade in one year into the number of students enrolled in the same grade the next year and following. This ratio simply tells the difference between the size of groups in various years. This methodology does not track a single group through the years to determine the change in size. This variation in methodology is probably best used to determine kindergarten enrollments as described earlier. Such a set of projections could be used best for comparison purposes with other methods of projection.

The cohort survival method of projecting student enrollments is the most widely used method in the United States (Cary, 2011). Almost every state uses the cohort survival method to determine future enrollments because it is simple and easy to calculate. Data needed for the mathematical process is readily available. There is also a great deal of accuracy in this method. Although some demographers believe the regression analysis is more accurate than the survival ratio, an equal number believe the survival ratio method is just as accurate as the regression analysis. The survival ratio methodology accounts for the individual factors influencing enrollments, such as movement into and away from the school system, retention, death, annexation, housing change, and employment change. These factors, coupled with the ease of handling data and the universality of the method, speak for continued use of the methodology throughout the school systems in the country.

There are some disadvantages to the methodology, however. Sudden growth or decline in the community may be moderated to the point of not having sufficient influence upon growth patterns in the future. If a community is growing rapidly in the most recent years, a ten-year database may not identify or allow the real impact of recent growth or decline to influence future enrollment figures. In such cases, demographers must augment the cohort survival ratios with supporting community growth indices to corroborate the original findings or to modify the projections to account for previously unidentified community developments. In addition, unless the survival ratio is continually updated with current enrollment histories, any small margin of error is magnified in succeeding years. This is true of any set of projections regardless of the methodology.

Table 5.2 contains a set of projections derived through the grade level cohort survival ratio methodology. Table 5.3 illustrates the results of a linear cohort survival ratio methodology.

COMPUTER-DRIVEN PROJECTIONS PROGRAMS

At one time, all projections were completed by a person doing the computation by hand or with a calculator. This was a time consuming operation, but it was the only way projections could be done. Needless to say, there were many times mistakes were made. The likelihood of mistakes was present at all times. Even with the most sophisticated calculator, projections were a time-consuming operation that was subject to error.

With the advent of the computer, projections became a much easier job. The computer permitted demographers to handle larger sets of data and produce projections sooner. Computer software programs are currently on the market that can be used to project student enrollments on the school building level using the cohort survival methodology. Such programs are available from a number of commercial concerns and even universities. In addition, educational consultants can develop such software for a school system. Some school systems have developed indigenous-survival ratio programs to fit local concerns.

The programs developed by most commercial firms are what might be termed "generic software" in that they are developed with the mathematical

Table 5.2. School Enrollment Projections from Grade Level Cohort Survival Method, 2020–2029

Grade	2020	2021	2022	2023	2024	2025	2026	2027	2028	2029
K	216	242	200	213	241	240	240	239	238	238
1	335	269	275	248	249	291	290	290	289	288
2	272	297	265	270	237	239	280	279	279	279
3	279	285	300	276	259	237	239	280	279	279
4	334	282	281	294	278	261	238	240	282	280
5	234	320	280	295	282	273	257	234	236	277
6	288	259	332	301	316	263	254	239	218	220
7	309	265	251	311	288	307	256	247	232	212
8	364	318	262	256	327	289	308	257	248	233
9	311	337	321	271	275	324	287	306	255	246
10	266	238	257	239	238	222	262	232	247	206
11	280	229	208	229	247	214	200	236	209	223
12	221	252	214	204	246	237	206	192	227	200
Sp. Ed.	80	87	95	92	73	81	82	78	78	76
Total	**3,789**	**3,682**	**3,541**	**3,514**	**3,556**	**3,478**	**3,399**	**3,348**	**3,317**	**3,257**

Table 5.3. School Enrollment Projections from Linear Cohort Survival Method, 2020–2029

Grade	2020	2021	2022	2023	2024	2025	2026	2027	2028	2029
K	216	242	200	213	241	240	239	238	238	238
1	335	269	275	248	249	246	243	239	217	212
2	272	297	265	270	237	232	227	222	217	212
3	279	285	300	276	259	250	241	233	225	217
4	334	282	281	294	278	272	269	264	259	254
5	234	230	280	295	282	280	278	276	274	272
6	288	259	332	301	316	313	310	307	304	301
7	309	265	251	311	288	285	282	278	275	272
8	364	318	262	256	327	329	271	269	267	265
9	311	337	321	271	275	273	271	269	267	265
10	266	238	257	239	238	237	237	236	236	235
11	280	229	208	229	247	254	261	268	275	282
12	221	254	214	204	246	255	264	274	284	295
Sp.Ed.	80	87	95	92	73	83	82	83	82	2
Total	3,789	3,682	3,541	3,514	3,556	3,549	3,536	3,523	3,507	3,596

processes to serve as many applications as possible with no modifications for local demographic factors or conditions. By using the mathematical process of the method alone, questionable projections may result. The mathematical projection of a set of enrollment figures may produce results out of proportion to what is perceived by knowledgeable local school personnel.

When a school system is in the market for a commercial software package, school personnel should determine the exact method of projection that will be used and whether or not the program can be modified to fit local conditions. Based upon answers to this question, school systems should be able to make an intelligent decision regarding applicability of the program. School systems may also wish to obtain the services of a knowledgeable educational consultant to assist in the evaluation. The school system may employ an educational consultant to develop a program that will fit the needs of the school system just as economically as purchasing commercial software.

FORECASTING BY USE OF GEOREFERENCED DATA

This method of projecting student enrollments is sometimes called the land-saturation analysis method because the line of projections proceeds to the time when all land in the school system is used for the intended zoning purpose, and a count of students can be made. This method is usually considered the most comprehensive of all methods of projecting student enrollments in a limited geographical area (Slagle, 2000). It is the most costly method to initiate and to maintain because of the need to keep the system up-to-date at all times.

The premise upon which this methodology is based is that eventually all land in a given geographical area will be used for some purpose and that projections can be made from that utilization. Each parcel of land in a school system has a designation for use given by the zoning board of the local government. This zoning designation allows the owner to use the land for the purpose requested and to build appropriate structures upon it to accommodate the purpose.

Thus, if a parcel of land has a zoning of R-1, the owner can build a single dwelling upon the site. The owner may not build a car wash or apartment on the site because of the zoning regulation. Zoning regulations cover all types of land use from farming to commercial and heavy industry to a variety of residential zoning designations. These regulations allow an owner to use the property for designated purposes and at the same time prohibit that person or company from using the land for purposes other than the designated one.

Land in the school system that contains some type of housing is of concern to school planners because these are certain types of property from which students are generated. Exact counts of individuals living in existing housing can be made through a census canvas. Base data for the georeferenced system comes from the census that a school system conducts. Almost every school system in the country is required to conduct some type of enumeration of youngsters in the service area. These canvasses may be performed on an annual, biannual, or triennial basis. Data obtained from each canvas provides the school system with base information about the makeup of the various sections of the school system.

Most school systems conduct a thorough enumeration of the residents and, as a result, have an excellent database. Unless diligence is exercised in gathering census data in these canvasses, the school system may be handicapped in trying to project student enrollment in the future. In some instances, particularly in large urban school systems, U.S. Census data is used as the database.

The reason for this is the enormity of the task of counting every individual in a large metropolitan area. The expense of the effort and the amount of time needed to organize and execute such an undertaking makes it mandatory to use U.S. Census data. There are problems, however, that must be overcome in using this data. In most situations, the boundaries of the census tracts do not match either the individual school building attendance area or the school system boundaries. Extrapolation and adjustments have to be made in the data to conform to the boundaries of the school system. Regardless of the source of data, an accurate count of individuals will provide invaluable data about the composition of the school system.

From this data, an index or factor can be developed describing the family that lives in each dwelling. Various family indices can be developed to reflect differences in type of housing. For instance, the family index may be different for families living in multiple-family units than in single-family units. A single-family dwelling unit on a one-acre tract might produce a different family composition index from a dwelling situated on one-tenth of an acre or on a five-acre tract. Each living unit type can produce a different family index. After analysis of the census data and the development of family indices, this factor can be used to project the number of students generated by new housing developments of any sort. Each dwelling unit is multiplied by the specific family composition index to determine the total number of individuals the new development will produce.

The family composition index should also indicate the breakdown within the housing unit. The index should describe the number of adults who are in the family and the number of dependents by age grouping. For instance, the school age grouping should show what percent of the family would be preschool aged, elementary school aged, and middle and secondary school aged. If the family composition index was 2.97, the breakdown should include what percent of that number would be in each age group—1.65 adults; 0.10 preschool child; 0.67 elementary school child; 0.45 middle school child; 0.10 high school child. These percentages can then be applied to new housing units to project the number of students that will be generated by that type of housing. In this manner, total student projections of sections of housing and of the entire school system can be developed.

Growth in the school system will result from changes in land use or development of vacant land. When land that is zoned residential is developed, such plans must come before the local governing body. Likewise, changes in zoning from one type to another must also be approved. Thus, sufficient notification of proposed changes in use or zoning of any tract of land can be detected by the school system by perusal of the official minutes of the local governing body. Changes in zoning designations can be made upon application to the proper governmental body and office. Application is usually made to the zoning board and, if approved, the local governing board ratifies the approval so that the comprehensive planning map of the area can be officially changed.

Such changes occur when economic conditions warrant a different use for the land. For instance, suburban farm owners may change the zoning designation of the farm to that of a residential area so that new housing can be constructed to accommodate a growing population. Such abrupt changes in zoning designation require more than a simple letter of request by the owner; when such changes occur, the development of the land by means of a plot plan is required by the zoning board. This document assures fidelity of the land development to requested changes in zoning ordinances. Each plot on the plan is examined to assure proper land coverage, utilities, traffic, land impaction, social and civic services, and other requirements. All such changes must first be passed by the zoning board and subsequently by the governing board so that such action may become public knowledge.

The success of a land-saturation analysis system of projecting student enrollments is predicated upon close cooperation between the local government offices and the school system. Proper and timely notification of changes in land use and zoning is essential if the school system is to obtain the type data needed to organize and keep the system up to date. Information on proposed changes is passed on to the school system through the official minutes of the zoning board and local governing board, copies of tentative tract maps, staff memoranda, and even informal communications. The land-saturation analysis system was originally developed to predict the rate and nature of residential growth in undeveloped school systems (Gilmore, 1974).

Other types of development, such as urban renewal, can also result in growth. Although the data regarding this type of development is area specific, it nevertheless needs to be monitored to provide a comprehensive view of the school system. The basic resource of community growth is residential development on zoned land, regardless of where it is situated in the school system. Specific data needed for land-saturation analysis may vary from one school system to another, but the basic information will include the following:

- Current zoning by parcel or study area
- Gross acres of undeveloped land by zoning type
- Net acres of undeveloped land by zoning type
- Projected number of dwelling units by parcel or study area predicted on zoning density allowances
- Estimated year of development for each tract
- Number and type of new dwelling units projected per year for planning time frame—five, ten, or fifteen years
- Number of bedrooms per dwelling unit
- Address and location description
- Developer's name and address
- Price range
- Rental range
- Critical development factors, such as sewer line extension, new roads, industry, flood plain work, annexation
- Yearly development estimate by study area
- Survey of proposed subdivisions under consideration
- Undeveloped acreage by school attendance area
- Breakdown of projected yearly dwelling units by attendance area
- Proposed general zoning plans, which could change density allowance
- Urban redevelopment master plan
- Survey of requested and issued building permits
- Survey of issued occupancy permits

Several advantages are associated with the land-saturation analysis methodology. A good deal of confidence can be placed in the accuracy of the projections. The nature of the increase in student enrollments and the direction of growth can be predicted with a high degree of accuracy. The timing of the growth can also be anticipated to a high degree based upon estimates of completion of housing developments and upon actual completions as verified by occupancy permits. Just as this may be an advantage, there is also a disadvantage in the timing because there is no way to predict precisely when a housing development will be completed and occupied.

Many factors outside the control of the developer govern the sale of property, particularly housing.

There are, likewise, some disadvantages to this methodology that limit its use. Firstly, such a system works only where zoning ordinances exist. As strange as it may seem, many rural areas in the country do not have official zoning ordinances to govern land development. Obviously, where such zoning does not exist, a georeferenced system cannot be used. The land-saturation analysis would probably be inappropriate in a large rural area where there is little or limited housing development. Most likely, the most beneficial application of such a system would be in a growing suburban area, although an urban area could most certainly put such a system to good use (Gilmore, 1974).

Another disadvantage of the georeferenced system is the cost to implement and maintain the database used for making projections. Unless the system is constantly updated with current data, the system becomes obsolete in a matter of days or weeks. A school system must commit sufficient resources to have a first-rate system; otherwise the funds are not well spent. Obviously, a good computer hardware and software system is needed, and this increases the cost, but the personnel costs needed to implement and maintain the system are perhaps the most expensive. The availability of good data for decision-making by school personnel, however, should more than compensate for such costs.

In addition, the extension of the georeferenced system into other areas of administrative decision-making of the school system could well justify the cost of the system. There are many possibilities for extending the land-saturation analysis system into a more sophisticated system of management information that could assist in areas other than student enrollment projections. The land-saturation analysis system data is attached to each parcel of land in the school system and also to the people who inhabit the structure on that parcel. The kinds of data attached to the dwelling and subsequently to the individuals can be as extensive as needed. The school system maintains considerable data on each student that could be attached to the dwelling in which the student lives. Listed below are examples of what such data might include:

- Schools in which the youngsters are enrolled
- Distance from elementary and secondary schools
- Numbers of the buses and routes used by students
- Types of programs in which students are enrolled
- Numbers and kinds of disabled persons
- Racial and sexual designations
- Grade levels

Other data about preschool children, school-aged youngsters, or even adults could be generated and attached to the family group, but all data would be attached to the dwelling in which the family is located. Data about the structure in which the family lives could also be useful for planning purposes. Data about the housing could include:

- Size of the building lots in acres and square feet
- Size and shape of all structures
- Assessed valuation/true market value of the structure
- Additions to the original and date of construction
- Utilities available and used
- Type of zoning

Other types of data about the dwelling might be identified and used, depending upon the planning needs of the school system.

An information system such as this tie selected student and census data to demographic and geographic data forming a comprehensive information system, which is sometimes referred to as a geocoded or georeferenced system. From such a system, many administrative and management decisions could be addressed. For instance, proposed changes in the bus routes caused by student increase could be analyzed through data manipulation. Proposed decisions could be developed and the implications of such decisions analyzed before being implemented. Location of new school buildings could be identified easier through such a data system.

In addition, the closing of a school building, with all of the ramifications, could be analyzed before the fact so that all exigencies could be anticipated. Savings of time and effort could result with the availability of such data, and decisions could be enhanced greatly because of the amount of data (Cooper, 2003).

The heart of any land-saturation or georeferenced information system is the data related to each parcel of land and its location. Much of this data can be obtained through the U.S. Census Bureau's DIME (Dual Independent Map Encoding) file (Gilmore, 1974). This is a geographic base file defining a street network in terms of segments, nodes, enclosed areas, and non-street features such as railroad tracks, municipal boundaries, and rivers. By matching the addresses of students and other demographic data with DIME street segments, the coordinates of a student's house can be interpolated into the system. This enables the system to identify and isolate each dwelling by location for further analysis. Each of the codes can be tied into the existing school attendance areas for compilation into school building groups on elementary, middle school, and high school levels. In addition, the Geographic

Information System contains the same information and is readily available to everyone using a website.

Much of the data needed for each student is currently available within the information system of the school system. This data can be hooked into the geocoded database. The technology and databases needed to implement a georeferenced information system are currently available. All that is needed is to tie the two systems together, which can best be done by marrying the U.S. Census DIME file to the information the school system currently has to form an integrated information system.

STUDENT YIELD INDEX IN
PLANNING FOR STUDENT GROWTH

The cohort survival method is the traditional approach used to project student enrollment. This approach looks at the real numbers of students currently in school and those who have been born within the past five years. This type of projection is relatively accurate when student mobility is low and population trends are relatively stable. The methodology is less accurate, however, where student mobility is high, community development is accelerated, school census data are flawed, or school attendance zones and student entry dates change frequently.

When projecting future enrollment, planners usually can assume that as communities grow the school population grows. But this rule of thumb is not always applicable. Some communities are desirable locations for second homes or retirement complexes, which may increase the population but not necessarily the number of students.

Projecting Enrollments

It is unusual, but happens occasionally in a local school system, that a community experiences growth in the general population and a decline in student population. In areas where it is desirable to have second homes, the local school system will find a growth in the general population, yet also find a decrease in student population. In such instances, the cohort survival method of projecting student populations may not be as accurate as desired.

Also, in communities where there are pockets of development, the school authorities need to know how many students such pockets of growth will produce. This would call for the use of the student yield index to determine the potential student population in the community being developed.

Normally, a student yield index can be developed using data from the county or city government office responsible for maintaining an official listing of all real estate transactions. That local county office maintains a listing of all residences by address, assessed value of the residence, and other demographic data relevant to government needs. Unfortunately, in some localities this data may not be available to school personnel because of privacy concerns held by the county or city office. Therefore, planners might have to look to other data to help them project enrollment.

An alternative source of data could well be the building permits issued for new residences by the county or city government. Building permits for the past five years might be valuable data because they would accurately represent recent demographic development of the county or city.

The first step in developing a student yield index is to obtain the building permits that were issued for housing of any sort. Building permits without a street address are not usable because it is unknown if the permit is for housing or commercial construction. In addition, the permit cannot be traced to a student address.

The pool of building permits with street addresses are then classified according to the value of the building. The local school board can determine the different categories of value of the building permit to form a classification of housing from the least expensive to the most expensive. In many instances a four or five category designation of residences can be acceptable. These categories might be something on the order of the folowing categories:

- $0–$100,000
- $100,001–$200,000
- $200,001–$300,000
- $300,001+

The next step is to match the street addresses of the residences from the building permits with the street addresses of the students enrolled in the schools. This process needs to be completed by local school system personnel because of privacy concerns. A specially designed computer program will need to be developed for this task. The result is a single listing of residences within the value categories and with addresses identified where students live and addresses where there are no students enrolled in the local public school system.

The next procedure is to enumerate the total number of students in each value category of the building permits and divide this number into the total number of residences within the category. This computation will give the student yield according to the value of residence, which is basically the average number of students who live in a certain type of residence. This is done for each value category of residences.

It is also beneficial to know the grade level of each student. To obtain this data the indices needs to be further broken down into elementary and second-ary students by applying the percentage of elementary and secondary students currently enrolled in the schools to the total enrollment of the school system. By applying these elementary and secondary indices to new housing, the lo-cal school system can approximate the number of each level of student being generated by new housing (Earthman, 2006).

Obstacles to Accuracy

School officials face challenges with this methodology for the following reasons:

- In most states, the local school system is independent of the local govern-ment; a local school system must rely on the cooperation of the local gov-ernment to obtain the information.
- In some cases, the data available is not up-to-date or accurate. Errors tend to creep into data that is not kept current on a monthly basis.
- In those states where local school systems are organized on a district level, the data may not be as discrete as it would be if the school system was organized on a municipal or county basis.
- Merging two sets of data can be challenging. The data set from the local school system must align in some fashion to the data from the local govern-ment office. County or city data focuses mainly on the property owned by individuals within the county. Thus, this data is tied directly to the address of a piece of property or real estate. The data may also be divided into magisterial districts for certain tax purposes. On the other hand, the local school system data is aggregated based on school attendance areas. One government unit might use a complete address and the other government unit may use abbreviations of some sort or not require a street address, so matching may be a problem.
- Whoever submits the building application can ascribe any amount of value to the construction project. In other words, a developer can state the value of a residence will be $160,000 whereas the developer will eventually sell the residences for a much higher price when it is completed. As a result, an accurate count of the number of residences in specific value categories is impossible for such cases (Earthman, 2006).

The most profitable use of student yield indices is in localities that are expe-riencing rapid growth and where the normal cohort survival method cannot keep up with such growth (Gilmore, 1974).

The student yield index cannot take the place of a more conventional projection method such as the cohort survival method, but it can be used to augment the results of the projection method. In addition, the student yield index can identify student growth in specific geographic areas that are smaller than the usual school attendance zone. Being able to project the number of new students in a subarea of a specific school attendance zone would be helpful to educational planners because the cohort survival method could not project for such a specific area.

The student yield index cannot be specific in projecting the exact age or grade level of students, yet it can be modified to permit identification of elementary and secondary school students. Therefore, the student yield index is a very useful tool for the educational planner to use as a supplement to conventional methods of projecting student populations.

The importance of student enrollment projections to the planning process of a school system cannot be emphasized enough. Such data is necessary for all types of decisions, including where and when new school buildings are needed. In addition, decisions in other areas of the school enterprise use future student numbers as a basis. The prudent administrator, however, recognizes the limitations of any set of student enrollment projections. All such projections are based upon certain assumptions about the development of an identified geopolitical area. For the most part, demographers assume that future development will reflect past development.

To the extent that assumption is correct, a great deal of reliability can be placed in the projections. This reliability can be enhanced by having current data, but there are always limitations that should be placed upon use of exact numbers contained in projections. Although projections give an idea of the numbers of students involved and the direction and rate of growth, school planners should observe caution in using the results of any set of projections for decision-making.

SUMMARY

Educators need to know how many students will always be enrolled in the schools to provide the needed learning spaces for them. This is ever more important to know about future enrollments in order to give the school system enough time to provide the physical learning space to accommodate the student body. In this chapter, four methods of projecting student enrollments were discussed: forecasting by analogy, forecasting from total population, forecasting by cohort survival ratios, and forecasting by using georeferenced data. Each method has advantages and disadvantages that should be recognized.

In addition, the Student Yield Index was suggested for projections of a small geographical area. While there is no one best system, neither is one method necessarily the most accurate, although some methods have more promise than others. Each method is used by school planners and has a place in the planning process. The cohort survival method is probably the most widely used method of projecting students. State departments of education almost universally use this method of projecting student populations.

Chapter 6

Long-Range Planning
Evaluation of Existing Facilities

The long-range plan contains a description of the educational program to be offered in the school system in the present and over the next few years. In addition, the plan projects present and future student populations that need to be housed. Once the program and the anticipated number of students are set, the next task is to determine how students will be housed. One aspect of this task is determining what buildings are currently available and what will be needed for future changes in the educational program and number of students entering school.

Long-range planning can only be done by evaluating all the buildings used for educational purposes. This evaluation should establish the capability of each building to sustain the program needs and student population of the school system. For example, if a school system decides to convert to a middle school program, there are strong implications for building change. All intermediate or junior high school buildings in the school system will have to be evaluated for possible structural changes and conversions to accommodate the educational program change.

If the program change is to be accomplished within the period of the long-range plan, building changes must be made in a timely fashion. This way the program can be implemented before the end of the current long-range plan. In addition, the grade configuration change from a junior high or intermediate organization to a middle school organization may affect the capacity of the buildings scheduled for change. This inextricable tie between educational program, number of students, and building must always be recognized (Earthman, 1990).

Each structure must be evaluated to understand how the present inventory of school buildings can fit the expected program. The purpose of evaluating the existing buildings are to:

- determine which existing facilities will be able to accommodate the desired program with the given number of students
- ascertain what improvements to any buildings are necessary to enable the facility to work better
- develop a list of building improvements and maintenance items to be included in the capital improvement program
- provide data on which to base subsequent designs of new buildings or additions
- determine the extent each facility aids in desegregation and reacts to population shifts and declines
- verify existing available teaching spaces in the school system or to gather data to implement such an inventory (Earthman, 1990)

EVALUATION TEAMS

A team headed by a representative of the school facilities department should carry out the building evaluations. Team members should include the principal and selected teachers from the particular building. Team members should be knowledgeable about instructional methodology, curriculum, educational technology, and structural and mechanical engineering.

The team should have a representative from the central administration curriculum and instruction office as well. It is important that the central administration be represented because of possible educational program changes that will be implemented system wide during the long-range plan. In addition, representatives from the architecture and construction section of the facilities department should be included (if such personnel are available). Small school systems that do not have such personnel may wish to employ an outside educational consultant to assist with the evaluation. This practice is common in both large and small school systems.

If the task warrants, this evaluation team can be augmented by curriculum specialists drawn from various sources. The task of the team is to evaluate the building to gather data for use in improving it. In extreme cases data can be gathered to assist the school board in deciding whether to keep the building in service or to convert it for other purposes.

FREQUENCY OF EVALUATION

The frequency of evaluation depends on the purpose of the evaluation. Several levels of evaluation should be performed during the life of the school building. Repeated evaluations throughout the life of the building ensure the building is maintained and that it adequately houses the students and educational programs over the years.

The initial building evaluation is conducted when the building is first constructed, then, periodically, the building must be completely reevaluated in terms of number of students and type of program housed. At the beginning of every long-range program, each building in the school system should be assessed by an evaluation team as described above. The basis of the evaluation is the program description in the long-range plan, but the general condition of the building should also be inspected. All the systems in the building should be inspected and evaluated to determine their current condition and any need for improvement.

Systems such as heating, ventilation and air conditioning, lighting, plumbing, and communication should be reviewed for efficiency or need for improvement. Basic structural components like the roof, floors, walls, and fenestration should be reviewed as well. Such an evaluation will require the services of an architect and engineer. If the school system does not have such services on the staff, a consultant must be retained.

Some systems also think it wise to obtain the services of an educational consultant, especially if their staff is relatively small. Outside educational consultants bring a sense of objectivity that district employees cannot and, according to research findings, outside consultants better identify facility changes needed to accommodate the given educational program than can the building principal.

MAINTENANCE EVALUATION

Another level of appraisal is the annual evaluation for maintenance needs. The building principal, custodian, and a representative of the teaching faculty should perform this evaluation. There may be times when the principal desires the services of a subject matter specialist or other expert from the central administration to assist in the evaluation. This might be appropriate when there are educational program changes in the offing (Earthman and Lemasters, 2004).

This annual review should be used to identify maintenance items that have developed during the year but which are not of an emergency nature. Emergency repairs such as broken windows, clogged plumbing, broken doors, and the like, of course, require immediate attention and are handled through a different system. Items that might be addressed in the annual evaluation include conversion of a room, construction of shelves, change of lighting, or additional water service.

Items identified through this evaluation are sent to the office in charge of the capital improvement plan for inclusion on the list of changes and improvements scheduled for that building. Next, the items are again prioritized cooperatively by the central administration and building principal and become part of the capital improvement program.

SPECIAL EVALUATIONS

At times, a special evaluation of a facility needs to be made outside of the regular appraisals conducted in conjunction with development of the long-range plan. Rapid changes in student population, major changes in educational programs, or structural building failures are all reasons for a special appraisal. Depending upon the circumstances, the school system may need new data on several buildings, all buildings, or just one building. Sometimes special evaluative instruments are used to gather the data. These occasions may require the services of an educational consultant to construct an appraisal survey and conduct the evaluation. This is frequently the case when a school system has failed to conduct frequent and periodic evaluations of its buildings and the effort becomes a bootstrap operation to bring the school system up to current expectations.

APPRAISAL INSTRUMENT

To evaluate a building effectively, an appropriate appraisal instrument is needed. Building evaluation instruments assist the team in reporting the condition of the facility by summarizing and organizing what the evaluators should observe. Items covered include the configuration of the building, furniture and equipment available, lighting, temperature, general conditions, specific features needed for specialized programs, accessibility by handicapped persons, numbers and kinds of spaces available, technology systems, and support services, just to mention a few (CEFPI, 2004).

Building evaluation instruments have been developed by states, individual school systems, professional organizations, and individuals. Examples can be found in any textbook on school facility planning or numerous websites. Examples of appraisal instruments include:

- *CDW-G 21st Century Classroom Assessment Tool* (2010)
- Collaborative for High Performance Schools Operations Report Card (2010), Collaborative for High Performance Schools, San Francisco, CA
- Facility Inspection Tool Guidelines (2009), Coalition for School Housing, Sacramento, CA
- Master Facilities Plan Evaluation Checklist (2008), 21st Century School Fund, Washington, DC

These guides can serve as a starting point for a building evaluation. Each must be modified to meet the particular needs and desires of the local school system as well as the regulations mandated by the state in which the school system is located.

INDIGENOUS EVALUATION INSTRUMENTS

In order to take into consideration local conditions, many school systems develop an instrument for local use, such as facility demands or local pedagogical practices. Many states require large tracts of land for school sites; however, urban school systems must accommodate buildings on small, heavily impacted sites. Locally developed instruments can take this disparity into account. A locally developed evaluative instrument can be used over a period of years, providing consistent data on each school building in the system. Development of such an instrument can be done by the school district's facilities department. Appendix A contains a building evaluation form developed by a school system.

Most standard evaluative instruments use a predetermined number of items that are given a numerical score to indicate how well the item meets certain requirements. The most commonly used scale ranges from 1 to 5. Such a scale ensures uniformity of evaluation because each space in the building, as well as the site, has a specified number of items to evaluate, and each item requires a score. Such a scale allows a person to check the appropriate evaluation and arrive at a total.

This uniformity is further enhanced by listing each space with predetermined items to evaluate. In this way, such instruments enable successive evaluators to consider the same items using the same scale. This permits the school system to have a certain degree of uniformity in the evaluations for each building over time.

EVALUATION DATA

Each evaluation produces data about each building in the school system. The data consists of a list of projects or tasks to be completed to keep the school building in a state of good repair and to provide the kinds of spaces and accoutrements that enable the educational program to function properly. These projects need to be incorporated into the capital improvement program.

Most school systems separate regular maintenance projects on existing buildings from other capital improvement projects such as additions to existing buildings and new buildings. Often, the maintenance program is separate from the regular capital program and even funded differently from the operational budget of the school system. In unusual circumstances, maintenance projects may be funded through bond funds, however, this may not be the best use of these funds because of the long-term payback and the interest costs over a period of years and the short-term nature of the project. Major maintenance projects such as new roofs and heating systems may well be funded under capital funds because of the long life of these items. The periodic and annual evaluations of school facilities will produce items that can be classified as typical maintenance projects and at the same time identify needed capital improvements to the building. All these must be prioritized if included in the maintenance list.

Central administration and building personnel should work together to prioritize items, deciding which to fund first and which to fund later. Some items identified by the central administration staff may have priority over other items because of prior knowledge of the condition of the building or because of a district-wide preventative maintenance program. In other cases, items related to various programs or particular circumstances in the local school organization may determine the priority. In any event, both the building principal and staff and the central administration personnel must be satisfied with the final priority list.

Following this, the items are placed on the maintenance list or schedule of the school system and funded in order of the priorities set. The funding pattern may well extend throughout the entire five to seven years of the long-range plan. Both the annual and periodic evaluation of the school building should include an appraisal of the following areas:

- ability to support the educational program
- adaptability of the building
- aesthetic quality of the building
- structural soundness
- site conditions

- operational and maintenance efficiency
- condition of mechanical systems
- compliance with safety rules (Earthman and Lemasters, 2004)

Only through a system of periodic and annual evaluations will the school system identify projects needed to maintain its facilities in good repair. Through prioritization, the items on the maintenance schedule will be accomplished in a timely fashion. In this manner, the facility needs of the school system can be met within the resources available. School facilities are a valuable community resource that needs to be kept in the best possible condition at all times. Proper evaluation of the facilities will provide the necessary data to assist school personnel in completing this task.

SUMMARY

Long-range planning can only be done by evaluating all buildings used for educational purposes. This evaluation should establish the capability of each building to sustain the program needs and student population of the school system. To understand properly how the present inventory of school buildings can fit the expected program, each structure must be evaluated. The team that conducts the evaluation should be headed by someone from central administration and should also include the principal and selected teachers. Additionally, curriculum specialists may assist in the evaluation of the buildings. The frequency of evaluation will depend upon the size of the student body and curricular changes. There is also a need for a building evaluation to determine maintenance needs to keep the building in good working order. The evaluative instrument can be either on the market or an indigenous instrument designed for local needs. Data from the evaluation should be utilized to form the list of facility needs for the future or in the case of maintenance needs to form the maintenance schedule.

Chapter 7

Long-Range Planning

Financial Planning

The financial considerations for a long-range plan should be coordinated with other planning efforts. The success of any plan is defined by having the necessary financial support exactly when it is needed to pay for implementation. Without this coordination, the planning effort is severely blunted and becomes an expensive exercise for the school system.

Individuals and offices responsible for the financial support of the long-range plan should provide their input to the planning process from the onset. Beyond initial planning, advice on the financial resources and constraints of the school system is always needed by school planners at crucial points along the planning schedule. Coordination of efforts is best done through a planning council of the school district. The planning council usually reports directly to the superintendent of schools. In small- and medium-sized school systems, the planning council might be a small group representing the major areas of responsibility in the school system.

Periodic meetings of the council keep members current with the process of the planning effort and, at the same time, address problems. The coordinating mechanism of the planning council assists the school system in producing tightly written long-range plans that reflect the needs and resources of the school system and its clientele.

The financial portion of the long-range plan must identify resources for both operational and capital projects. This means that both the annual and longer-term funding of capital projects is addressed. Even though the long-range plan covers several years, only one year of the plan is funded at a time. Consequently, the financial portion of the long-range plan deals with resources for two major aspects of operation: the day-by-day running of the school system and the longer-term capital projects.

The idea behind the funding package of the long-range plan is to know the sources of revenues and how to apply them and then to put this together into a cohesive plan of action. Funding for the operational portion of the long-range plan comes from state contributions through some type of formula, local contributions from taxation, and whatever federal funding that is available.

Capital project funding is developed in much the same fashion. The local financial planner must be knowledgeable about the types and sources of funding for capital projects in the particular state and how to obtain them. The success of not only the long-range plan but also the capital improvement budget depends on the availability of sufficient funding at the proper time to complete each project.

The funding for capital projects can come from a variety of sources: a new school building may be financed from a single bond issue while an addition to an existing building might be funded from the annual operations budget of the school system. Both projects, however, are considered capital projects. Operational funds could also fund major renovations and the purchase of school sites, buses, and major equipment. All these projects are capital expenditures. A school system could construct, if resources were available, a new school building from the annual operating budget. Such expenditures, however, are extremely rare because the large cost of a new school means that such a financial impact could not be sustained. However, these examples do show the flexibility in the use of operational funds. Capital funds do not have that flexibility of use.

The designation of capital and operational funds is derived from the manner in which the funds are obtained and expended. Both funds come from state and local tax revenues. Operational funds are obtained through annual tax collections on both levels, while capital funds are derived from the local school system going into debt for a specific purpose or through some form of state aid. When this is done, the funds obtained can be spent for only the stated purpose: constructing a building or completing a similar project.

Funds left over from the project, if any, must be returned to the taxpayer unless the school board can legally reallocate them to another capital project that can be completed with the excess funds. In some states, this action must be taken only through a referendum of the voters. In this manner, the control of capital funds is derived from how funds are obtained. Capital funds cannot be used for operational purposes such as the daily operation of the school system.

The entire maintenance program of the school system is funded through the annual operational budget. Maintenance projects identified through the school building evaluation completed for the long-range plan are included in a maintenance and alternations schedule that is tied into the funding package of the long-range plan. Some of these projects are quite substantial in scope and cost, but if the projects are to keep the building in a state of good repair, they should be funded under the operational budget (Chan and Richardson, 2005; Holt, 2002).

There is an inextricable tie between the long-range plan of the school system and the capital improvement plan developed to house the educational program. The long-range plan follows a logical pattern of development to describe the type of educational program offered in a geographic area. The long-range plan further describes how many students will be involved in the educational program, which gives a clue to the number of facilities that will be needed to house properly the number of students. After an evaluation of the existing buildings to determine how many students can be accommodated, the deficit (if any) in classroom space must be recognized and eliminated by constructing new space.

This correlation between programs offered, number of students enrolled, and available spaces produces the number of new school buildings or classrooms that will need to be constructed. This need for new construction must be addressed through the financial portion of the long-range plan. School systems receive funding for programs from many sources, including all three levels of government. In addition, sources other than the government contribute to the operation of the public school systems of the country. Such is not the case for capital project funding. The sources of funding for such projects are very limited.

FEDERAL GOVERNMENT FUNDING

The federal government provides limited funding of public schools because it does not have the responsibility for educating citizens. Federal funding is usually restricted to program initiatives and personnel development programs. Even in these instances, the programs that are assisted financially are ones that impinge directly upon the welfare of the country. This rather unique position results from provisions within the U.S. Constitution. The Tenth Amendment to the Constitution, known as the Reserve Clause, reserves to the states any power not designated by the Constitution to the federal government (Alexander and Alexander, 2012). Education, or the responsibility for providing an education, is not mentioned in the Constitution, and is therefore a responsibility of the states and not the federal government.

It is important to keep this in mind when considering the financial effort of that level of government in assisting local school systems in housing educational programs. Because of this clause, the federal government has not been noted for providing construction funds to local school systems on a general basis. Only in very specific cases has that branch of the government provided funds of any consequence for such an effort.

Undoubtedly, the Northwest Ordinance of 1797 was the first effort of the federal government to assist local school systems in building schoolhouses under which the sixteenth and thirty-second townships of government lands were donated for local purposes (Alexander and Alexander, 2012). This could be considered the offering of a site for a school building. Such offers were made to each territory when it became a state, and many local school systems were organized around that geographic location.

Perhaps the most recent effort to assist local school systems with school building problems was during and immediately after World War II. Under the Impact Aid Program of the Landrum Act of 1941, the federal government provided funds to local school systems to purchase sites, construct buildings, pay for fees, and equip the schools. Only school systems that were affected by the impaction of federal workers in the area were eligible for such funds; the vast majority of school systems were not eligible. School systems near military bases, armament factories, or other war efforts were the only ones to receive assistance. The greatest funding for this program was during the war years, with the effort dwindling as the need lessened. In 1943, $80 million was appropriated for this program, but one year later, in 1944, only $20 million was allocated. As the war ended, the need subsided, and the act was subsequently not funded and expired.

The federal government has provided, from time to time, construction funds for vocational schools. In 1963, Congress passed the Regional Vocational High School Act that provided funds for planning and constructing regional vocational schools throughout the country. Originally, planning funds were available, with the possibility of matching funds for construction following. The act was not sufficiently funded to complete the planned projects, and the lack of local funding on a regional basis meant that very few buildings were constructed.

In the same vein, the government provided construction funding for vocational schools in selected impoverished areas. Under the Appalachian Regional Development Act of 1965, construction funds were allocated for such institutions. Only limited funds were allocated each year. In 1976, for example, just $10 million was available for the entire Appalachian region, insufficient to make an impact upon the diverse population in such a large geographical area. Since then, no construction funds have been available under that legislation.

Another piece of special-purpose legislation was the Emergency Relief Act of 1974 and 1983. The latter version of this act provided construction funds to localities to rebuild governmental and public buildings destroyed by flood conditions in Virginia and West Virginia. In this area, the damage to the local infrastructure was so complete that the federal government felt compelled to provide funding under the general welfare clause of the Constitution. School building replacement was included under this program of restoring the local infrastructure. This one-time program is no longer funded.

The removal of asbestos from public buildings is considered a national problem that deserves attention from the federal government. The asbestos removal program funded by the federal government provided planning funds to allow local school systems to identify sources of asbestos and develop a plan for its removal. Funding for the actual removal of asbestos in the public schools, however, was extremely limited, which forced local school systems to provide matching funds. The mandatory provisions of the legislation that require asbestos removal provided a strong impetus to sanitize quickly every building. Most school systems have completed such a program for elimination of asbestos in the school buildings.

The federal government also has an interest in the education of special populations. Most of the funding has been for educational programs of various sorts and for personnel retraining. The government, however, has taken the lead in ensuring that buildings are accessible to the handicapped. Through the Education for All Handicapped Children Act of 1976 and Section 504 of the Rehabilitation Act, the federal government has made provision for handicapped students to have access to buildings owned and operated by local school systems. Funds available through these acts, however, are for planning purposes, and not for the actual renovation of the building. These pieces of legislation have not been funded at a sufficient level to provide relief to local school systems in complying with the mandatory provisions of the acts.

One of the most far-reaching pieces of federal legislation concerning school facilities was the Housing and Community Development Act of 1968. Under this act, local school systems were reimbursed for certain costs associated with land banking of school sites identified in the long-range plan and purchased in advance of need. Funds were available for reimbursement of settlement costs, relocation costs, and interest on bonds used to purchase parcels of land. The concept of acquisition of sites in advance of actual need was quite far-reaching and encouraged long-range planning by the local school system. School systems apparently did not take advantage of this opportunity because the 1973 Capital Improvement Budget document of the School District of Philadelphia stated that only one other locality than themselves had made an application for funds under this act. This legislation was not funded in subsequent years.

The federal government has provided funds for new construction on college and university campuses at different times. Such legislation, however, has been for special disciplines. The Higher Education Facilities Act of 1992 provided funds for the construction of science and mathematics buildings. In the implementation stage, $230 million was appropriated for a three-year period for such projects throughout the country for both public and private institutions of higher education. Subsequent revisions to that legislation in 1992 reduced the amount available to colleges and universities.

From time to time, every governmental level has surplus property that must be disposed. The federal government began such a program shortly after World War II, when it divested a great quantity of war-produced material and equipment. Under the Federal Surplus Property Act of 1941 all types of property were transferred to different levels of government and to individual private citizens. Real property was disposed of by offering sites to other governmental levels first, and then disposing of them to the private sector. Several military camps, arsenals, training sites, and similar facilities were transferred to local school systems. This program is still in operation, but there is virtually no real property included as surplus today.

During the most recent downturn in the economy, special stimulus funds were appropriated for the improvement of educational physical facilities. The Great Recession of 2008 prompted Congress to enact legislation designed to help stimulate the economy. The most notable piece of legislation was the American Recovery and Reinvestment Act (ARRA) of 2009 (P.L. 115-5). This act provided funds to businesses, states, individuals, and even local school systems. Funds appropriated under this act were for businesses in hope to stimulate the stagnate economy. The important provision for education, however, was Section 2.3. This section provided approximately $21 billion of funds to states and local school systems for school modernization.

At the present time those funds have already been appropriated to the states and local school systems. The economic recovery since the enactment of ARRA has not been robust and economists predict a slow recovery. In this light, the prognosis of further funding under this act is rather slim at best, given the current political atmosphere.

In recent years, the federal government has provided limited assistance to improving school facilities by enacting tax credit bond programs. Under these programs the federal government provides tax relief to holders of bonds issued to pay for school facilities. The school systems in turn do not have to pay the interest on the bonds issued to build facilities. This provides some relief to the local school system. Some tax credit bond programs include:

- Qualified School Construction Bonds—Funds to states and local government to repair school facilities

- Qualified Zone Academy Bonds—Funds to local school systems to repair school facilities
- Qualified Energy Conservation Bonds—Funds to local school systems to reduce energy consumption
- Build America Bonds—Low interest bonds to be used to finance construction and modernization of school facilities

School systems must apply for these bond programs, and in some cases must qualify before they can apply. Saving on the bond interest will in many cases enable the school system to construct needed school facilities. Depending upon the interest rate of the bond, the local school system may save up to one-third of the total cost of a new school building over the twenty year period of the bond issue.

For the Qualified School Construction Bonds issuance dated 2010–2012, there were four hundred school systems and states that issued such bonds. This is not a large percentage of the total number of local school systems in the country.

The federal government enacted legislation, the American Recovery and Reinvestment Act of 2009, which provided funds for the emergency repair and modernization of school facilities in response to the economic downturn of 2008. Under provisions of this legislation states and local school systems could apply for grants to repair and modernize school facilities (P.L. 111-5, Section 805).

STATE GOVERNMENT FUNDING

Each state has the responsibility for providing some form of education for all citizens. As a result, each state has developed a system of local schools and a scheme for funding them. Naturally, the funding system reflects the importance citizens place upon education. In addition, each state has made a decision regarding the extent of funding for school buildings. Not all state legislatures have opted to provide state funds to the local school systems for school buildings.

If the financial commitment for school buildings provided by all states could be averaged, the conclusion would be that states do not provide a significant amount to local school systems for school construction. There are several reasons for this. First, there is the belief that the localities should provide housing for students, rather than the state. This belief is rooted in the colonial period, when each family in a locality had to make provision for housing the schoolmaster. Second, the title to the school building is usually held by the locality and it is understood that state funds should not go into property that is owned by the local government.

These reasons may seem trivial in light of present day thinking. Yet, for centuries, these beliefs have governed the actions (or inaction) of state legislatures. The idea of equity among programs and facilities is a recent phenomenon that is only now struggling for acceptance. Likewise, the philosophy that the state government is responsible for providing equality on the local scene is yet to be fully implemented throughout the country.

The amount of assistance a state gives local school systems for new school construction ranges from absolutely no state funds in twelve states to full funding of capital projects in Hawaii. Hawaii, however, has only one local school system and the funding scheme from the state reflects this single entity. Approximately 75 percent of the states provide some type of state assistance that confirms the idea that most states believe in some sort of shared responsibility for providing housing to students.

There are many plans for providing state assistance, but such assistance generally falls into two basic categories: grants-in-aid and loans. Grants are funds that are given outright to the local school system. Loans must be paid back to the state agency; the locality uses state funds for a period, usually under favorable conditions.

Grants-in-Aid

Under this type of assistance, the state funds are given to the local school system and do not have to be paid back. Grants may be outright gifts with no qualifications of the recipient school system. In this instance, each school system qualifies for a certain amount of assistance. Usually grants are on a per-pupil basis, such as a certain amount of capital funds received by the local school system for each student in membership.

Grants can also be made on a classroom basis, where the funds are distributed according to the total number of students divided by a set number of students per classroom unit. For instance, twenty-five students may be the factor used to decide the number of units a school system has, with payment based upon the number of classroom units into which the total student body can be divided. Educational program grants can also be awarded in like manner for state support, but this funding is separate from capital funding.

Grants-in-aid can also be awarded according to some qualification of the school system on a matching basis. Under this provision, a local school system may qualify for a set amount of funds, but that would have to be matched with local capital funds. In some states, the original amount of state funds would be determined by the amount of square feet in the building, certain building components, number of students to be housed, or similar criteria.

In addition, a financial aid factor may compensate for wealth or lack of wealth in a local school system. Under these programs, school systems classified as poor would receive additional compensation over and above the normal grant amount. Twenty-seven percent of the states have enacted grants-in-aid programs to provide state assistance to local school systems. There is an equalized grants program in sixteen states, and the rest have either a flat or matching grants provision (Camp, 1983).

Grants can be given for capital outlay or for debt service. In the latter case, school systems must go into debt and construct the building before any funds are available. Under this type of program, the state provides a grant for the debt thus created upon application by the local school system. These grants go to pay off debt. Under the capital outlay grants programs, the school system usually has to expend funds up front before receiving aid from the state. Some sort of grants program for debt service, equalized, matching, or flat, exists in sixteen states (Educational Writers Association, 1989).

Some states provide grants to local school systems for capital construction based upon a per-pupil count. These grants are awarded regardless of need. Usually the grant amount is very low and, as a result, the school system must advance considerable local funds for any major construction project.

Loan Programs

The second way local school systems receive state assistance for capital projects is through loan programs. Under these programs, a fund is established from which school systems may secure loans. The loans are secured by the title to the property on which the school is located. The local school system may borrow a set amount of money to be used in constructing a school building. The payback for the loan is usually over a twenty-year period.

The interest rates of state loan programs are usually below the rates obtainable on the open market, in some cases as much as three percentage points below. Both low interest rates and favorable payback conditions make this a favored program. The amount of funds that can be secured under these programs is usually limited. As a result, school systems must contribute local funds to complete the project.

SCHOOL BUILDING AUTHORITIES

School Authorities are vehicles to circumvent certain restrictive legislation. An authority is a quasi-governmental corporation incorporated under the laws of the state and with state backing (Camp, 1983). These are single-purpose organizations with a public governance structure appointed by the governor, legislature, mayor, or city council. A building authority can do two things: (1) raise funds for local school systems, or (2) actually construct buildings for the system and lease them back.

The Virginia Public School Building Authority raises funds for local school systems. The authority can get a better rate of interest on a large bond issue than a small school system could get with a small bond issue. The authority can usually command a better credit rating than small school systems, which also results in better interest rates.

Some building authorities plan, design, and construct buildings for the government. The Chicago Public Building Authority, for example, does all of the work entailed with having a building constructed to the exact specifications of the school system, including obtaining the site and site development. The authority then enters into a long-term lease with the school system to pay back the cost of the building. At the end of a specified period, the building's title reverts to the local school district and the authority uses the funds received to construct other buildings. This is in effect a turnkey project for the school system.

LOCAL GOVERNMENT FUNDING

The local school system has the largest responsibility for funding school construction. In addition, the local school system has a limited tax base upon which to secure needed funding for capital construction. The local real estate tax is the sole source of revenue for school systems for both operational capital funds.

This places a heavy burden upon the citizens of the locality. Most schemes for raising funds for school buildings rely upon debt to be paid over a period of years. This seems to be the most equitable method because the payment for the building is assumed by not just one generation. Not all methods of raising funds for school buildings are legal in all states, and the school administrator should make certain, through legal advice, which ways are acceptable for raising funds.

Pay-As-You-Go

The pay-as-you-go method of raising funds for school buildings stipulates that building will take place only when funds are available. Under this method, funds must be provided through the operational budget. Paying for construction when funds are available saves money that is normally spent on interest payments, which can represent from 40 to 200 percent of the cost of construction. Saving this much money is indeed a sizable gain.

At the turn of the twentieth century, this was a popular method of financing public schools. Of course, school buildings at that time did not approach the cost of such facilities today. There are not many school systems these days that can allocate sufficient funds from day-to-day operations to pay for a new school building. Today, no school system uses this method of raising construction funds.

Sinking Funds

The sinking funds method is also called the capital reserve fund. A sinking or reserve fund is much like a savings account: funds are placed in an account for future construction, and when the amount needed to build a school is reached, planning and construction take place. A specific amount of money is set aside each year to build the sinking fund for the amount of funds needed. Since this spreads the cost of the building over a number of years, high interest payments are avoided.

There are two reasons school systems do not use this form of raising revenue. First, it takes many years to accumulate sufficient money to pay for a new building. If the student population increases rapidly, before there are sufficient funds to construct a building, the school system faces a housing problem that may consume more funds than are in the sinking fund.

Second, the money in the sinking fund can only be invested in suitable governmental investment instruments. The interest paid on these types of savings usually does not keep up with inflation. As a result, the sinking fund can never grow large enough to cover the cost of construction. At one time, this was a common method of raising revenue for school buildings, but today it is not seen as a viable method. In fact, in some states, the sinking fund is not legal.

General Obligation Bonds

General obligation bonds, or municipal bonds, are the traditional method school systems use to finance capital construction. The proceeds from the sale of general obligation bonds can be used for any purpose involved with planning, designing, and constructing a building: contracting planning expertise, design work, construction, equipment, site purchase, the employment of in-house educational planners, and so on.

The municipal bond is a debt instrument backed by the full faith and credit of the local government unit or school system. It is not a lien against the property of the school system, rather it is an obligated debt of the government. The authority for issuing these debt instruments is obtained by a public referendum of the voters. Voter approval of the sale of bonds indicates it is the wish of the community to go into debt.

When a school system decides to go into debt, certain actions must be taken. A bond referendum must be held so that the voters have an opportunity to express their wishes. The school board and administration must observe the legal procedures involved with the process of going into debt. This includes limitations of indebtedness, vote of approval, type of bonds to be issued, payment of the principal, maximum term of payment, maximum rate of interest, restrictions on the sale of the bonds, tax rate, time limits for election notices, and voting procedures.

The first step is for the school board to pass a resolution that a bond referendum is to be conducted. In some states, the school board must request a local court to conduct the bond election. Upon official notice from the school board, the court makes all preparation to conduct the election. Tellers are appointed, polling places established, ballots printed, ballot boxes readied, election dates and times established and posted, and official notices of the election posted and printed in the newspaper. The court conducts all the steps (Holt, 2002). After the election, the court notifies the school board and publishes the results.

In many states, the local school board can actually conduct the election. In these locales, the school board does everything listed above. The results of the election are then certified to the local court and to the office of the city or county treasurer. School systems fiscally dependent upon a local government must have approval from that body before going into debt by conducting a bond referendum.

The ballot is a simple statement asking voters if they approve going into debt for the stated amount of money. In most states, a simple majority of the votes cast—50 percent plus one vote—is needed to pass a capital bond referendum. In some states, majorities of up to 60 or 66 percent of the voters are required to pass a bond issue.

There are some limited exceptions to the normal method of going into debt through a referendum. In some instances, school boards or city councils can bond themselves to a certain limitation of the assessed value of the property. In Virginia, if the school board uses either state loan funds or funds from the public school building authority, voter approval is not required. In some communities, the city charter permits local city councils to go into debt without voter approval. However, these are the exceptions to the rule of voter approval for debt (Holt, 2002).

When a school board first seeks a referendum, it secures the services of a bond attorney. Such services can be obtained through a reputable bonding house—a company that buys and sells bonds and other debt instruments. The bond attorney determines the legality of the bond by investigating the procedure used by the school board to go into debt. The bond counsel also assists in preparing the actual bonds and makes certain the correct terminology is used. Once these preliminary actions are completed, the bonds are printed. Each bond is a valuable, negotiable commodity and must be personally signed by a legal representative of the school board (Holt, 2002).

When the bonds are delivered, they are sold at public bidding. The school board sells the bonds to a commercial firm that, in turn, sells the bonds to the public. A notice to bid on the sale of the bonds is submitted to the legal newspaper of the locality. The time and date for receiving the bids are contained in the notice. When the bids are received and opened, the best offer to purchase the bonds is accepted by the school board.

Usually, the best bid is for the lowest percent of interest for the school board to pay on the bonds. The bank, investment house, syndicate, or brokerage firm that submits the lowest bid is awarded the sale of the bonds to the public. That company in turn puts the bonds on the public market for open sale. Many pension funds invest regularly in such municipal bonds. Mutual funds devoted to the purchase of tax-free bonds are also firms that purchase such bonds. People invest in these pension funds or mutual funds and receive the benefit of tax-free income.

Municipal or general obligation bonds are usually offered in $5,000 denominations. At that price, few people can afford to purchase them. That is why mutual funds offering access to these investments are popular. In some unusual circumstances, municipal bonds may be offered in the $1,000 denomination—specifically designed for those individuals who might want to purchase this type of investment.

Types of Bonds #13

There are four types of bonds that local governmental agencies can choose from: term, sinking fund, serial, and amortized bonds each use a different method for repayment. Only one type of bond is printed under an issue, as the method of payment should be uniform over the life of the bond.

Term Bonds

Term bonds are issued for a predetermined period, at the end of which all bonds are redeemed. The interest on the bonds is paid during the term of the bond. At the end of the term, the school system must raise the entire amount of the bond issue to redeem the bonds. This balloon payment at the end of the term is often a sizable amount and difficult to raise.

Sometimes this leads to issuing additional bonds to finance the original issue, which can lead to permanent debt. Most schools do not issue this type of bond because of the difficulty in raising the entire bond amount at the end of the term. Payment of the principal amount of the bond issue often places the burden of payment on the next generation of taxpayers.

Sinking Fund Bonds

Sinking fund bonds are term bonds, in that the principal of the bond issue is paid at the end of the term. A set amount of the principal of the bond issue is set aside each year and placed in a sinking fund to draw interest during the life of the bond. At the redemption date, the full amount of the bond issue is paid. Interest accrued during the life of the bond is used to reduce the amount of principal the school system has to raise for redemption. In some states, this type of bond is not legal.

Serial Bonds

Serial bonds are redeemed at various times during the life of the bond issue. A set number of bonds are redeemed during the first five years, another group in the next five years, and so on, until the entire issue is retired. Interest is paid on the bond until it is redeemed. With several maturity dates, the school board can raise sufficient funds to retire a portion of the total bond issue without the burden of raising the entire sum at one time.

The serial bond is the most favored type of bonding used by school systems. One reason is that a large balloon payment is avoided and, at the least, the various payments are not excessive. The repayment of the entire bond issue, including principal and interest, is spread over the time of the bond issue. This permits the school system to determine a set annual tax rate to repay. The burden of repayment is shared equally over the life of the bond. Investors like this type of bond because of the varying dates of maturity.

Amortization Bonds

These bonds are like serial bonds in that there are no balloon payments. The repayment schedule for these bonds provides for retiring part of the principal of each bond over the life of the bond. A semiannual payment to the investor contains the earned interest plus part of the principal. The payment schedule on this bond is much like a government-backed housing mortgage, where principal and interest are returned with each payment. An additional advantage with this mortgage is that, with each payment, the debt load of the school system is reduced proportionately.

CREDIT RATING

The interest rate on a bond is directly related to the credit rating of the school system. The lower the credit rating, the higher the interest the school system has to pay the investor holding the bond because the bond is considered more at risk. Each school system that has bonds for sale has a credit rating developed by one or more of the major credit-reporting agencies (Holt, 2002).

The common agencies are Moody's Investors Service, Standard & Poor's, and Fitch Investors Service. These agencies rate school systems and other branches of government according to their ability to repay debts. These ratings and the factors used in establishing them are much like the credit rating of an individual. Many items enter into the rating for the school system, such as amount of current debt, ratio of debt to assets, history of repaying debt, ratio of assessed valuation of property to number of students in school, number of outstanding bills, record of payment of bills, stability of leadership, history of successful bond referenda, and even the percentage of favorable votes on the last bond referendum.

Credit-rating scales of the school system are indicated by letters from high (AAA, Aaa, A) to low (CCC, Ccc, C, D). In this manner, the bonds then carry the rating of the school system. Credit ratings are important to the school system, and everything that is possible should be done to keep the rating as high as possible.

SCHOOL SYSTEM BOND CAPACITY

Each school system has a debt limit that is called a bond capacity. This means the system can go into debt to a certain limit through offering bonds for sale. Either the constitution or statutes of the state most often define the bond capacity of local school systems. These limits may be a certain percentage of the assessed value of the taxable real estate in the school system. The limits range from a low of 5 percent to a high of 15 percent. In some cases, school systems may exceed the debt limit by appealing to the state legislature or some other state office for approval.

MANAGEMENT OF BOND PROCEEDS

The proceeds of a bond issue are not always used immediately. The planning and design work for a new school must precede the actual construction. Thus, the bulk of a bond issue may not be needed for two years after the bonds are sold and the proceeds realized by the school system.

Prudent administration of these funds indicates that the funds are kept in a safe place but one where some interest can be gained. It is not unlawful for school systems to invest part or all of the proceeds of a bond issue into interest-bearing instruments. There is a limit, however, as to the type of instrument that can be used. All investments must be into an instrument issued by another governmental agency. For instance, local school systems could invest in state or federal government bonds, notes, or bills. School boards may not invest in any instrument that places the principal amount of the investment at risk. In addition, school boards may not engage in arbitrage of any sort. Arbitrage is the practice of making money on speculative instruments.

ALTERNATIVE FUNDING PLANS

The majority of capital improvement projects are funded through the issuance of general obligation bonds. These are usually called municipal bonds because they are issued by a local governmental agency. Over the decades, this type of funding has generally been adequate to fund the needs of school systems.

In recent years, with the growing need to upgrade existing school facilities and accommodate a growing student population, many school systems are in a financial situation where they have difficulty in properly financing all their capital needs. In addition, the large increase in the cost of school facilities has created a strain on the financial resources of school systems. One report on the finances needed to upgrade all schools in the country placed the amount at $322 billion (National Education Association, 2000). This amount is just what it would take to get all existing school buildings to satisfactory condition. In addition, this report is nineteen years old and the cost has increased considerably. A report published by the U.S. Department of Education (2014) indicates that 67 percent of all schools needed repair or modernization to bring buildings up to standard condition, and the cost for that would be $197 billion. The difference between the two figures indicates the difference in the population of school buildings in the survey. Although both these reports are dated, the cost of bringing all school buildings up to standard condition is a tremendous financial burden for local school systems.

These reports do not address the need for new school buildings in certain school systems that are experiencing student growth. This large financial burden cannot be borne entirely by local school systems. To remedy this situation, many local school systems and states have tried a number of alternative funding plans to relieve the financial burden of providing adequate school buildings. The American Society of Civil Engineers (2017) published a report giving U.S. schools a grade of D+, with 24 percent of the structures rated as being in poor condition. The report also states that the United States continues to underinvest in school facilities in the amount of $38 billion each year.

Alternative funding sources have become popular in selected localities. Some creative ways of using streams of dedicated revenue to leverage debt or other enhancements have been successfully used. In addition, some models of alternative funding from sources other than school systems have been modified. Modification of financial schemes in other segments of the government have been implemented in certain localities.

Some caution has to be used in discussing alternative schemes to fund educational capital improvement projects. The first caution is that most alternative funding plans are site or place specific. In other words, the alternative funding plan can be used for a specific school building but cannot be used universally for other school sites in the school system or school systems in other locations. Moreover, most alternative funding plans cannot raise the entire cost of a single capital improvement project. In addition, funds realized under any alternative funding plan are usually limited in the amount raised.

Nevertheless, such alternative funding plans as are applicable to capital improvement projects should be used to the fullest advantage. This means that administrators need to be aware of possible plans that may be available to their particular state and locality because not all plans are universally applicable. What might be permissible to employ in one state may not be in another.

STATE REVOLVING FUNDS

State revolving funds are an effective mechanism for attaining low-cost financing to meet community needs. These funding mechanisms are also considered loan programs in that the state loans funds to local school systems to pay for capital improvement projects. The return of principal and interest from the local community builds up an ever-larger fund balance. Under such plans, the state lends the funds at below-market levels with favorable repayment rates. A revolving fund is a loan and is technically not a debt that could be counted against the debt limit of the school system.

Several states currently have provisions for loan programs to local school systems. The rate of interest charged by the state is usually low and the term of the loan may be upward of twenty years. These are indeed favorable repayment terms. Most states have restrictions on the amount a school system can borrow, and there is usually a backlog of requests for the limited capitalized loan fund. Even with these limitations, state loan funds are very attractive and useful to the school system.

There are some variations of this scheme in that some authorities are suggesting that the federal government provide each state with matching grants to capitalize the state revolving fund. A state could create an independent revolving loan fund to facilitate the same end. In either case, the return payments would increase the total capitalization of the fund and provide an increasing supply of money to lend to local school systems (Council of Infrastructure Financing Authorities, 1998).

State Credit-Enhancement Programs

These types of programs use the credit rating of the state rather than the local school system to sell bonds (Standard & Poor's, 1998). Due to a number of factors, most local governmental units, such as the schools, have a lower credit rating than the state in which it they are located. Therefore, the local school system would pay higher interest rates on bonds they issued. State credit-enhancement plans are essentially the substitution of the credit rating of the state for the local governmental agency to sell bonds. Significant benefits in lower interest payments can be realized through this substitution. Credit-substitution programs are created through a state constitution provision, legislative statute, or both. This legal basis ensures payment by a state government.

One major factor in these programs is that, through the legal provisions of enhancement, the state provides a cure for default on the part of a locality. The state, in essence, pays for any default on the part of the school system. This cure may be in the form of withholding state aid from the local school system, or, the debt may be paid through a state school building fund. Thus, the bondholder is assured that the debt will be paid in a timely fashion. While credit ratings assess the probability of full and timely payment of the debt based on economic, financial, management, and debt factors, credit enhancement plans can also reflect legal provisions of public law that protect bondholders from possible default.

The extent of credit enhancement depends upon the exact nature of the program of the state. In some instances, the state guarantees payment to avoid default by the local school system. In other states, the responsibility of debt repayment rests with a state aid intercept program that diverts standard education payments from the school system to make debt payments. Both of these methods of payment are an effective way to guarantee payment. School boards and administrators should explore the use of credit enhancement programs when contemplating the issuance of bonds.

Tax Credit Plans

Under a tax credit, plan bondholders are rewarded for purchasing municipal bonds by allowing them credits against possible tax liability. In these plans, tax credits can be used against federal tax liabilities and are substituted for the interest bondholders would normally receive from the school systems. One such plan that was approved by Congress under the Taxpayer Relief Act of 1997 is the Qualified Zone Academy Bond. There are variations of this plan proposed in other legislative measures. This act was ultimately not funded by Congress.

Under the Taxpayer Relief Act of 1997, a new category of no-interest bonds were created. State and local governments were to be able to issue qualified zone academy bonds to fund the improvement of eligible public school buildings. An eligible holder of a qualified zone academy bond would receive annual federal income tax credits in lieu of interest payments from the school system. These annual credits would compensate the holder for lending money and, therefore, would be treated like taxable interest payments for federal tax purposes. The benefit of these bonds would be that the school system would not have to pay interest to the bondholders. This would in effect reduce the overall cost of the building. In many cases, the interest payments for any construction project normally exceed the original cost of construction by at least two times. Thus, over a twenty-year period, considerable revenue could be saved. Although the idea of these tax credits is viable, Congress has not funded this act.

Impact Fees

Almost every local government can enact ordinances relating to the proper development and use of land. These ordinances can take the form of imposing an impact fee on a developer to pay for public services such as schools. An impact fee is different from a tax because the fee is based upon the enforcement of the government to regulate private activity to protect public health, safety, and welfare. Impact fees are a form of development extraction, where an extraction is a condition of permission that requires a public facility or improvement to be provided at the expense of the developer.

An impact fee is

1. in the form of a predetermined money payment.
2. assessed as a condition to the issuance of a building permit, an occupancy permit, or plat approval.
3. pursuant to local government powers to regulate new growth and development and provide for adequate public facilities.
4. levied to fund large-scale facilities to serve new development (Ducker, 1994).

ALTERNATIVES TO NEW CONSTRUCTION

It is natural to think that whenever additional students need to be housed, the school system should construct a building, but such thinking may not result in the best solution. For the most part, it is a good solution to construct a school building, but each situation should be evaluated to determine if other options might be more beneficial to the school system. Several alternatives to new construction are available to school systems and should be considered.

Long-Term Leasing

In certain situations, it may be more economical to lease a facility rather than build a new one. Comparing the initial cost of building a facility, the interest payments, and the cost of ownership to the cost of a leased facility for twenty years, may be to the advantage of the school system. Only by completing such studies will the school board know which decision to make. Such studies employ a life-cycle comparison of owned versus leased facilities. This is where all costs of the facility are used for the comparison.

There are many available spaces that would lend themselves to a lease arrangement. Church educational classrooms, speculative buildings, and private school facilities may be used to great advantage to both the school system and the owner.

Long-term leasing of facilities is legal in all states and should be considered a viable alternative. Leasing permits the school system the use of school facilities without the burdensome debt that can negatively influence their credit rating because costs for leasing come from a different section of the operational budget than debt service. Another advantage to leasing is that the building remains on the tax rolls and the school system receives tax revenues paid by the owner.

Conversion of Existing Buildings

Some existing buildings can make good school facilities. Conversion of an existing building to fit the needs of a school is a good alternative to consider. Buildings that have large, open spaces make excellent schools. Warehouses, shopping areas, and supermarkets are all good spaces in which to put a school because, with a minimum of conversion, the facilities could house students. If the structure and systems are in good working order, then with the installation of carpeting or other appropriate floor covering, wall treatments, lowered ceilings, and lighting system, the facility is ready. The cost of conversion of the existing building is many times less than constructing a new building on a new site. Such building conversions make good primary or elementary school facilities.

One drawback to such a solution is that existing buildings often are not located where the bulk of students live. When this happens, additional transportation is necessary, which adds to the total cost of housing students. In urban areas where a site is either not available or the costs are prohibitive, conversion of an existing building could be a good solution.

Inexpensive Buildings

Inexpensive buildings are not cheap buildings. These are buildings constructed with material that makes them inexpensive. One example is an air structure, which is actually a balloon supported by air pressure. A typical building foundation is laid, which might rise to four to six feet above the ground, and, above this, a balloon structure is attached, and the building is maintained by air pressure. Auxiliary pumps are in place in case of failure of the main air pumps.

Such a structure could cover large expanses, such as a swimming pool, tennis courts, and even a practice soccer field. Several applications of this type of building have been used for several decades. This solution, however, has limited application.

Systems Buildings

Some school systems have tried to reduce the cost of a school building by using what have been called modular structures. Such buildings are composed of various systems that are constructed in the factory and then assembled at the site. This combination seems to reduce the overall cost of a building. Factory-built components can be constructed faster because there are no stoppages of work because of weather, and an assembly line can be created for the construction process.

There are constraints on the use of modular buildings. One is that the spaces within the structure are either a square or a rectangle. In addition, most modular buildings are single story; however, there are some companies that can produce a multistory building.

USE OF COMMUNITY FACILITIES

It is common for students to use community facilities in their education. Field trips have been a part of education since the early part of this century. However, the idea of locating classes of students in community-owned facilities is quite different. However, every community has space in both commercial and public buildings that are vacant and could be used to house a class of students. Municipal buildings, libraries, museums, and commercial buildings are examples of places where space can be found to house students.

The School District of Philadelphia housed five hundred students in such facilities within the city during the 1960s. This was known as the Parkway School. A rented office space served as the headquarters and homeroom for the students, but the subject-matter classes were taught in such facilities as a newspaper building, courtroom, science museum, and insurance office. All the facilities were close enough for students to move from one building to another in much the same fashion as college students. This solution, however, may have limited applications.

CONTRACTING FOR SERVICE

In some localities, housing developers must provide either a school site or, in its place, a monetary consideration to the school system to have their development plan adopted. In some cases, a developer can construct a school building less expensively than a school system can. The developer could then lease the building to the school system for their use. The building would be built to the specifications of the school system.

The economy would come from the fact that the developer has the equipment and workforce already on site. Tax write-off advantages would accrue to the developer, the land would still be on the tax rolls, and the school system would have a school ready when the children arrive. Further, the school system would not have incurred a debt, but, at some point in the future, the school system could purchase the building, if needed.

A further extension of this concept might be not only to lease the school building from the developer, but also to contract to provide the entire educational program. The school system could enter into an agreement with the developer, who would provide not only the building but also the staff, materials, and supplies. The curriculum would be provided by the school system. Such an agreement is legal in all states and, in some special situations, might be a viable economic solution.

SUMMARY

The financial portion of the long-range plan must identify resources for both operational and capital projects. This means that both the annual and longer-term funding of capital projects is addressed. There are a number of ways school systems can obtain funds for either new construction or major reformations. The federal government does have some plans that school systems can utilize, but these schemes are limited and provide merge funding. The state is a major funding source of local schools in some states. In other states the state provides no funding. The major funding source for capital projects is the local school system. In the majority of states the locality is the sole source of funding of capital projects with a variety of bonding vehicles. Recently, school systems have utilized a variety of different methods of funding capital projects. There are also alternatives to housing students in acceptable facilities than a regulation school-owned building.

Chapter 8

Development of the Capital Improvement Program

The long-range plan of the school system is the basis of other plans or activities, which are called action plans, as explained in chapter 3. The long-range plan serves as a general guide, so the entire organization can work cooperatively toward the identified goals. Because of the size of the long-range plan, additional and more manageable plans must be developed. The enormous tasks identified in the long-range plan are broken into component plans that can be completed.

The actual work detail needed to complete the long-range plan is contained in subsequent plans developed by various offices and departments after the final adoption of the plan. These offices and departments then assume responsibility for executing the plans for which they have responsibility. Each department or segment of the organization contributes to the long-range plan during the formulation stage for those areas in which the department has responsibility and expertise. After the plan is adopted, it assumes responsibility for execution of that portion.

For example, part of the long-range plan describes the instructional and classified staff needed to implement the desired educational program. This description of needed staff is comprehensive in that types and numbers of staff are identified, even according to the level of instruction. Based upon the description of the staff needed in the plan, the human resources office must fashion a development plan to secure the number of teachers, administrators, and staff members needed. This action plan covers the same time span as the long-range plan and must be completed at the same time as that document. Over the years, the personnel department will systematically implement the human resource development plan in support of the long-range plan. This will happen in other departments of the school system as well.

The long-range plan also stipulates the educational program to be carried on and the number of students expected over the years. These factors determine the scope and size of the school system program. In addition, the plan describes the number of classrooms this combination of program and students will need to be properly housed in adequate facilities. The previously completed evaluation of existing facilities owned and operated by the school system identified the current inventory of classroom spaces available. The difference, if any, between the number of classroom spaces available and those needed for the given student body represents the number of new classrooms that need to be constructed. In addition, the distribution of the student population will indicate where the additional classrooms will need to be located.

In school systems experiencing a decline in student enrollment, the problem of surplus space and usage of that space will be identified in this section of the document. All this represents data needed to produce a plan to provide suitable housing for students.

Just as the long-range plan is the basis of subsequent action plans to employ the needed teaching staff, develop curricular materials, retrain staff, and other efforts, it is also the basis of the capital improvement plan of the school system. Data for the capital improvement program are derived from the previously conducted evaluation of all facilities, which have been described in previous chapters.

If a comprehensive evaluation of all facilities has been conducted and complete data on facility needs obtained, the necessary ingredients for a capital improvement program are available. The implementation plan, which is called the capital improvement program, is developed as a response to the need for classroom space.

CAPITAL IMPROVEMENT PLAN

The capital improvement plan (CIP) is a set of proposed actions to provide housing for students of the school system (Tanner and Lackey, 2005). The written document that details the plan is often called the capital improvement program. The plan or program covers the work of several years, and its span coincides with the time span of the long-range plan.

The completed program will consist of a number of different kinds of capital projects, including new school buildings, additions to existing schools, major renovations of older schools, the purchase of sites or buildings, and major improvements to schools. The program will also list the surplus classrooms when the school system is declining in student enrollments.

A school system always has more capital improvement projects than funds to complete them, so each project must receive a ranking for when it will be completed. Many factors enter into setting the timing for each project. When prioritizing, the most important factor is the need to house either a growing or declining population. If a school system is growing rapidly, the construction of new schools may take precedent over all other projects. In different circumstances, other factors may carry more weight.

The exact timing of the project is determined by a cooperative effort between the school facilities department and the superintendent. The fiscal officers of the school system also participate in this process because they can give advice on the availability of funds.

An office must be responsible for actually compiling the program document and having it published. This office may be in the school facilities department if there is sufficient financial expertise. In large school systems, there is generally an office devoted just to the preparation of the capital improvement program. This office provides coordination services to other departments and offices that have a direct input into the prioritizing process. This office also has a direct relationship to the department responsible for development of the capital improvement budget, which is the instrument used to complete capital projects. In a small school system, this responsibility may be assigned to a director in the central administration or in a very small school system to a single person.

CAPITAL IMPROVEMENT BUDGET

The capital improvement program lists all capital projects the school system wishes to complete over five to seven years. These projects are described in the long-range plan developed by the department. Each project has a description of the scope of and need for the project. In addition, the cost estimates for each part of the project are obtained, either through an estimator on the school staff, or, in the case of small school systems, through the expertise of an outside architectural or construction consultant. The description tells how this project fits into the overall scheme for the school system. The various components of the project are listed as well as the suggested time for completing them. Not every project contains the same components, but a new school building project would include purchasing a site, obtaining some educational planning, securing architectural services, contracting for construction services, and obtaining furniture and equipment to complete the building. The listing of each capital project would look somewhat like Table 8.1.

Table 8.1. Capital Improvement Project Description

Cost Element	Total	2019	2020	2021	2022	2023
Plan/design	2,400	800	980	420	100	100
Land	4,000	4,000				
Site improvement	2,000		2,000			
Construction	44,750			44,750		
Furniture/equipment	3,362					3,362
Technology	3,187				700	2,487
Total	**59,699**	**4,800**	**2,980**	**45,170**	**800**	**5,949**

Note: figures in millions of dollars.

Project B0156
Potomac High School
Description: A project is required to plan and construct a sixty-station high school in the northern Potomac area to be completed by the year 2021.
Justification: Rapid residential housing construction in the area to be served has required construction of five schools in the last four years. Enrollments are projected to increase in the next five years.
(Expenditure Schedule [in thousands of dollars])

The capital improvement described in Table 8.1 shows the total anticipated expenditures for the project over the five years and the suggested outlay of funds needed to complete it. A total of $59,699,000 is proposed for the construction of a new high school. The design work is spread out over a number of years and shows the heaviest concentration of work in the year immediately preceding construction. The site is purchased two years in advance of the beginning of construction, sufficient time for preparation of the site. The last major purchase is for technology, loose furniture, and equipment. In as much as this last amount of $5,949,000 is not needed until the beginning of the fifth year of the project, that amount can be invested in proper instruments to realize some funds with which to offset inflation for the period. Even the $45 million for construction will not be needed until the beginning of the third year, and an investment strategy can be developed to realize some funds for that period. A proper investment program for all funds should be established based upon the expenditure schedule.

CAPITAL IMPROVEMENT PROGRAM APPROVAL

There are several levels of approval for CIP. The points of approval are both within and outside of the school system. The initial level of approval is with the central administrative staff, which has the responsibility for compiling the document. This level of approval is the first hurdle for CIP.

The basis for prioritizing all the projects suggested for CIP is the need to house students properly in modern school buildings. Growth in student enrollments in a school system can mandate the priority system, or a program initiative in a stable school system can be the deciding factor. There is always the pull in prioritizing projects between the need to implement a new program and to provide sufficient classrooms for the student body. Undoubtedly, in a growing school system, that need takes precedence over new program implementation, if it is a matter of only one being served properly, but there is always the need to provide the right kinds of facilities so a program can function properly.

Nevertheless, initially central staff has to put each project into proper sequence, considering everything needed. After the document is put together with the suggested prioritization, it is reviewed by the administrative council, team, or cabinet of the superintendent for their approval. This body of administrators is very knowledgeable about the needs of the school system as a whole and about the political environment in particular. This group may suggest changes in priority, but for the most part, such changes will have very little influence over the overall thrust of the capital improvement program.

Following this internal review and approval, the superintendent recommends the capital improvement program to the school board for their formal approval. After the document is explained to the school board in sufficient detail, a series of public hearings is set. The school board conducts these hearings for citizen input. There may be one or several meetings throughout the school system. In some states, there are rules and legal regulations regarding the public hearings on all programs that must be observed, but the public hearing for a capital improvement program or plan is different from the public hearing on a proposed capital improvement budget. The budget represents a public expenditure of funds, whereas the capital improvement program is simply anticipated actions based upon prioritization.

Following the public hearing meetings, the school board meets in regular session and approves the program by resolution. This approval simply gives the staff the right to proceed with the projects in the order listed but does not give authorization for the expenditure of funds. The approved program, however, becomes the official document to judge progress in completing the work of the school facilities department (Oates and Burch, 2002).

In some states and localities governmental agencies other than the school system may have either approval responsibilities over the capital improvement program or a review capability. Such agencies as the art commission or the city/county planning commission may have review capability. Even if these agencies do not have any responsibility for reviewing or approving the document, they should be brought into the process to provide a review. The more widespread the review of the capital improvement program is, the better the dissemination of information throughout the school system.

CAPITAL IMPROVEMENT BUDGET

The capital improvement budget is a different document from the capital improvement program. The capital improvement program is a set of proposed actions to provide housing for students in the school system and can be classified as a plan for doing certain things. The capital improvement budget, on the other hand, is a document that authorizes actions through the expenditure of funds. The capital improvement budget is an approved expenditure plan for capital projects (Oates and Burch, 2002).

Any budget is defined as an adopted expenditure plan along with a revenue plan, and the capital improvement budget deals specifically with funding for school buildings. Without the budget, the school system staff would have no authority to spend funds for any project no matter how worthy. Capital improvement budgets that are being offered to the school board for consideration are, in fact, *proposed* capital improvement budgets. Only after the document is approved by the school board and proper authorities can the document be called a budget in the true sense.

The proposed capital improvement budget is developed from the capital improvement program. In a school system that has many capital improvement projects, the various projects in the capital improvement program are spread over several years to allow for the orderly development of each project and completion of every phase in a timely fashion (Montgomery County, 2008). In addition, the projects are spaced over several years so that school staff can handle the projects without being overburdened.

The projects listed in the first year of the capital improvement program then become the projects to be funded through the capital improvement budget. In the example of the capital improvement program discussed earlier in this chapter, first-year projects, including the purchase of a site and employment of an architect, would become the projects funded in the capital improvement budget. All budgets for a school system are for one year at a time and do not carry approval for more than one year. The appropriations in a budget document are only for the year in which the budget was approved.

At the end of the first year, all of the projects in the capital improvement budget should be completed. When that happens, the projects listed for the second year become the projects in the proposed capital improvement budget for the following year. This process of completing projects listed in one year and then proceeding to the following years in systematic order allows the school system to complete the capital improvement program.

The process of approval for the proposed capital improvement budget is the same as for the program. The state usually has legal requirements for public hearings. The hearings normally must be held ten days prior to consideration by the school board. When such hearings are completed, the school board approves the budget by resolution. The approved capital improvement budget becomes the authority by which school staff can commit funds to projects. Until the budget is approved, contracts cannot be signed, materials and supplies cannot be purchased, nor can employees be hired.

MAINTENANCE SCHEDULE

During the annual evaluation of a school building by the principal and/or central staff, many items needing repair are identified. These items may be as simple as a door not working correctly or a broken light switch or as major as a roof replacement or mechanical system improvement. Lists of all projects—big and small—are gathered into one master list for each school building. Items needed for preventative maintenance are also included. All items, regardless of source, become part of the maintenance schedule of the school system (Chan and Richardson, 2005).

Most school systems have a program for preventative maintenance (PM) and replacement of major systems in a school building (Kowalski, 2001). Such programs rely upon regular servicing of equipment to prevent untimely obsolescence and breakdown. In addition, specified replacement of equipment and parts of buildings prevents interruption of the use of the building by school personnel and students.

School systems usually develop a list of items in a building that will need replacement after a specified period. For instance, heating systems usually have a definite lifetime. After that, the system will undoubtedly fail. To forestall that happening, school systems regularly replace the systems—as well as roofs, lighting, and other systems—at the end of their useful life, regardless of condition. This allows the maintenance staff to replace the system at the convenience of the school staff and not cause an interruption in service.

As with most organizations, maintenance needs of a school system are more than can be completed in one year. Thus, the school staff has to develop a maintenance schedule for a certain period of time, usually a five-year period, although the schedule can be for a shorter period.

The maintenance schedule is ongoing and never completed. As soon as all the items for one year are completed, there is another group of items to be added to the schedule so that it is extended for another year. This process of constantly adding maintenance projects to the schedule continues throughout the life of the school (Chan and Richardson, 2005).

The central administrative staff and individual school building staff prioritize each item. After this prioritization and approval internally, the schedule is submitted to the school board for their review. The school board does not have to formally approve the maintenance schedule specifically, nor does it need to have any public hearings, because this is an internal matter. The funding of the maintenance schedule, however, depends upon the operational budget that the school board has to approve.

During the operational budget approval process, all budget categories, including maintenance, are open for public review. However, only the amount of funds proposed for maintenance work is identified, not specific projects. The funding provided for maintenance projects depends on the school board. Sometimes limitations are put on the amount of maintenance funds available because of certain factors that have nothing to do with maintenance work (Earthman and Lemasters, 2004).

In school systems with a high regard for the school buildings and the investment they represent to the community, sufficient maintenance funds are always available for needed work. Sometimes during financial emergencies the school board seeks to conserve limited funds for the program of the school by reducing the amount of maintenance funds. This action is shortsighted both in the immediate and long-range future. Proper maintenance of school facilities demands a focused program of identification of need and completion of task with appropriate funding. Only in this manner can the buildings of the school system be kept in a state of good repair.

Normally, a certain present of the value of the school building should be spent on every building each year for maintenance needs to keep the building current. This percent of funds should be at least 2 percent of the assessed value of the school building. In this manner, over fifty years the school system will have spent funds in the amount equal to the assessed value of the building to keep it in good repair.

SUMMARY

The Capital Improvement Plan (CIP) is an outgrowth of the long-range plan and serves as the document to guide for the school system in completion of capital programs. This document lists all of the major capital projects the school system intends on completing within a period of time. Normally, the CIP covers a period of six to ten years depending upon the extent of the plan and must be approved by the school board. The Capital Improvement Budget is derived from the CIP. Usually, the first year of the CIP is considered the first year of the Capital Improvement Budget. The Capital Improvement Budget must also be approved by the school board and after approval becomes the instrument for the capital expenditure of funds by school employees.

The Maintenance Schedule is made up of all needed improvements to the school building to keep it in good working order. All of the needed items or projects to be completed are listed for every building and included in the schedule. Each year a portion of the Maintenance Schedule is completed. The Maintenance Schedule is never entirely completed because new items are added each year as the need arises.

Chapter 9

Developing Educational Specifications

Educators must make many difficult decisions in planning a school facility. One of the most difficult sets of decisions to make in this process is to define the type of program that will be carried on in the new facility and to relate this program to building needs. Sometimes referred to as programming the school, this activity identifies the school's educational program and then relates these components to certain aspects of school planning such as the amount of space needed, relationship among spaces, furniture and equipment required, and various services and utilities needed. The completion of this task requires a person well versed in educational programs and methodology and at the same time knowledgeable of state requirements for space.

Educational specifications are a set of statements that describe to the architect the types and kinds of educational activities that will take place in the proposed building and relate these activities to school planning factors such as spaces, square footage, and relationships (Hill, 2005). These statements are contained in a document that is used by the architect to design the building. Educational specifications should be clear, concise, and exact in what is requested in the building (Earthman, 1976).

Needless to say, interpreting the needs of those who will use the completed facility is not an easy task. Developing these specifications demands a reasoned approach to school planning and a systematic procedure involving many people inside and outside the school system. The procedure enables people to have input into the new program that will become the basis for the architect's design.

It is no small task to write a set of educational specifications, and many times school systems do not devote sufficient time, energy, and funds to complete a good job. There are several reasons why this occurs.

Perhaps the main reason for not developing a good set of educational specifications may be the lack of leadership on the part of the educators responsible for the task. When educators do not exercise leadership, a vacuum exists and there is always someone who is willing to step into the leadership vacuum and provide some direction to get the job done. The architect has a contract to complete a design project by a given date and needs certain specifications to complete the work. When these specifications are not forthcoming from the educators, the only thing that can be done is to complete the task that an educator should have completed. In such a situation, the architect feels compelled to provide some leadership and fill that vacuum.

Sometimes educators feel the task of writing educational specifications to be the responsibility of the architect because it has been done that way in the past. The custom of letting the architect complete the educational specifications is still practiced in some regions of the country. Sometimes there is a vague demarcation of responsibility in the minds of the educator and architect that results in the task being assumed by the architect. Again, some architects have a desire to provide extra services in exchange for a building commission and will try to write a set of educational specifications. Architects are the first to admit that they are not versed in the educational program to be offered and should not be the ones to write the educational specifications for the project.

Many times educators also hold the mistaken belief that the school system does not have the capacity or the staff to do the task and cannot afford to purchase outside assistance. The expenditure of staff time or funds to hire competent outside educational consultant services to develop a set of educational specifications is quite small compared to the amount of benefit the school system receives from well-planned facilities. In addition, the actual amount of money spent is a very small proportion of the total amount of funds spent on the project. Some educators feel they do not know how to guide the process of developing a set of educational specifications. All these conditions underscore the point that educators need to exercise leadership in guiding the process of developing a good set of educational specifications. This leadership must be demonstrated by designating a member of the school staff to write the document or by obtaining the services of an educational consultant.

When a new building or an addition to an existing building is planned, many questions need to be answered. The answers to these questions are then written so that everyone will know what they are, and the questions will not have to be asked repeatedly. Out of the process of answering these questions will come a document that will serve as a planning tool for both the educator and architect (Ohio School Facilities Commission, 2008).

The following are typical questions relating to new facilities that need to be answered:

- How many students will the facility serve?
- What are the age groupings, backgrounds, needs, and capabilities of the students who will occupy the facility?
- What subjects will be taught?
- What methods of teaching will be used?
- What type of educational technology will be used, and where?
- What will be the configuration of the classrooms?
- What special areas are needed, and for whom?
- What kinds of teacher work areas will there be?
- How long will the school day be?
- How many students will eat lunch or breakfast?
- Will the program offer drama, music, and sports?
- Will the community utilize the building?
- What kind of media center should the facility have?
- Will the program include science, mathematics, and vocational subjects?

These are just a few of the questions that need to be answered for the architect to design a facility needed by the school system. The answers become the basis of a set of educational specifications.

At least two processes are in operation at all times in a classroom or instructional space. One concerns the activities a teacher goes through in teaching students. The other is the activities that a student engages in to learn something. Each of these processes is separate but complementary. Describing these activities is important to the architect because this type of information allows the architect to design the kind of environment that will support the activities.

For instance, if a kindergarten teacher wants a group of students to sit on the floor to engage in a reading activity, then the floor should have a soft covering. On the other hand, if the students will engage in an activity such as watercolor painting or woodworking, a floor covering that can be easily cleaned should be specified. In addition, teachers need certain equipment, spaces, and accoutrements in order to teach effectively. Only by clearly describing all these types of activities, both teacher and student initiated, can the educator hope to communicate facility needs to the architect successfully.

DEVELOPMENT PROCESS

The preparation of the educational specifications for a school facility is clearly the responsibility of the school system, whether someone on the staff or an outside educational consultant prepares the document. The superintendent in a medium-sized school or the assistant superintendent for facilities in a larger system must assume this responsibility. However, this responsibility is discharged by actually designating an office or person to take charge of the process.

In a large school system, someone from the school programming section of the school facilities department is usually designated with the responsibility. That person takes on the project as part of the workload. In some school systems where many school projects are planned simultaneously, there may be more than one school planner in that section. Projects are then assigned to individuals by either geographic area or by rotation. In medium or small school systems, a principal can be released from a school assignment to complete the task, or a supervisor or other central staff person can assume the responsibility.

In addition to assigning responsibility, the school system must assign resources to complete the task. This may mean providing office space, secretarial, duplication, and communication services, travel funds, and other resources. News of the task and the person responsible must be communicated throughout the school system so that everyone will know who will be working on the project.

Having one individual actually write the educational specifications is a wise idea because of the various input sources. One author can give the document sufficient focus and at the same time clearly state the needs of the users. This also centralizes responsibility for the document. The old adage that a committee cannot write a good report is undoubtedly true in this case. There will be, however, much committee input into the material of the document, but this will be through the interactive process.

As stated earlier, the process of developing a set of educational specifications is a fact-finding activity. In effect, the person writing the document must meet with many people to gain their input. How these meetings may be organized and conducted is debatable, but some meetings should be on an individual basis. This would be particularly true of specialists, such as people responsible for maintenance and operations, cafeteria, computer services, and transportation. Meetings with parents and teachers may be group sessions. If the project is for a school replacement, there may be a series of meetings with parents and teachers.

The first group meeting should define the project and responsibilities of the planner. The staff and community are made aware of the scope of the project, if they do not already know it. Input may be requested and obtained at the initial meeting and/or at subsequent meetings. The planner then tries to put together all the identified needs of the potential users of the school facility. Some needs of the potential users may result from a desire to implement a new program or may arise because the school system is beginning a new program for all schools. In any event, all the needs are sifted and put together within the confines of the financial budget for the school building.

Appendix B contains a checklist for developing a set of educational specifications. This checklist was developed for a rather large school system where many school projects are developed simultaneously. The checklist is to be followed by a planner who is developing a set of educational specifications. All of the contact points in the large system are identified so that the planner will not omit one. This checklist requires the school planner to complete eighteen different tasks, and he or she will need to meet many more times with groups and individuals in order to do so. In the school system where this checklist is used, the school organization is subdivided into school districts with a district superintendent in charge. In this situation, there is a three-tiered organization—school building, district, and total school system—which must be brought together for closure on the specifications for a new building.

Obviously, there are general parameters for all school buildings that originate from the total school system (Rollins, 2012). These may be related to certain educational programs to be implemented or they may arise from certain commonalities within the school system. For instance, school systems may specify that every school should contain certain elements, such as a particular size of library, types of heating plants, standardized kitchens, or maybe grade organizations. In addition, some program needs may be identified on the level beneath the total school system, when the school system is divided into subgroups such as areas or districts.

Finally, some programmatic needs stem from the local school building organization, regardless of whether the project is a new school or a replacement. All these needs must be merged into one program description with accompanying facility needs. After the final writing, but prior to duplicating the document, the groups and individuals that had input may want to review the specifications for a last approval.

SCHOOL BOARD APPROVAL

The final approval for the educational specifications should be by the school board. It is important that the educational specifications be presented to the school board for its review and approval because the specifications will be used as the final arbiter for what will be in the building. School board approval represents school policy in that changes in the educational specifications cannot be made by someone in the school system that thinks this or that should be included or excluded. In addition, school board approval of the set of educational specifications limits the size of the building to what can be accomplished through the budget.

CONTENT OF EDUCATIONAL SPECIFICATIONS

As stated above, the educational specifications contain answers to questions about the building so that the architect can design what is needed. The people who know the most about the educational program must supply the answers to all questions regarding the program that will be housed in the building. In the absence of any clearly written document, architects must guess or rely upon previous solutions to design problems.

No predetermined subject areas must be included in the document, but general practice indicates that the following areas should be addressed:

- educational situation and student body
- description of the community to be served
- the site and site development
- educational philosophy of the school system
- educational program to be offered
- educational trends in subject matter and methodology
- implementation of technology
- space requirements in square footage
- functional relationships of the facility
- specialized facilities for vocational education, science, physical education, home arts, technology education, and music
- indoor and outdoor recreational facilities
- building communications and utility requirements
- furniture and equipment
- plant service area and facilities
- parking and vehicular traffic
- site and plant security
- community use of the facility (Earthman, 1976)

Other areas may be addressed, depending upon local circumstances, but the list is comprehensive enough to cover almost every area. Even though the educational specifications may be clearly written, they may need to be interpreted to the architect during the design stage.

The task in this phase of the planning process for school buildings is to describe the educational program that will take place in the new building and to specify the types and kinds of spaces needed to house it adequately. In order to do this, educators must show a great deal of leadership in developing the educational specifications that will be used by the architect.

BUILDING CAPACITY AND UTILIZATION

One of the most important items that need to be discussed in a set of educational specifications for either new buildings or the renovation of existing buildings is the matter of capacity of the building. The capacity addresses the first item in a set of educational specifications. How many students will the building serve? This must be determined first of all and the reason for this is twofold. First, the population of any given area in the school system must be properly housed in the facility and the number of students in that area determines how large the building will be. Second, the cost of the building is determined by how large the facility is and that is determined by capacity.

Capacity relates directly to the budget of the project. How the building is utilized also relates to the capacity of the building. Educators and programmers must determine how the building will be utilized to account for all variations of scheduling the student body so that there are sufficient spaces for all of the students who will be enrolled. Utilization of the building in essence determines the ultimate capacity of the building. In elementary schools the utilization of the building is very close to the design capacity, meaning that the actual number of student spaces in the classrooms is the number of students that the building can accommodate. In secondary school buildings the utilization rate of the building does not approach the high utilization rate of elementary school buildings. This is because of the movement of students from classroom to classroom depending upon the subject taught in the classrooms or laboratories.

The two terms are related in that they deal with the number of students that can be placed in a school building at one time. Building design capacity can be defined as the actual number of students a school building can accommodate at one period of time. This is usually the design capacity. Capacity is based upon a predetermined amount of space that is required for either an individual person or an activity. The absolute design capacity of a building can easily be determined by counting the number of student spaces allocated to the building.

For example, in an elementary school of twenty classrooms with a student to teacher ratio of 25:1 the capacity of the school would be five hundred students. The five hundred students would need, in addition to the base classroom, a library, cafeteria space, a physical education space, and even separate spaces for art, music, and special education classes as the case may be. These latter spaces, in an elementary school, would not be counted into the absolute capacity of the building because students in a classroom would move from the base classroom to these other spaces for specialized instruction by a different teacher. The base classroom would be vacant during this time of instruction, but the students would return to the base classroom for instruction the remainder of the school day.

If the special education program specified a resource room for students in this program to go to for specialized instruction, these classrooms would not be included in the absolute capacity because the students would be pulled out of the regular classroom for this kind of instruction and return to the base classroom. Thus, the basis for the absolute capacity of the school building is the base classroom space using the predetermined pupil-teacher ratio. If the pupil-teacher ratio changes by either increases or decreases, then the capacity of the building would change accordingly.

For buildings housing secondary education students and programs the design capacity is determined by the total number of student spaces in the building that the design professional designated. But determining how many students a secondary school building can hold would be determined by how the building is utilized. This is because secondary students move from classroom to classroom to specialized classrooms and laboratories for instruction. This movement of students from one classroom to another must be accounted for by an increase in the number of classrooms.

For instance, the student space in specialized classrooms and laboratories are included in the design capacity, but because not every classroom or laboratory holds twenty-five students every period of the day, some accommodation for low enrolled classes must be made. To account for that, a certain number of additional classroom spaces must be factored into the building. This additional classroom space addresses the utilization rate of a school. The reason for this is the rostering practice of secondary schools. It is not possible to successfully roster twenty-five students in every class section for the entire school day. To accommodate this factor, some secondary schools utilize every classroom and laboratory only 85 percent of the time. In some very tight scheduling practices, the school might be utilized 90 percent of the entire school day, but this is not common.

The end result of this is that when planning a new secondary building, programmers plan on 10–15 percent extra classrooms or laboratories to accommodate the student population.

Coupled with the above is the demand for physical space within a classroom. The standard formula used by design professionals is 35 square feet per pupil. If the pupil-teacher ratio is 25:1 then the architects multiplies the number of students by the predetermined 35 square feet of space, resulting in a classroom of 875 square feet of space. Most states have certain space requirements for general purpose classrooms. These classroom requirements vary from a low of 650 square feet of space to 850 square feet for a standard classroom. For specialized laboratories and spaces, the amount of space would be from 1,400 to 2,000 square feet of space. The former requirement is very small for the modern educational program and the latter requirement is more fitting. Design professional are guided by these requirements or suggestions and design the building accordingly. There are other space requirements that have been developed to serve in designing specialized spaces in a new school building. These requirements are for specialized classrooms and laboratories. Many of these requirements have been developed by trade experts or other specialized experts.

The eventual size of the school building then is determined by the number of student spaces incorporated into the building plus the required square foot allocation for each student. This combination is oftentimes represented by a single digit. For instance, many school systems allocate a certain square foot allocation per student to represent all of the space needs for the building, including circulation space. Some of these allocations are used for programming the school building.

As an example a school system may allocate a total of 250 square feet of space for each student for which the building is planned. This represents the total space a student would need for all activities. If the school system is planning to house 500 elementary students in a building, school authorities would multiply the 250 square feet of space by the number of students for which the building is planned. In this case that would represent 250 x 500 students for a total of 125,000 square feet of space in the building. For the total space in a secondary building, programmers would need to add 15 percent additional space to account for the needed classrooms and laboratories. As a result a building of 125,000 square feet of space would need to be increased to 143,750 square feet of space.

#
16

SUMMARY

A set of Educational Specifications are statements describing the educational program to be carried on in the new school building. The specifications also list the number of students who will be in the school and the number, kinds, and types of learning spaces that will be needed. The specifications detail every space that is needed in the new building for it to work effectively and efficiently. The Educational Specifications are given to the architect to enable design work to proceed. The Educational Specifications are developed by the educators in the school system. In those cases where school system personnel are not available, the school board usually employs an educational consultant to develop the Educational Specifications. This document should be approved by the school board to provide for an approved set of statements describing what will be in the new structure.

Chapter 10

Site Selection and Acquisition

PROBLEMS SECURING A SITE

Selecting and acquiring an adequate school site is one of the most difficult tasks a school system must do in planning a new school. Over the years, this task has become increasingly more tedious because of several factors over which the school system has little or no control.

Some of the factors stem from the geographic area in which the school system is located; others stem from evolution of the educational program.

The natural increase in houses, industry, and commercial enterprises tends to reduce the number of adequate sites available to the school system. With the increase in program demands by the state, local school systems find themselves needing larger sites upon which to locate a school. The result is that there are fewer acceptable sites available from which the school system can choose.

Another factor is the increased price of land that has taken place. School systems are still paying for that increase. School systems with limited funds to purchase sites find it difficult to obtain suitable sites upon which to place a new building.

Because of this situation, school systems have been forced to come up with some rather creative and different solutions to the location of school buildings and students. Some school systems have located schools in existing commercial buildings no longer needed for their original purpose. Converting these structures to house a school has often proved to be a satisfactory solution to some difficult housing problems. Warehouse buildings, supermarkets, or other kinds of loft-type buildings have been converted to excellent school facilities. In recent years unusual weather conditions have destroyed many school buildings and such commercial structures have been converted to school use.

One problem with such facilities, however, is that the existing structure is usually not located where the students are located, necessitating busing of students to the facility. Sometimes the neighborhood in which the converted building is located is not the most desirable, and other social problems exist at that location or come about because of siting the school building there.

Nevertheless, the conversion of existing structures to school facilities is an excellent idea.

Other solutions to obtaining a site have been to use existing public buildings. A good example is the Parkway School in Philadelphia. This organization rented a small commercial building for the headquarters and home station for the students. Classes were then held in various rooms and spaces in public and private buildings. Buildings such as museums, municipal courthouses, art institutes, insurance offices, and newspaper buildings, for example, had spaces where classes could be held. These spaces and rooms were in a compact geographic area, so students could walk from building to building. A flexible schedule was used to allow students to have several classes in one building so that they did not have to walk great distances between classes (School District of Philadelphia, 1973).

Although the Parkway School no longer exists, it was an excellent example of using the community as a classroom space. This idea, or at least modifications of it, could be used in many communities to house students and programs if a little imaginative thinking is used.

Another practical idea for obtaining a site for a school building is to use property already owned by the city or county government, parks department, or recreation department. Although the idea of sharing a site between two governmental units is not new, its application is not as widespread as it could be. In many states, this is a rather novel idea, but placing a school building in a park already owned by another governmental unit is a good application of this idea. Benefits accrue to the community in two ways. First, the school system does not have to pay the purchase price of a new site. Second, less overall land is taken away from the community upon which to locate two governmental functions.

Another problem in finding adequate sites for new school buildings is the political consideration of new sites. Each possible school site must in some way be considered or approved by the political power structure in the community. This fact has been well documented in a study of the large school systems in the country (Earthman, 1976). This does not necessarily mean that members of the various power structures must meet and approve each site. What this does mean, however, is that each site selected by the school board must not be intended for some other larger community purpose nor intended for another use by someone or some community group in the local power structure. Most sites selected by school boards raise no general concern in the community as to the propriety of that use of the land, other than some community members who live near the selected site. However, occasionally, there is a concern raised that the site could be better used for some other purpose.

The matter then boils down to how the members of the community in the power structure that is affected believe the site should be used. Generally, members of the various power structures become knowledgeable of the possible sites under consideration because of informal interaction with school board members. Consequently, if no concern is raised by some group or groups, the school board then believes it should go ahead with the consideration of the particular sites in question.

School boards are not politically powerless in this matter, and sometimes it is possible to gather the strength of a community to press successfully for a particular site when groups oppose that action. School boards cannot always rely upon their political powers, but through compromises, solutions to site problems can be found.

LAND BANKING

To avoid the high cost of real estate, school systems need to plan for the future when selecting sites. Waiting until an area develops with new housing is not the time to purchase a site for a new school building. School systems need to be as forward thinking as the tract developer is. Traditionally, a school system waits until students are in evidence before planning for a new school building. This method leaves the school system reacting to situations and having to pay an inflated price for land. A few school systems do plan for the future by purchasing land in geographic areas of possible growth long before the growth takes place. This is usually called land banking.

It is quite possible in rapidly growing communities to identify and acquire sites for schools that will be used five to ten years in the future. This proactive planning can ensure the school system the best possible site for a school when the area does develop. Land-banked school sites that are not going to be used for a long period of time can be used in the interim for recreation. Park and recreation facilities can be constructed on the proposed school site and the community can use these facilities. Planned correctly, these facilities would in no way hinder the construction of a new building when the appropriate time comes.

A system of land banking future school sites requires a great deal of long-range planning by the school system. Such a system also requires a commitment by the school board to finance such a plan. Although the total cost of sites in this plan would be much less, it would be necessary to raise sufficient funds to carry this out, and it might be difficult to convince laypeople to support the plan.

Another problem encountered by school boards in trying to obtain sites for the future is the lack of appropriate legislation to control housing subdevelopment planning to ensure sites for schools. Proper legislation can come from either the state or local government. The state legislation would be simply enabling legislation for the local government to pass restrictive ordinances requiring dedication of land for municipal services.

It is the local government that needs to pass appropriate ordinances restricting the growth of subdevelopments so that schools are not inundated with new students. No one wants to control or hinder the growth of a community, but unbridled growth can cause considerable trouble for all levels of government, including the schools, in trying to provide services to new residences.

Some local governments enact ordinances that require housing developers to dedicate land for schools, as well as other municipal services, in every plan submitted for approval. This is a form of land banking that helps the developer sell houses and enables the school system to save appropriate land for school purposes. Such ordinances can be enacted in almost every locality.

A different approach to controlling subdevelopment growth has been taken by the state of Maryland. The Adequate Space Needs Act has provisions for partially controlling growth when public facilities are reaching a point of overcrowding. Under this act, school systems notify the local government when certain school buildings are overcrowded. The school system certifies that the buildings cannot accommodate any more students and that all available space in the building is being properly used. Based upon this certification, the local government notifies potential developers that their plans for a housing subdevelopment may not be approved, but that each individual building permit will be passed upon as it comes forward. This, in essence, controls all substantive planning by the developer until the school system can accommodate more students by either building new structures or redistricting for more space.

Each developer may get approval for a certain number of sites to be built upon, but each permit is voted upon as it effects school population. The county board of supervisors does not approve permits if approval means the schools will be overcrowded by the children from the family that occupies the house on the site. There is a two-year provision for an approved permit, and if the builder does not exercise it within that period, the approval expires. This moratorium on approval of permits may last until a new school building is constructed, which may be three years. Since this situation prevents developers from proceeding with planning, this delay undoubtedly causes them considerable damage. The only recourse in this situation, therefore, is to turn to political solutions in an attempt to move the appropriate governmental unit to provide funds for construction of new schools.

Another problem associated with site selection is the need for the local school board to consider innovative approaches to housing educational programs. Legislation is needed in every state to allow school systems to try different approaches to meeting school building needs. The use of air rights over an existing site is one approach that could be investigated. Use of the air rights over a site by a commercial firm could enable the school system to help pay for a new building. Multiple uses of space on a school site or within an existing building is another approach to assisting school systems in financing building costs for new sites.

SITE ACQUISITION

School systems may obtain a new site for a building in several ways. Here are the most common methods:

- purchase from the owner
- a gift from a donor
- exercising the power of eminent domain
- receipt of surplus governmental property

The first method of obtaining a site is the most common way for all governmental agencies. Under this approach, the owner of a site is contacted for possible sale. When the school board decides to purchase the site, a resolution is passed that states that fact along with a contracted amount of money. Following this action, the legal counsel of the school board approaches the owner to complete the negotiations and consummate the sale. A contract is drawn up, signed, and executed. A title is then obtained through the local governmental office that records deeds.

There are times when a piece of real estate is given to the local school board as a gift. The gift may be from a patron of the school system, a commercial firm, or an estate. Regardless of the source of the gift, school boards may accept such offers. Sometimes the gifts come with conditions attached. Perhaps the giver stipulates that the land can be used only for a school building, and if a school building is not constructed on it the property reverts back to the owner. There may be other conditions regarding use of the site or what can be placed on it. In such cases, the school board must abide by the conditions if the gift is accepted. A school board does not have to accept a gift, and in some instances, the school board would be wise to refuse the gift.

If the gift comes with no conditions, the school board may treat the offer of real estate as any other gift and use it as it sees fit: it may use the property for a school building or sell the property and use the proceeds for any program or activity in the school system. Sometimes real estate developers will offer the school system a parcel of land in a new housing development as a school site. Such gifts often carry a condition that a building has to be placed upon it. Then the school board must decide whether or not that site will fit into the overall capital improvement program. The timing of the receipt of a gift is out of the hands of the school board and many times does not fit the needs of the capital improvement program. In cases where the gift comes from an estate, legal entanglements can take considerable staff and legal counsel time for disposition of the real estate.

All local school systems are an extension of the state government. Because of this, every school system has the right of eminent domain. This simply means that the school system, through the school board, may condemn property for educational purposes. This is the legal act of taking the property of a citizen for public purposes, in this case, education, with just compensation for the property.

This legal right may seem rather easy and simple, but in actuality, this is the most difficult and emotional method of obtaining property. State highway departments use this method much more than school systems because of the large tracts of land necessary for highway construction. It is almost a routine practice for that department and seems to be accepted more generally than if a school system uses this method. This method of obtaining sites is rarely used by school systems and only in those cases where a particular site is needed and the owner is not willing to sell at what seems to be a fair offer by the school system.

To exercise this right, a school board must pass a resolution stating that this site is needed for educational purposes. The matter is brought before the local district court or usually the lowest court in the local government. The matter to be heard is the determination of the fair price for the property. Several methods can be used to determine this. The court may appoint two or three appraisers to determine a fair price. The court can then take whichever price it decides is proper.

Alternatively, the court can ask each party to present estimates of the price, and the court again decides the final price. The reason the court is involved is to make certain the property owner receives a fair price for the property under consideration. The fair price set by the court may be higher than what the school system originally determined it to be. In that case, the school system has to pay the owner whatever price the court finally stipulates.

This is the chance the school system has to take when entering this procedure. In addition to the price of the land, there may be other costs associated with condemnation, such as possible damages. These damages may be in the form of additional money to compensate a business for losses, costs of relocation, and payments to homeowners for purchase of homes of equal value. All of these may be in addition to the land costs. Thus, sometimes condemnation may be the most expensive method of acquiring a site. The school board must also gauge the possible emotional upset within the community for taking homes. Typically, the homes taken in a condemnation proceeding belong to owners who can least afford to move, financially, socially, and emotionally.

The last way for a school system to obtain a site for a school would be for one other governmental unit to declare a site they owned to be surplus. This, in effect, is transferring a piece of property from one governmental unit to another. Such programs began shortly after World War II, when the federal government began selling war furniture and equipment and even began giving away war property and sites acquired previously. The selling of government property is very common and such property can range from typewriters and furniture to camps and even air bases. Most often, real estate, rather than equipment or furniture, is declared surplus and available for transfer to another agency.

In these cases, the owner of the property notifies other governmental units that a certain piece of property is redundant. Following this, interested units can apply. The owner determines which unit is to receive title to the property and the transfer is made. Surplus property usually has no cost attached to the receiver, other than supplying a fee simple title to the property.

Although there may be some exceptions, most land declared surplus by a government agency is limited in its usefulness to the school system. In other words, the location of the property, the amount of land, or the characteristics of the land usually contribute to make the surplus property unsuitable for school use.

SCHOOL SITE STANDARDS

Many states have mandatory standards for minimum acreage for school sites. States that do not have mandatory standards do recommend certain minimums for school sites. Each school system should know what the state requires as far as the minimum site is concerned and observe that in acquiring a site. More importantly, the school system should ascertain the amount of land needed for a school site through analysis of the program that will be located there and then acquire a site to fit the program. Based on a careful study, the Council of Educational Facility Planners International (2004) has developed site standards, stated here:

- elementary school—ten acres, plus one acre for each one hundred students
- middle school—twenty acres, plus one acre for each one hundred students
- high school—thirty acres, plus one acre for each one hundred students

An elementary school of 500 students would require fifteen acres using this formula. A high school of 1,200 students would require forty-two acres.

These standards were developed through a study of the types of activities carried on by a student body in the particular type of school. The larger secondary school sites reflect the need for different playing fields such as soccer, softball, baseball, football, and track. The elementary school site size reflects the type of outdoor physical education program that is common on that level. These standards were also developed under the presumption that land would be available for school purposes.

In urban areas, such requirements are impossible to meet. Indeed, if such sites were even available, the price would be far beyond the financial capabilities of the school system. One school system located in a large urban area (School District of Philadelphia, 1973) developed the following minimum standards for their school sites, with maximum numbers of students, following an exhaustive study of the type of physical needs in the urban setting:

- elementary school—two and one-half acres: 900 students
- middle school—five acres: 1,500 students
- high school—ten acres: 3,000 students

Of course, not every urban school is located on a site as large as these. In large cities, a five-acre tract of land could well demand a price of $10 to $20 million per acre, which is undoubtedly beyond the resources of the school system.

Existing urban school buildings are very seldom located on a site as large as those recommended, and school buildings thirty years or older are almost never situated on a site that large. This applies to those school buildings located in the suburbs and rural areas as well. The need for more space to accommodate the modern physical education program has been a recent phenomenon in all school systems.

SITE SELECTION PROCESS

Selecting a site for a new school building is a volatile task because everyone wants a new building but no one wants a school located next to their house or business. This is a natural feeling because of the amount of traffic that is normally around a school. Both pedestrian and vehicular traffic are problems a neighborhood must tolerate if a school building is located where students live. If students are bused to the school, there is morning and afternoon traffic bringing students to and taking them from the building. In addition, students do not always use the sidewalks or paths to go directly home. Students wandering around the neighborhood present problems to some communities. In spite of this, a new school building and its occupants do not usually cause an intolerable amount of disturbance in the neighborhood, and the building can serve as a focus for the entire community (ICCMA, 2008).

Some people claim a school building may lower property values in the immediate neighborhood. Such has not been the case. In fact, schools tend to hold the community together. Early research has shown that the location of a school improved not only the value of the surrounding properties, but also the entire neighborhood; in fact, the school enhanced the economic health of the community. Grabe (1975) found this to be the case in a study of school sites in Michigan. The school building served as a central point of interest for the community because of the many activities, in addition to the day school, that took place there. Subsequent research has confirmed these findings (Neilson and Zimmerman, 2011). These researchers also found that as a result of school construction activities, student achievement scores in reading and math increased.

Very few school buildings are related to only one neighborhood. Rather, they are tied into several different ones that comprise the community. Only in dense city areas can a school relate to only one neighborhood. The school building should then relate to a service area composed of a variety of neighborhoods. This is especially true of high school buildings where attendance is very large.

The question of who to involve in the site selection process must be answered before the actual process is begun. Again, school board policies should be researched to determine the extent of involvement of various parties, particularly community involvement. Some school systems exclude community involvement as a matter of policy. In a survey of large school systems, the majority indicated the community was systematically excluded from the process of site selection (Earthman, 1976). The reason given was that parents and community groups could delay selection and acquisition of the site because of their objections to a particular site.

Urban areas typically face the prospect of an inordinate amount of time being spent on acquiring a site; with parental objections, resolution of the question might be years from the date the site is needed. Such exclusion from the site selection process, however, might not be acceptable in a great number of school systems throughout the country. As stated above, the person responsible for leading the site selection process should refer to the school board policies for guidance in community involvement before initiating the process.

If the community is involved in this process, their role may well be that of a learner rather than anything else. Laypersons generally do not have a good grasp of the amount of land needed by a school for a modern educational program. Nor are they conversant with other criteria that should be applied in trying to select a site, or even the selection process itself. This does not mean, however, that they serve as a rubber stamp for the school administration.

Quite the contrary, community members can help by lobbying for certain sites, identifying certain sites, and even mediating between competing groups. Involvement in this process can also result in a group of people who are more knowledgeable about what kinds of sites are needed and the process that a school system goes through to obtain one. The bottom line for community involvement, however, is what the school board policies stipulate.

The process of selecting a site may seem like a simple task of identifying a piece of land by driving around the area and then presenting a recommendation to the school board. Such is simply not the case.

In the first place, identification of potential sites is completed more scientifically than that. Identification of potential sites has input from a number of sources both inside and outside of the school system. The general area of the school system to be served by this site is identified through analysis of the projection of student population; transportation system; and the configuration of the county, district, township, or city. The resources of not only the school system, but also the city/county planning commission and state highway department are used to locate potential sites.

The involvement and cooperation of other departments in the school system and other governmental agencies must be assured at the start of the process. Selecting the site necessitates many meetings with school system personnel, community leaders, and local government officials. Obtaining some type of consensus through these meetings may require that the process lasts from six to eight months at least, and may extend to as long as a year. The various steps identified in the selection process include the following:

- The site selection team is assembled by the superintendent.
- The team meets with appropriate school department heads to initiate the project and begin to develop criteria.
- Planning parameters of the search are established.
- The site team meets with the local community to obtain their input into developing criteria.
- The site team meets with the local planning commission to talk about available sites and criteria.

- The site team develops a list of potential sites.
- Data on all potential sites are gathered.
- The site selection team physically inspects all sites.
- The site team meets with the community and lets them know the potential sites and how the criteria was applied.
- The site team meets with appropriate school departments to bring them up to date on the process.
- The site team meets with the local planning commission to seek approval of potential sites.
- Recommendations are made to the superintendent, who then makes recommendations to the school board.
- The school board passes a resolution to acquire the site, after discussions.
- The legal counsel for the school board draws up a contract for the purchase of the site and negotiates with the owner.
- The legal counsel examines the title, removes any liens, and produces a fee simple title for the school board (Earthman, 1990).

In some of the larger school systems, this procedure is much more complicated and lengthier because of the increased number of people, departments, and governmental agencies that are included in the process. Delays in public hearings or any other meetings may cause the procedure to acquire a site to extend to a year or more. In a large school system, it is not unusual to begin the site selection process two years in advance of the time of construction for the building.

SITE SELECTION CRITERIA

Potential school sites are evaluated by the site selection team using criteria developed by them and adopted by the school board. In some cases, these criteria are written into school board policies. However developed, the criteria are used to evaluate all the potential sites in order to recommend the best site to the school board. Here are some of the criteria that may be suggested:

- proximity to centers of student population
- adequate size and shape for the present and future enrollment
- accessibility to the site
- any existing traffic hazards and nearness to industrial areas
- utility services available near the site
- suitability of soil—percolation tests
- price within range of the school system budget

- contour of land to allow for drainage
- consideration of urban/suburban planning
- environment conducive for a school
- aesthetic appeal of the site
- favorable zoning regulations
- close proximity to community resources
- close proximity to safety facilities
- suitable for construction
- sufficient space for adequate parking
- the amount of usable land on the site
- easements of any nature
- sufficient free space to support anticipated educational programs
- safety of the site
- no geographical or topographic features that would present construction problems
- recreational facilities and areas near the site
- site development costs within the school budget
- site helps the desegregation program of the school system
- using this site for a school does not remove desirable housing from the market

All these criteria are important in evaluating a site, but, in the final analysis, the total cost of the site may be the one criterion that determines whether the school system can obtain it or not. The cost to purchase the property from the owners is relatively simple to determine, but the total cost of the site should also include the cost of site development. It is necessary to calculate not only the initial cost but also the cost of land development and the cost of maintenance.

Land development costs can be estimated in several ways. Professional landscape architects, building architects, and construction engineers can provide the school system with cost estimates for developing a particular site. In evaluating the development costs, estimates of the cost of the following tasks should be made by the appropriate landscape architect:

- clearing and grubbing
- demolition and removal
- earth moving
- rock removal
- under drainage
- electrical service
- athletic and other facilities

- storm drainage
- water supply
- sewage disposal
- walks, drives, and paving
- sodding, topsoil, and planting
- fencing, gates, and barriers

The total cost of these items, along with the cost to acquire the property, should give a reasonable estimate of the total cost of the site in question. A school system may wish to use other criteria to fit local conditions. The application of the above criteria to the site should constitute the evaluation procedure. Each of these items can be placed on a rating scale and a judgment then made on each item using that scale. The above items can also be converted to questions, which might help the site selection team members apply the rating in a uniform manner.

SITE EVALUATION

Each site is evaluated by each member of the site selection team. A profile and total score is developed, following inspection of the site. Site evaluation is a difficult job, especially when many members are doing the task. The simplest method, however, is to use a standard rating scale developed by the school system, with each member of the site team conducting an independent evaluation.

The initial judgment of each member of the team is recorded and compared to determine the degree of consensus. Since a high degree of consensus is desired on the final evaluation, disparity in results should be identified and discussed. After these discussions, consensus should be reached for each site and all the sites should be ranked, ordered from the first to the last based upon the profile and total score. The site with the best evaluation should be the first recommendation to the school board.

Shown here is an evaluation for a recommended site from a large city school system. The results of the evaluation can easily be seen and identified. This type of recommendation is presented to the school board following all the staff evaluations. In this example, the city school system plans to put two secondary school buildings on one site to economize on the cost of two sites for the two schools. The evaluation form refers to the site standards for high schools used in this city, in this case the maximum acreage that is in keeping with densely populated urban areas.

Washington County Public Schools
Washington City

#19

SITE EVALUATION FOR PROPOSED HIGH SCHOOL Description: The area bounded by Frankford Avenue, Hegerman Street (unopened) and a line parallel to and approximately 750 feet northeast of Stevenson Lane; parcel to be shared with proposed Vocational Skill Center.

Characteristics:
Size: 24.3 acres (to be shared with Skill Center)
Right of Way Affected: None
Physical Characteristics: Wooded, vacant, triangular, gently sloping
Estimated Cost: $4,950,000
Availability: Unknown
Service Area: Well located to serve anticipated school population
Transportation: Buses 66 and 84 adjacent, Penn Central station .6 mile away
Community Facilities: City golf course and recreation center 2 miles away
Relocation: None
Planning Comm. Review: Approved, Open Session, May 4, 2019
Community Reaction: Acceptable

Advantages
Size: Excellent
Rights of Way Affected: None
Physical Characteristics: Very Good
Estimated Cost: Low Service Area

Good Disadvantages
Availability: Unknown
Transportation: Good
Community Facilities: Fair
Industrial Facilities: Good
Relocation: None
Conclusions: At 24.3 acres, Site A could easily accommodate both the high school and the vocational skill center. The skill center would require approximately 4 to 5 acres, leaving about 20 acres for high school use. The site is quite close to the School District maximum standard of 21.5 acres. Considerable benefits—operational, physical, and financial—would be produced by this arrangement. Shared heating, air conditioning, cafeteria, and other services, plus reduced site acquisition costs are examples. Site A is well located with respect to most of the

major industrial area of the far northeast and offers excellent physical characteristics. The School Facilities Department of the School District recommends Site A to the school board.

While this process is occurring, the various power groups of the community should be apprised of the potential sites to ensure acceptance by all segments of the community. Naturally, it would be a waste of time and effort not to acquire political acquiescence for a site long before it is presented to the school board as a recommended site.

Although school board members may not be members of all power groups, each member does have access to members who are high in the various power structures of the community and in that manner can obtain information. As a result, school board members can obtain a feel from the power groups concerning the advisability of acquiring a particular site for a school. In most cases, school board members do not have to go so far as to request a review of particular sites or even ask about the site; rather the absence of questions and expressed concern by members of the power groups indicates acceptance, or at least acquiescence. In order to talk intelligently to power group members about potential school sites, school board members must be aware of the sites being seriously considered by the site selection team.

SITE SELECTION RESOURCES

Several resources are available to the site selection team in identifying and evaluating potential sites for new schools. Most of these resources are located in the office of the local government, specifically in the city/county planning commission. There also are some useful resources in the tax assessor's office. The following resources can be useful in identifying possible school sites:

- comprehensive plan of city/county
- topographic maps
- highway maps
- geographic information systems (GIS) (Coopers, 2003)

The comprehensive land plan of the geographic area served by the local government is maintained by the planning commission. No matter what level of government, such a map or plan is maintained in every locality. The map is the official document that shows all the land and the applicable zoning. It also contains the projected use of land in the future. All the present and future use of land is documented in this map.

Some localities even project on this map where future public services such as fire stations, libraries, schools, recreation facilities, parks, and governmental offices will be located when that area is developed. At the same time, these maps show where vacant tracts of land in a particular development or area are situated that could be used for school purposes. The office of the planning commission should be the first resource that is used in the search for usable school sites.

Topographic maps show the terrain and physical features of a geographic area and are useful not in finding potential sites so much as identifying physical features of an area under consideration. These maps show elevation and characteristics of the land. Topographic maps may be obtained from the state highway department, the federal government, or any cartographic outlet.

The highway department of each state maintains a large selection of maps covering the entire state. Most of the maps are used for development of the transportation system; however, they can be useful in locating possible school sites. Maps showing present and future utility installations are valuable for determining availability of these services. Highway personnel are always pleased to work with school system personnel in site selection because of the heavy traffic impact schools have upon surrounding areas.

The above are but the most common resources that are available to the site selection team in trying to identify and evaluate possible sites. The Office of the Assessor will also contain data needed by the site selection team. In this office, the owners of every tract of land are recorded, as well as the exact amount of land contained in a certain tract. These two pieces of data are extremely important for the school system.

Each piece of property in the governmental unit is listed in this office, along with the assessed value of that property. If the state or county/city practice frequent reappraisal of property, the current market value is then not hard to determine; this is very important for the school system. If the state does not reappraise property periodically, this piece of information is of very little use. Then it might be necessary to obtain the services of a land appraiser to determine the market price of the property in question because the school system needs to know this information to negotiate with the owner for a possible sale. Additionally, the school board needs to know if the property value is beyond the resources available to the school system for purchasing a site.

SITE TITLE

Every school board needs to have a clear title to all property owned and operated by the school system. The title needs to be a fee simple title, meaning a title that is clear of any liens or assessments. Following the decision of the school board to purchase a piece of property, the legal counsel must negotiate the contract to purchase the tract. Then the legal counsel must examine the title in the county or city Recorder of Deeds office. If the title is clear, with no liens or attachments, then a new fee simple title can be written for the school board for the school system.

The school board needs to hold the title to all property because no major construction can take place on the site if the school board does not legally own the property. In addition, in those states where financial aid is given to local school systems for construction purposes, the state has to be sure the school system actually owns the land. Otherwise, whoever owns the property then owns the building constructed upon the site and that owner can make decisions about use and disposition of the building. Almost all states that give assistance for construction insist that the local school system own outright the property for which aid is given.

SITE USE AND DEVELOPMENT

Proper use of the school site is extremely important to the community. The school system needs to utilize the site so that all educational and community needs are accommodated. To ensure this, a plan of development needs to be promulgated. This plan is sometimes called a master site plan. Specifications for this plan are developed by educators and approved by the school board, in much the same way educational specifications for the facility are developed at a later date. The architect uses these specifications to lay out and define areas on the site where different activities can be accommodated. A master site plan is especially needed for those sites where more than one educational facility will be located in order to fully utilize the site and provide for all activities.

For those sites where only one school facility will be located, such as a high school, a site development plan should be made based upon the needs of the educational program. These specifications are usually contained in the set of educational specifications developed for the facility itself. The educational specifications should describe in detail the numbers and kinds of playing fields, courts, and auxiliary spaces needed for the type of educational program at the facility.

JOINT-USE SITES

Quite frequently the school board and some other local jurisdiction, such as the recreation department or library board, may join in the use of a school site. There are several applications of this concept. The school board may be able to purchase a site larger than needed for the type and size school that will be placed there. This would then allow the other party to develop the site for a particular use. The recreation department might develop playing fields and erect equipment for their after-school program that could be used by the school during the day.

The school board and other local jurisdictions could also purchase sites that are contiguous that go together to form a site large enough for both functions. This practice is generally more accepted because one jurisdiction usually is not able to fund the site purchase for the other jurisdiction. In addition, the school board must have a fee simple deed to the land upon which the school is located for loan purposes.

Joint purchases of a site need considerable lead time in order for each jurisdiction to budget sufficient funds and have those available at the time of purchase. This facilitates joint purchase of sites by two or more jurisdictions in that those funds can be budgeted in advance of actual need. Some counties utilize an advanced land acquisition policy to help identify possible joint-use sites for future purchase. Such advanced notice serves the budgetary process very well.

SUMMARY

The selection and acquisition of a site for the new school building are difficult tasks because of factors not under control by the school system. In addition, curricular demands of the educational program require additional acreage to be contained in the site. The usual method of obtaining a site is through purchase from the owner, however, there are other methods including condemnation through eminent domain processes. This process is seldom utilized.

The school system must first of all determine what the site needs are, meaning size, location, and transportation requirements, among other things. There are several site location programs that are utilized by school systems to locate a site. Once the proper site has been located and evaluated as to its usefulness, the school system agrees to purchase the site. The school system must hold a lien-free title to the site in order to build upon it.

Chapter 11

Employing the Architect

One of the most important actors in the planning/designing/construction process for a new school building, for an addition to an existing building, or for a major renovation is the architect. This person puts into form what the educators need and desire to house the stated educational program. As a result, considerable staff time and effort should be expended to secure the services of an architect that can serve the school system well.

Some large school systems have architects on staff. Architects do design work for the school system, but seldom, if ever, design entire school buildings. This is because, to complete the project, an architect designing an entire building needs considerable support staff, such as consulting engineers and technicians. Support staff, along with sufficient workspace, would have to be provided by the school system in order to design a major building project. This is rather difficult to do because of limitations of staff and the volume of new work completed in these systems.

Usually, staff architects are used to design small renovation projects or additions to existing buildings. Some staff architects supervise the development of design work by outside architects under contract. This supervision is very crucial to the development of an appropriate, timely design for a new school in a large system.

There are five basic services that can be expected from an architect upon being hired:

1. schematic design
2. design development
3. construction document development

4. bidding advisement
5. construction monitoring

Some architectural firms can provide other services to a client, such as pre-planning, evaluation, feasibility studies, programming activities, and orientation to the building. However, all the services outside the basic services, which are covered by the contract, come at an additional cost (Tanner and Lackey, 2005).

Sometimes, architectural firms will offer to provide educational consultant services as part of their total package. Although this is one way for a school system to obtain needed educational consultation on a certain project, the cost of such additional services are borne by the architectural firm, which in turn bills the school system for these services. It is often far better for the school system to hire its own educational consultant to ensure the type of services needed and the objectivity required.

School administrators may think the educational consultation received through the architect is a free service taken out of the total cost of the architect's fees, but this is not true. All the services outside the basic five cost the school system extra. Whatever additional services the school system needs should be discussed and decided upon at the time of contract negotiations so that the responsibility for the cost can be determined early.

 ## SCHEMATIC DESIGN PROCESS

At the schematic design stage, the architect develops a concept for the building and works to place all the components within the structure, observing proper relationships between the components of the building. The concept is developed and refined through repeated reviews of the initial work. At the end of this stage, the architect has a drawing of the building showing all spaces within the building, relationships between spaces and functions, and the general configuration of the building (Brubaker, 1998).

Completion of the schematic design represents the first milestone for architectural design work. This is a crucial stage because the perimeter of the building is set at this time. Further changes to the exterior of the building could demand a redesign at extra fees. Interior design can change during the design development stage, but basically the outside walls of the school building and the basic shape of the structure are set at the conclusion of this stage. In addition, the building has been located on the site and circulation patterns established. When the school board has approved the schematic design, the architect will have completed approximately 10 to 15 percent of the total work of the project and is paid accordingly.

DESIGN DEVELOPMENT STAGE

After the schematic design has been approved, the entire scheme needs to be further developed and refined. This is where the fine points of the design are established. Systems other than structural, such as electrical, plumbing, and HVAC, are designed and refined.

During this process, some of the spaces within the building may change shape or size, but the building's configuration remains intact. At the end of his stage, final drawings are complete. This phase represents approximately 20 percent of the total work effort of the architectural team.

CONSTRUCTION DOCUMENT DEVELOPMENT

The construction document development stage of work proceeds at the same time as design development. The construction documents consist of the final or completed drawings and a set of technical specifications that lists all the materials used in the construction of the building. This phase represents approximately 40 percent of the total work effort and is usually completed by architects, engineers, and technicians who are familiar with the properties of the materials used in the design and who can describe them in functional terms (Vickery, 1998).

BIDDING ADVERTISEMENT

As part of the agreement, the architect will provide services during the bidding process for hiring the contractor. Such services might include helping the school system to secure an adequate number of viable bidders for the project, evaluating the bid in terms of the budget and the capability of the bidder, recommending areas where reductions in the project may be made when a bid is over the budgeted amount, and recommending to the school staff whether or not to accept a bid or to negotiate with the lowest bidder. These services represent 5 percent of the effort and are well within the scope of responsibility of the architect.

CONSTRUCTION MONITORING

Construction monitoring takes place after the bidding and while the contractor is building the structure. The task consists of providing periodic review of the status of the building project and onsite supervision of the work of the contractor. Developing shop drawings and providing material review is also included in this phase. Both a clerk of the works and the architect provide this service, the former on a periodic basis, such as weekly or biweekly, and the latter at certain stages of construction. Approximately 20 percent of the total work on the project is expended in this phase.

SELECTION METHOD

Several methods are available for selecting the architect or any other professional for service to the school system:

- noncompetitive method
- comparison selection
- design competition

The most frequently used method of selection is the comparison of several candidate firms; the least used is the design competition. All the methods are used at some time by school systems throughout the country.

Noncompetitive Method

This method of selection is also called direct employment because a school system usually employs an architect who has done satisfactory work for the system before or is the only architect available because of geographic location. Some school administrators find it easier to continue to work with the same architect who previously worked for them. There is no review of candidates or their credentials because the evidence of a good building is already located in the school system.

Some school systems, because of their rural and isolated location, find it necessary to employ the only architectural services available. Additionally, the architect might know the school system and school board, which could greatly facilitate development of the design and approval of it. There are many cases where architects have successfully served a school system over a period of years and this method of selection of an architect continues today.

In spite of the ease of selecting an architect through the direct method, there are some decided drawbacks. The most important disadvantage is the likelihood that the architect who does repeat business in a school system might tend to repeat the same solution to building problems. This means the architect tends to design the same building regardless of the location, specific educational requirements, or the type of program offered. The school system then tends to end up with one type of building throughout the system.

When the school system uses one architect to the exclusion of others, sometimes the school system may have to wait on a design if the firm is heavily engaged in other large projects. Such reliance leaves the school system at the behest of the architect when a building is needed. These are sufficient reasons not to use this type of architectural selection, wherever possible, in favor of one that will allow the school system to employ different architects to design buildings for the school system.

Comparison Selection

This method of selecting an architect compares several different firms for possible employment. A school system uses this same type of selection procedure in hiring other professionals such as teachers, administrators, and other staff. After a rigorous selection process, an architectural firm is selected based upon a comparison of the credentials of its employees.

Design Competition

This method of selecting an architect is based upon preliminary work that the architect has done. A school system selects firms to participate in the competition or may open the competition to all firms that want to participate. The educational specifications of the new building under consideration are developed and given to the architects who will be in the competition. The architects develop a preliminary design and several elevations—sketches of what the building will look like. The school board or a panel of educators evaluate the designs and choose one as the winner.

The architect who submits the winning design then receives a commission to develop that design further. In this manner, the architect is then chosen. The chosen architect then proceeds in the normal manner to refine the design and bring the project to bid.

On the surface, this method looks extremely promising for the school system and ought to encourage the best architects to enter the competition. However, this is perhaps the worst way to select an architect as far as both school system and architect are concerned. The architect must put considerable resources into the design of the model that will be submitted. These resources are up front, and if the architect is not a winner, these resources might be lost.

In an AIA competition, however, each of the submitting firms are compensated a fixed amount. These costs may not cover the expenses of the architects but are factored into the total cost of the project to the school system.

The chance of a particular architect winning depends on the number of architects entered into the competition. The design work of the architect cannot be used in any other project because the educational program will undoubtedly be different. The combination of high initial cost, the chances of not being selected, and the waste of design effort if not chosen weigh heavily upon not entering a competition. Most architects will not enter such a contest for a school building commission unless there will be some benefit even if the commission is not obtained.

This method of selecting an architect is even more disastrous for the school system. If the competition is conducted according to rules of a design competition, the school staff cannot see or critique the design of the architect before it is submitted to the panel, and after the design is chosen, few changes can be made to the design because that was the basis of selection. The school system is then committed to that particular design.

One of the most crucial periods in the design stage is the conceptualization of the building done by the architect early in the work when the school personnel should have extensive, direct input. The architect needs to have such input to be sure the design is being true to the educational specifications. Without it, the architect is left to translate the specifications alone.

This is not a desirable situation for the school system because interaction with school staff is desperately needed in the initial stage of design. Further, the architect knows that an eye-catching elevation or sketch can oftentimes sway a panel of judges and may design with that in mind. This, coupled with the fact that the design cannot be changed, makes this method less than desirable for both the architect and school system.

SELECTION PROCESS

Assuming the school system will select an architect through the comparison method, several steps must be taken to assure that an orderly process is used to make the selection. Several questions have to be answered by the school board in order to set parameters for the staff. These questions deal with whom should be involved, the degree of involvement, the criteria to be used, the materials to be evaluated, and the method of evaluation and final determination.

The school system administrative staff should recommend to the school board the process to be used in identifying, evaluating, and selecting the architect. The process should be no more complicated than the school staff can administer properly, but it should be comprehensive. Those responsible for conducting the process should be identified.

In a large system, the office that has the responsibility for supervision of the architect should administer the process and involve appropriate personnel outside that office. This might be the office of the director of Architectural Services or director of Architecture and Construction under the assistant superintendent for School Facilities.

In a medium-sized school system, the person or office responsible might be the director of Buildings and Grounds under the assistant superintendent for Business Affairs. In small school systems, the person responsible for administering this process might be an assistant superintendent or the administrative assistant to the superintendent. It is not unheard of to have an outside educational consultant assist the school system in the architect selection process.

The process of selection should follow the board policies devoted to architect selection and to personnel selection because much of what is done in the process is directly related to what a school system does when other professionals are employed. A review of the school board policies is the first order of business in developing the process.

Once the staff has developed the process, it should be approved by the school board to serve as the official guide for the staff to conduct the selection process. The process should be published for staff purposes and given to each architect who is a prospective candidate for selection.

Personnel Involvement

The first question to be resolved is who to involve in the architect selection process. This applies to both school staff as well as people outside the school system. As stated above, one office or person in the school system should be responsible for conducting the process, keeping relevant documentation and ensuring a timely completion. Staff members other than the responsible office should be brought into the selection process as needed.

Some school systems believe community members should be involved in selecting an architect. There are both pros and cons to this issue. Those who believe in community involvement feel that the community has a stake in the building and should help with the selection. This argument could well be used for any phase of the educational enterprise and thus, community members should be involved in selecting teachers, principals, superintendents, custodians, cafeteria workers, maintenance workers, textbooks, educational materials, buses, cleaning material, and on and on. The absurdity of this argument is clear.

The real question about community involvement is whether or not community patrons can bring to the process some different insight than the school staff who will work with the firm, or even if these people have a compelling interest in this service. There is little doubt that few community members know what makes a good architect or what to look for in evaluating an architectural firm.

If such is the case, then perhaps involvement is more showcase than substance. If involvement of community patrons does not slow down the process or violate any employment confidentiality or protocol, then it would be permissible to involve them; otherwise, community patrons should not be involved. The involvement of community patrons might be at best a learning situation for them and a chance to be exposed to the processes used by the school system. Outside of that, the value of their contribution to the process is questionable.

Developing Criteria

Once the question of involvement is decided, the next task is to develop criteria for evaluating the architect. The leadership for this step is taken by the office responsible for the process. Developing criteria can involve many people both inside and outside the school system. If people outside the school organization are used in this process, the office responsible within the school system usually organizes the effort through a series of meetings. These meetings often are held in the neighborhood of where the new school is to be built or in the school where an addition or renovation is to be done.

The central staff administrator will need to suggest possible criteria to initiate the process of criteria development. While discussing what the architect will do on this project, criteria can be developed as to what the community would like in the architect. From there, a logical extension of criteria would ensue. The following are suggested criteria for choosing an architect. A local school system may add other criteria deemed important in their situation.

All architects must be registered by the state in which they are working. Usually, this registration is obtained by passing an examination following the completion of a degree from an approved university program. Registration is important. Without it, an architect could not use the drawings that were created for a project because architects must put their registration number on every drawing to indicate that it was created by a state-approved professional (Vickery, 1998). Registration is granted on a state-by-state basis, and an architect from out of state must gain registration in the state in which work is to be done.

Architects can be recognized by their professional organization for outstanding work in their field by being granted membership in the American Institute of Architects (AIA). These initials are used at the end of the name of the architect to show such membership, an indication that the profession deems the architect worthy of distinction. A further designation of outstanding work is election to the College of Fellows of the AIA (FAIA).

Other organizations to which architects belong enhance their stature. Some architects who design many school buildings or are at least interested in designing such structures belong to the Association 4Learning Environments (A4LE). This organization is composed of individuals in educational organizations interested in facility planning, architects interested in school facility design, private educational consultants, and professors who teach educational facility planning. Membership in this organization tells the school system that the architect is interested in designing school buildings and wants to keep abreast of the field.

Another standard that can be used under this criterion is that of design awards. Some architects submit schools they have designed to organizations that give awards for outstanding buildings. Organizations that sponsor such programs include the American Association of School Administrators, the National School Boards Association, the Association 4Learning Environments, Association of Physical Plant Administrators, and the Association of School Business Officials International. Annually, these organizations recognize architects who have designed what they consider outstanding buildings. Architects are usually proud of these awards and list them in their achievements. School system personnel should evaluate these awards for what they are—recognition of good performance by the firm.

Experience

This criterion tells the school system much about the architect because the whole history of accomplishments of the firm are displayed in written form. A review of this list indicates how much work the firm has done and how much of it was done in school systems as compared to work outside the field of education.

A firm may have designed only one school building in its history and that may have been several years or decades ago. This would be revealing to the school system that was looking for a firm with considerable educational experience.

This listing should indicate not only the kind of experience, but also the size of the projects that the firm has undertaken in the past. In addition, some projects entail considerable creative design work because of certain constraints of the site or situation. What the architect did to solve this problem can be recognized through the project lists and description. This criterion is important in recognizing what the architect has done in the past and will indicate what the architect will do in the future.

Quality of Work

This is an extremely difficult criterion to evaluate because of the many factors that enter it (Rollins, 2012). Every architect would like to design buildings using only first-class material, but that is not always possible because of budget constraints placed upon the architect in designing the building. In many instances, school boards or owners are interested only in initial costs and in keeping these costs down; therefore, the architect is constrained to meet these demands.

This was the case in many school buildings designed and constructed in the 1950s. School systems at that time were hard pressed to keep up with the growing population and, at the same time, to keep down the cost of buildings. As a result, many architects designed buildings that are not aesthetically pleasing, but even more importantly, are not holding up under use. However, the architects who designed these buildings cannot be held solely accountable for the deterioration. The lack of quality in construction material could easily have been caused by the decisions of the school boards and the school staffs. The architects simply met their specifications.

The architect should tell the school system personnel the circumstances under which each building was designed so that the constraints can be understood. Architects should be able, however, to show examples of quality buildings that were designed over a period of time. School system personnel should look at examples of good quality buildings and even at some marginal quality buildings.

Staffing and Facilities

Architects usually indicate the staff available to them for projects. This gives the school system an idea of the ability of the firm to complete the project under consideration. For a large project, such as a middle or high school, a considerably larger staff is needed than for a small project. The size of the architectural staff is related to the number of projects or the size of the projects in the office under design. If a firm has a very small staff, they will need to expand to accommodate even a small elementary school building project. The number and kinds of professionals on the staff will tell the school system whether or not the architectural firm can perform the necessary design work.

The amount of space available to the firm is also a good indication of how the firm can accommodate an expanded staff to complete the design and engineering work demanded. There must be enough space to house an expanded staff, unless the existing staff can complete the work, which might mean the firm is not fully employed at the present time. This might give some indication of the health of the firm.

Method of Operation

Methods of operations refers to how a firm operates or interfaces with the client, that is the school system. Designing a school facility is not exactly like any other design project. There are two reasons for this:

1. There are many more approvals by offices and people within and outside the school system than for non-school projects.
2. The architect must present and defend ideas and concepts to many individuals and groups.

An architect must feel comfortable in dealing with large numbers of individuals and groups and must be able to listen to what they say and at the same time not be overly influenced by their arguments.

Sometimes, the ability to work under these conditions comes only through experience, and this is one reason some school systems insist that the architect they employ has had such experiences. This is not to say that an architect without such experience cannot perform nicely under these circumstances. Quite the contrary, there are many architects who feel comfortable under these situations.

If an architect who is employed has not had experience in the school system, it is incumbent upon the school system to orient the architect to the system and provide whatever help is needed to allow the architect to perform successfully. In this manner, both the school system and the architect will achieve good results.

Interest in the Project #21

Interest in the project is a subjective judgment at best, but there are many indicators that can be used to ascertain the degree of interest. Simply talking with the architect will inform school personnel how interested the person is in the project. If the person talks about other projects to the exclusion of the proposed project, perhaps interest in the project may not be sustained throughout the length of the project.

On the other hand, a school administrator will be able to recognize the person who has considerable and genuine interest. A visit to the offices of the architect may also give school personnel an idea of how other employees feel about the proposed project. Obviously, the architectural staff should not think the proposed project a burden on top of an already busy schedule.

References

References that the architect provides are very important. The school system will want to speak to these people about whom the architect worked with on their staff and how well the architect completed the project. If the references contain former school system clients, the local school system should interview the people who worked with the architect and staff in designing a building. The interviews should cover not only how well the architect worked with the staff, but also whether or not the architect kept within the budget, the number of change orders, and the effectiveness of the building itself.

Some people may want to include creativity and imagination in the selection criteria. In the first place, such criteria are very difficult to evaluate. Second, judgments regarding creativity and imagination are extremely subjective. What seems to be creative and imaginative in a building to some people may not seem so to others. The perception of creativity may be based simply upon individual likes and dislikes.

There is no real way to evaluate creativity and imagination in a person. True, there are some measuring instruments that are administered to children and youngsters for instructional purposes, but similar evaluative instruments for adult architects do not exist. As a result, creativity and imagination might be low in selection criteria because of lack of any agreeable method of measurement. On the other hand, some indices can show up in the work of the architect that might give a person a clue as to how creative and imaginative the person is.

If an architectural firm has a ready-made solution to the design problem a new building presents, this may indicate that the firm is not high on creativity and imagination and is relying on previous experiences to solve a current problem. Perhaps creativity and imagination should refer more to a fresh approach to designing a building project rather than solving the problem with previous solutions. Creativity and imagination do not, in school building projects, refer to radical design or strange building configurations.

Such buildings may not be functional on the interior, which is of the highest importance to a good educational program. Educational buildings are used for many decades. The building, therefore, must look just as good thirty or fifty years in the future as it does today. The building must also work just as well in the future as it does in the present. Sound judgments on building design and configuration by the architect produce those kinds of buildings.

In some places, school systems use the fee an architect proposes to charge as a criterion for judging a firm. Such a criterion, if used at all, should be the last consideration, and not bear the same weight as other items. In as much as the school system is the party requesting services, it can set the fee, regardless of what the architectural firm offers; however, negotiations between the school board and architect should allow for a fee acceptable to both parties.

Consideration of the fee in employing a firm leads to the practice of trying to bid for a commission. Such practices do not help the school system obtain the best architectural services but encourage practices that might lead to undercutting of services. School systems should offer a reasonable fee where the firm can make a sound profit without cutting services to survive a low-fee contract.

ARCHITECTURAL POOL

The first task in the process of selection is to develop a pool of possible applicants. This can best be done by contacting the local, regional, or state American Institute of Architects chapter and requesting names of members who might be interested in receiving a commission for a school construction project (Vickery, 1998). The AIA chapter will undoubtedly send a complete list of members with no definition as to field of specialty. This list will at least, however, be useful to the school system in making initial contact with interested firms. Architects are even listed in the yellow pages of the local telephone directory. In some cases, the advertisement there may provide some information on a firm. In some small communities that do not have access to large numbers of architects, the yellow pages may be a good source of architectural firms.

Larger school systems usually have a rather extensive listing of architects developed through inquiry by the firms rather than by the school system. Some school systems are interested in architects who have had experience or considerable work in designing educational facilities. There is very good reason for this criterion and school systems may well make it the most important criterion for selection.

Once the list of potential candidates is developed, an initial letter is sent to each firm. The letter states that architectural services are needed for a project that is described (see Appendix C). The letter goes on to state that if the firm is interested in being considered for the commission, certain material and data are to be sent to the school system for evaluation.

Once the school system has received the data and material from the architectural firm, they have to be evaluated. Someone who has some knowledge of architectural work can best do this evaluation. If the school system has an architect on the staff, that person might be the first one to evaluate the data and material. Other people on the central administrative staff might also evaluate this same data and material. The data requested by the school system asks for past performance of the firm, the capability of the firm to complete the proposed project, financial capability, and staff available to, or working in, the firm.

The material the architect submits, in addition to the above, usually consists of information about the firm, the number of projects completed, the type of projects, pictures and drawings of projects, and cost figures. When the firm has had experience in designing educational facilities, there will be mock-ups, elevations, and drawings of the building as well as supporting data on type of program, square footage, and costs. These are offered in an attempt to help the school system personnel see the type and kind of previous work done by the firm.

All of the data and material are the basis for making an evaluation of the firm for further consideration. When there are not a large number of firms to be considered, all the firms that responded to the initial letter are interviewed. If a large number of firms submit materials, the next step is to reduce the number of firms into a group that can be adequately interviewed and visited. This is done through an intermediate step of evaluating the data and material submitted by the architectural firms to reduce the total number of candidates.

An instrument can be developed and used to rank the firms in uniform manner by evaluating the material they have submitted. The instrument should take into consideration the size of the firm, number of engineers or availability of consulting engineers, years of experience, number of school projects designed, awards won by the firm, location of the firm, registration of the architects, costs of the school projects and the efficiency ratio of each project, and size of projects designed. Other items may be considered important by the school system and evaluated in addition to these.

If ten or more firms submit letters of interest and supporting material, the school board might have difficulty in interviewing that number of firms and adequately interpreting the results of those interviews. This would necessitate eliminating some of the firms in order to reach a final group of three to five firms that are of interest to the school board.

No ironclad rules exist for the number of architectural firms that can be interviewed. School boards have been known to interview all the firms that submit letters of interest. In larger school systems, time constraints prevent the school board from interviewing many candidates. In this case, the staff must gather data and eliminate some of the firms in order to utilize best the time available to the school board to interview the most likely candidate firms. The administrative staff must carry on the process of elimination. In rare instances, a committee of the school board with administrative staff support may conduct the first evaluation to reduce the group to a manageable size.

A group of no more than five architectural firms is about the right size for a school board to interview for a single project. There are situations where a school system will be designing several school projects over the course of a few years or where several school projects are under the same bond issue, where the school board may employ several architectural firms at once. In those cases, a larger number of firms must be interviewed and the first level of evaluation empowered to select a larger number of firms than stated above.

OFFICE AND SITE VISITS

After the first round of elimination has taken place, the next step is to gather further data on the firms to present to the school board. This can best be done by visiting the offices of the firms and some of the buildings they designed. There are several reasons to visit the firms' offices.

The first is to ascertain the level of staff support and their surroundings. In spite of the fact that educators cannot adequately evaluate the offices of another profession, certain observations can be made that will tell something about the firm. Although these may be subjective judgments, they nevertheless are valid assessments of the firm. Items that may be observed include the following:

• amount of space devoted to employees
• kinds of space used by staff
• number of employees that are currently working
• types and number of projects on which the office is currently working
• extent and kinds of technology employed in the design process
• how the staff feels about taking on another project
• reaction of the staff to a prospective employer

Subjective judgments about these items are no different from other judgments made by professionals in determining the ability of a firm to complete a project satisfactorily. Some school systems require an architectural firm to have a local office if their headquarters is in a different city or state. This visitation then gives the school system an opportunity to see if that requirement is met. Most often, a firm that has an office out of city or state will associate with a local firm so that the local staff and office can be used. This is usually a satisfactory arrangement for both firms and for the school system as there is a local contact that is known and can be reached.

The school system personnel will want to visit some of the buildings the architects designed to learn about the architectural work completed. One thing school personnel want to find out is how well the building has stood up over the years. School buildings are subject to relentless heavy usage by students. How well a building sustains such usage is of considerable interest to school personnel.

The users of the building should be interviewed to ascertain how the building fits the use. Caution must be observed here, however, because sometimes the usage is not what was intended. In other words, a room can be designed for twenty students and the principal assigns twenty-five or thirty. Obviously, the room is overcrowded, but not as a result of the architect's design.

Likewise, a space can be designed for a certain activity and now a different activity is assigned there. The space cannot support the new activity because it was not designed for it. The fault is not in the architectural design but rather in the use of the space. Such conversions, however, give an indication of how the building can be modified, if indeed it can. Following visitations to these facilities, school staff can make judgments about these situations that will be to the benefit of the school system.

SCHOOL BOARD INTERVIEW

Once the visits to the office and the various buildings recommended by the architect are made and the data gathered by the school system have been evaluated, the school staff usually makes a recommendation to the school board. Sometimes this recommendation consists of one firm, while in other instances there may be three to five firms that are included in the recommendation. In small school systems, the school board sometimes interviews all the firms and then makes the selection. School boards in large systems cannot afford to spend that much time interviewing architects because of the press of other decisions. In these cases, the number of firms that may be interviewed would be around three, at most. A letter requesting the architect to make a presentation is sent to all firms that will be interviewed. See Appendix D for a letter requesting the architect to make a presentation.

The interviews consist of a presentation by the members of the architectural firm to the school board to demonstrate their capability and experience. When more than one firm is interviewed, each firm is allotted a certain amount of time to make its presentation and respond to questions.

If questions are to be asked of the architectural firm, a predetermined set of questions should be developed and asked by board members. In the interest of fairness, all firms should be asked the same questions and given time to respond. Following the interviews, the school board then decides which firm they will employ. This can be done formally or informally without a vote, but once the board decides upon a firm, they must vote to enter into a contract with the firm that is selected. A resolution is introduced and passed by the majority of the members to enter into such a contract.

This is a legal action the school board must take, and that action must also be recorded in the minutes of the meeting as a public record. This action gives the legal counsel of the board authority to prepare such a document and to execute it. In many cases, the contract may call for an initial payment to the architect of a token amount to seal the contract.

ARCHITECTURAL CONTRACT

Architectural services are secured through a contract signed by a representative of the firm and the appropriate person to represent the school board. This legal document states precisely what services the architectural firm will give to the school system and the amount of money the architectural firm will receive for those services. As stated above, the school board must pass a resolution to enter into a contract with the architectural firm for a stated amount of money. The AIA has developed a prototype contract that can be used by the school system. The provisions of that document follow the usual services that are offered by architects. A delineation of responsibilities and liabilities is included in the contract so that each party will understand these areas.

A school system can develop its own contract through its legal counsel. Almost all large school systems develop their own contract so that provisions that are particular to the local school system or state can be incorporated into the document. Important safeguards for the school system can also be built into the contract that might not be in other contracts. Of particular interest might be the area of construction supervision. Appendix E contains a copy of a contract developed by a school system to secure architectural services.

The standard AIA contract states that periodic supervision will be given to the project by the clerk of the works who is an employee of the architectural firm. In small school systems, this might be construed to mean daily or even twenty-four-hour supervision, whereas to the architect it means a biweekly visit or occasionally a weekly visit. When the school system has a contract written for it, such differences can be accounted for and adjusted accordingly. It is much more preferable for the school system to develop an indigenous contract that will cover specifics needed to be included.

The contract, regardless of what type used, will stipulate the method of payment to the architect, who is paid based upon an invoice stipulating the amount of work completed. During the design stage and into the bidding and construction monitoring phases, the architect is paid on a monthly schedule based upon the amount of work done. Payments usually reflect the following schedule of completed phases and represent a percentage of the total fee that has been paid:

- schematic design—15 percent
- design development—35 percent

- document completion—75 percent
- bidding phase—80 percent
- construction phase—100 percent

By the time the architectural firm has completed the schematic design phase, 15 percent of the total amount of the fees payable will have been paid. Likewise, when the construction phase is completed, 100 percent of the fee will have been paid (Brubaker, 1998).

Some school systems retain a small portion of the architectural fees for a year after the building is completed as a surety. If this practice is desired by the school system, the contract with the firm will have to stipulate this from the beginning.

The contractual relationship between the school board and the architectural firm is no different from any other relationship in which a commercial firm provides certain services to the school system. The architects and engineers of the firm are simply members of a larger team of professional experts who are working to plan, design, and construct a building project. Architects and engineers are not decision makers in the school system.

The school board retains the right to accept and reject any product developed by the architects, and the firm is employed at the pleasure of the school board. Architects must not be forced into the role of decision makers by the educators and school board members. The absence of clear and concise directions and leadership might make the architect believe some decisions must be made to keep the project going. Such absence of leadership on the part of the educators and school board members should not happen.

TIME OF EMPLOYING THE ARCHITECT

The architect should be employed early in the planning process for a school project. Some school systems employ the architect before a site is selected so that the architect can provide some service in the actual selection process. These services are, however, beyond the usual conditions of the contract and must be paid by the school system. For a school system that does not have a great deal of expertise on the staff to deal with selecting a site, it might be a wise idea to employ the architect before that process begins. The architect might also provide some predesign planning services to the school system, which is usually beyond the contract fee. If a school system needs predesign planning, the exact nature of the planning task needs to be analyzed to determine whether it is a task that can properly be done by an architect or should be done by an educational consultant.

As an example, many times the school system needs some educational programming for spaces in a newly planned school. This particular task is clearly in the realm of the educational consultant because the programming of school spaces needs the expertise of an educator. This task entails the analysis of the educational program to determine the kinds of spaces needed, the size of these spaces, and the relationship of these spaces to other educational units.

SUMMARY

One of the most important actions the school board must take in building a new building or renovating an existing building is the employment of the architect of record. This person is responsible for designing the structure to the needs of the client. The identification, selection, evaluation, and employment of the architect is a responsibility of the school board aided by the work of the school staff in providing the school board with sufficient information about the prospective candidates to make an intelligent decision. The work the architect performs is contained in five stages of design work: schematic design, design development, document preparation, bidding, and construction monitoring. The architect is contracted by the school system to design the project and is under the direct supervision of school system personnel who need to provide guidance to the work of the architect. The best method of obtaining superior architectural services is to use the competitive method of employment where the credentials of all prospective candidates are evaluated.

Chapter 12

Monitoring the Design Phase

After the educational specifications have been approved by the school board, the architect is officially given the document to begin design work. This document becomes the program the architect uses to design the building and should be studied by the staff of the architectural firm in preparation for a kick-off meeting to get the design project started. Architectural firm representatives who will be working on the project and appropriate school personnel will attend the meeting. At this initial meeting, parameters of the project are given, questions about any phase of the project are answered by the school staff, communication lines are discussed, and the design schedule is approved. The conclusion of this meeting indicates the beginning of the design phase.

DESIGN TEAM

The people in the architectural firm who will be responsible for the design of the building form a working team. This group of individuals will work with the project to the end and will be termed the Design Team. This team is headed by the project architect and supported by other individuals. In rare instances, more than one architect may be on the team, but usually one person is the architect of record and responsible for determining the basic concept of the building, giving direction to the team, and making final decisions on the design.

The project architect also assumes responsibility for designing the building within the school system's budget. This last responsibility is very important because it will affect the final cost of the building. In essence, this person minds the purse strings so the project stays within budget.

The project architect is assisted by others both within and outside the architectural firm who provide engineering expertise. If the architectural firm is small, experts from other companies may collaborate with the project architect to form a Design Team to complete the project. In a larger firm, such expertise is employed by the staff. These support personnel usually follow the traditional disciplines associated with the building industry. An engineer is needed for the design of the basic structural work of the building. In addition, expertise is needed for other basic building systems such as the HVAC systems, plumbing, electricity, and technology. A group of experts in these areas serves as the basic component of the Design Team.

The Design Team may also be augmented by other experts in related fields from time to time. The design of a special area in the building may require added expertise. For instance, if a theater is to be designed, the Design Team may call upon the services of a theater consultant or an acoustical engineer for design advice. Someone well versed in the design of kitchens may be called upon to help with the design of that portion of the building. Likewise, experts in the fields of landscaping, library science, and gymnasium design may assist when needed.

DESIGN REVIEW TEAM

To assist the Design Team, the school system should appoint a Design Review Team consisting of the school personnel who are responsible for managing the design phase of the project. Specifically, this team is responsible for monitoring the work of the Design Team, assisting in the interpretation of the educational specifications, and giving approval to all parts of the design of the building (Earthman, 1994). This team is the counterpart of the Design Team and represents the owner, which is the school board.

The Design Review Team should be composed of a small group of individuals who will form the core and will stay with the project to the end of the design phase. The head of this group should be the staff member who wrote the educational specifications for the design project. In a large school system, this may be someone in the School Facilities Department at the director or supervisor level and may be designated an educational planner or school planner. In a smaller school system, the person may be a principal relieved of responsibilities to complete this planning project. If the school system employed an educational consultant to write the specifications, that person may well be the head of the Design Review Team.

Regardless of the designation, the person who actually wrote the specifications should provide direction for the Design Review Team. The second person on that team should be from the cabinet, council, or team of the superintendent. This person should be able to make decisions about the design work and have that decision hold without constant review by the superintendent or school board. That person should have the full confidence of the superintendent and school board to make everyday decisions without the need for review.

The third Design Review Team member should be a principal of a school building in the school system. The principal should know the workings of a school and how a school organization operates. In this manner, the principal should be able to anticipate the consequences of certain designs as far as student movement, access, program demands, and school organization requirements are concerned.

The basic core of the Design Review Team should be expanded at certain times to include other expertise in the school system. Expertise in selected areas such as maintenance and operations, cafeterias, libraries, vocational education laboratories, and gymnasiums might be needed when these sections of the building are under study. Directors, supervisors, or teachers of these subjects and areas could be brought into the Design Review Team at the appropriate time.

This group of secondary support personnel will eventually approve the design of that portion of the building for which they have either responsibility or expertise. For instance, the person in charge of libraries for the school system should be the one who eventually approves the layout of that area of the school. This applies to all other parts of the building.

The Design Review Team may expand from the basic unit when necessary and then contract to the three-member unit as the need may exist. It is not necessary for all persons in the school system to be involved in all phases of design review because they have neither the interest nor the expertise to provide sound advice.

The interface relationship between the Design Team and the Design Review Team is shown in Figure 12.1.

The Design Review Team closely monitors the design of the building from start to finish, reviewing all the work of the architect for acceptance. The review sessions usually begin with a presentation by the architect and then a question-and-answer period by the Design Review Team. Sometimes there are questions the architect has of the Design Review Team because a clarification is needed in the educational specifications. A resolution is made at the presentation by either approving what has been presented or by the architect agreeing to study the problem further and returning with a different solution.

These review sessions occur frequently during the middle of the design phase. In fact, the Design Review Team should not let more than two weeks pass without a review of some type. The sessions include examining architectural drawings of various parts of the building. Generally, the drawings that

Design Review Process

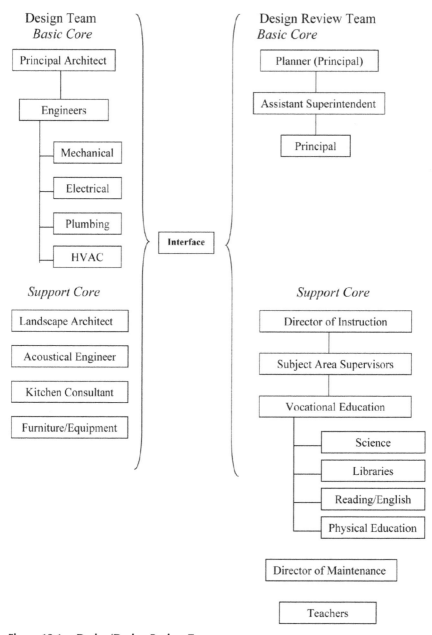

Design Team
Basic Core

Principal Architect

Engineers

- Mechanical
- Electrical
- Plumbing
- HVAC

Support Core

Landscape Architect

Acoustical Engineer

Kitchen Consultant

Furniture/Equipment

Interface

Design Review Team
Basic Core

Planner (Principal)

Assistant Superintendent

Principal

Support Core

Director of Instruction

Subject Area Supervisors

Vocational Education

- Science
- Libraries
- Reading/English
- Physical Education

Director of Maintenance

Teachers

Figure 12.1.   Design/Design Review Teams

are used in this review are 1/8" scale, but occasionally, when a detail is to be studied, a 1/4" drawing will be used.

DEVELOPING THE DESIGN

There needs to be a very close working relationship between the Design Team and the Design Review Team in this stage of development to guarantee fidelity to the set of Educational Specifications. This activity usually begins by locating the building on the site. After a thorough study of the site and the requirements of the educational program, the architect will suggest a specific location on the site for the building. In doing this, the architect will take into consideration the location of utilities, traffic patterns, parking needs, as well as the contour and aesthetics of the site. The building's location will be the first big decision to be approved.

The second decision will have to do with the concept the architect is trying to implement through the building design. The architect will develop a concept of the building, keeping in mind the scale of the neighborhood, the environment, type of surrounding architecture, certain site factors, the educational program, level of school, and even the idea of what a school is and the image the architect would like to project. All these elements comprise the architect's ideas in conceptualizing the school building. Within the concept, the architect has to fit all of the various components of the building that are needed to enable the educational program to function properly. The architect may develop more than one concept for study purposes, but only one idea is chosen to be further developed. The architect and Design Review Team agree upon the concept that allows further development.

Schematic Design

After the initial decisions have been made, the architect begins work on the schematic drawings. The schematic design is the point where the basic configuration of the building is determined. The architect seeks to define the concept internally by locating the various components of the school building. The relationship between these components has been defined exactly in the educational specifications, and the architect follows these directions in expanding the concept. Circulation of students, materials, and supplies within the building are also concerns at this stage of development.

The architect works to develop efficient lines of circulation within and outside the building. All these design problems are addressed at this stage of development. Approval points on all the work done in this phase take place at design review meetings where both the Design Team and Design Review Team meet to review the drawings. A series of weekly reviews and approvals leads to the completion of the schematic drawings.

When the Design Team has completed the work in this stage, the schematic drawings are formally presented to the school board. This consists of a review of the program and the actual design approved by the school staff. The school board should formally approve the schematic design of the architect. This can be done by resolution or by informal consensus of the school board. This approval is important because it gives the architect the signal to proceed to the next stage of design work.

The schematic design is also a milestone in the development of the design. At this point, the exterior of the building is set and should not be changed. The architect has reconciled the square footage of the building with the budget allocation for the building and, therefore, should be reasonably assured that the size of the building will not change after this approval. To change either the basic design of the building or to add or subtract from the size after this point in time would be cause for a redesign, which would cost the school board extra payments to the architect. Needless to say, to ensure the design is what they want, the Design Review Team should work closely with the Design Team. After school board approval, the Design Team is able to start the design development.

Design Development

The design development stage takes the longest amount of time because of the amount of exacting work that needs to be completed by the Design Team. Drawings of each segment of the building must be completed. Here again, weekly meetings between the Design Team and the Design Review Team are required to keep the project on schedule.

During this period of design work, many of the specialists on the school system staff are brought into the design process to review that portion of the building for which they have responsibility. Also during this stage, these specialists will eventually sign off on the drawings, indicating approval of the design. During this period, the furniture and equipment needed in the building is specified by either the school staff or by the architect. In very small school systems, the architect may take on this responsibility as a separate contract to assist the school system, but the school staff must approve of the type and kinds of furniture and equipment beforehand. In most other school systems, the school staff should write the specifications, conduct the bidding, and secure the loose furniture and equipment needed. This act saves the school system considerable funds in additional architectural fees.

During this stage, technical writers produce a document describing all the building materials that will be used to construct the building. This document is termed the technical specifications and, along with the final architectural drawings of the building, serves as the contract document from which bids are developed by contractors. The specifications in this document must be approved by the school staff if they did not write them. With the completion of the design and the technical specifications, the design development stage ends and the public bidding phase begins.

EVALUATING ARCHITECTURAL DESIGNS

In evaluating the work of the architect and the Design Team, school system personnel are placed in the position of having to review the work of a profession for which they have not had any training. The educators must decide if the design meets the needs of the organization that they are representing. This can be done successfully only if the people doing the review are well versed in the type of program that will be offered in the building. This is the first requirement in order to successfully review architectural plans.

The time frame for completing the design work for a new building varies depending upon the type of building involved, the size of the structure, the location, the availability of school staff to review designs, and the amount of staff the architect is able to employ on the project. Generally speaking, the design of a medium-sized elementary school should take approximately six to nine months, depending upon how much time the architect can devote to the project. On a large high school project, the design stage could well consume the better part of twelve months.

In planning for the opening of a new building, the school staff should anticipate these lengths of time for proper design work. There is a point when the design work can be pushed so fast that mistakes in reviewing the plans take place. Therefore, this possibility must be avoided at all costs. The proper and timely development of a good design for the new building is the first order of business.

Design Review

As described in the last section, educators are required to evaluate the work of a different profession, one for which they have not had any formal training. This presents a dilemma for those school staff that actually approve design work. These people will be required to read and interpret architectural drawings to approve the design and most school personnel have not been trained to do this. In fact, it is extremely rare for an educator to possess such background. Such expertise usually comes from experience in actually reviewing plans and not from any systematic study.

Actually reviewing plans is the best way to become familiar with architectural drawings. In addition, asking questions and listening to explanations is a good method of learning. Even if a question sounds simplistic, it should be asked, because that person is representing the owner of the new building, the school board. Design professionals are expert in being able to answer questions and are more than willing to do that. The responsibility for asking the question, however, rests with the school staff.

The basic question is what to look for when reviewing plans. One approach is to try to anticipate problems that may arise when a large number of youngsters are in the building trying to find classrooms and doing the work they are supposed to be doing. The Design Review Team members must be able to ask these questions to see if the plan works. If a principal is a member of the Design Review Team, that person can add valuable experience in looking at the proposed building. Another way is to follow a typical schedule of a student in the school for one day. Circulation patterns can be studied, relationships between building components can be evaluated, and student-grouping problems can be identified in this manner.

The basis for evaluation of any design is the set of educational specifications prepared for that particular building. This is the document that is to be used in evaluating every aspect of the building. All the descriptions given in that document must be found in the design of the building before approval can be granted. Questions generated from these descriptions can guide the design review sessions. The following list contains general questions that may be useful in evaluating architectural designs. These are but some of the questions members of the Design Review Team should raise at any review session.

1. Traffic patterns
   - Is the building barrier-free?
   - How do students enter a building, get to their lockers and classes?
   - Are there any hallways or intersections that might cause student traffic congestion?
   - Are the hallways sufficient to accommodate the numbers of students?
   - Is there a well-identified main entrance with reception lobby to help community users?
   - Do the hallways serve all areas with ease?
   - For high school buildings, is the circulation system compact enough to allow students to get from one area to another in the given amount of time between classes?

- Is the traffic flow from one building component to another efficient?
- Will areas that are not always opened be easily accessed so that they can be closed off when not in use?
- Does the main entrance have secure building elements to permit guarded entrance of visitors?
2. Relationships between components of the facility
   - Are the proper relationships between subject areas observed?
   - Are the general relationships of the building efficient?
   - Are the noise areas separated from other areas?
   - Are necessary relationships to outside facilities observed?
   - Are community spaces clustered together?
3. Numbers and types of instructional, administrative, and activity spaces
   - Are the numbers of teaching spaces called for in the educational specifications?
   - Are these spaces the right kind?
   - Are these spaces in the needed relationship to each other?
   - Are there the right kind and number of administrative spaces?
   - Are there the right kind and number of guidance/health spaces?
4. Size and shape of spaces
   - Was the ratio of 75 percent instructional and 25 percent noninstructional space observed throughout the plans?
   - Is each space sized correctly?
   - Are the teaching spaces the shape that will enhance the program?
   - Is there sufficient space to do what is necessary in the teaching program?
   - Are there any odd or irregular spaces being assigned as administrative space?
   - Has enough storage been provided in all administrative and instructional spaces?
   - Are there any triangular, oval, angular, or other similar spaces being assigned as teaching spaces?
   - Is there any wasted or non-assigned space?
5. Utility service
   - What type of energy source is being used?
   - Is there sufficient utility service to each area currently, and in case of expansion of the building?
   - Are there electric, natural gas, and water outlets where necessary?
   - How many electric outlets are there in the instructional spaces?
   - Are utilities zoned so that portions of the building can be heated and lighted independently?
   - Are there water and electrical services where custodians need them?
   - Is the building energy efficient?

6. Potential supervision problem areas
   • Are there any areas that may present a supervision problem?
   • Can students get onto the roof area?
   • Are there blind spots where students cannot be observed?
   • Are there places where trash can build up to present an eyesore?
   • Are there nooks, crevices, or indentions in the building that would allow undesirable hiding by people?
   • Are the restrooms free of problem areas and design features, such as low ceiling heights?
   • Are locker areas easily supervised? (Earthman, 1990)

The Design Review Team must also raise questions about other aspects of the building, such as types of building materials used in the structure, especially wall finishes. This is important because of heavy student usage that would generate maintenance problems later in the life of the building. In addition, the Design Review Team might want to raise questions about initial costs, maintenance costs, lifetime operating costs, energy conservation, and other design features. All these matters are within the purview of the Design Review Team.

KEEPING THE PROJECT WITHIN BUDGET

With all building projects, a major problem that must be faced is keeping the scope of the project within the given budget. This is true for each building project completed by the school system. The original budget for the project was established at the time of approval of the capital improvement program. Each year the project is in the program, the cost estimates are projected to account for inflation. In this manner, the project costs are considered current. When the design of the project is started, presumably, the budget is current and the architect can feel reasonably sure there are sufficient funds to complete the project.

During the design stage, the architect periodically prepares cost estimates for the school system to determine if the budget is sufficient for the project. The architect continues this process throughout the design stage until the project is put out for bid. All of this is to ensure that the school system has enough funds to complete the project. In a time of steep inflation, reserve funds may have to be set aside to complete the project.

There are several points at which control over the project is mandated to ensure the funds will be available to complete work. The first point of control is in the development of the educational specifications. Tight control over the allocation of space to each program area is necessary to ensure that the scope of the project will not exceed the funds and, at the same time, sufficient space is given to allow a program to function properly. The person developing the educational specifications must keep the project within the space allocated by the budget and not allow unreasonable requests to expand the project beyond what is available.

The second point of control is during the design stage. Many times requests for more space seem reasonable, but in trying to accommodate a program, the entire project is expanded to exceed appropriated funds. During the design stage, the educational specifications must be rigorously followed so that the scope of the building will not expand and thus exceed the available funds.

Another factor that impacts upon the total cost of the project is the materials that will be used in the building. The higher the quality of materials in the building, the higher the per square-foot cost and subsequently the entire building project. The original capital improvement budget cost estimate should allow for high-quality materials to be used in the building to reduce maintenance costs later in the life of the building. Changes in the quality of materials may have an adverse effect upon the total cost of the project.

When there are differences between cost estimates of the building at any stage and the budgeted amount, something has to be done to reconcile the difference. There are only two ways to accommodate a cost difference. Either more funds must be allocated to the project, or the project itself must be reduced in some fashion. When additional funds can be obtained from other projects or reserve funds, these can be applied. In some states, however, such fund reallocation is not possible (Earthman, 1994).

If the building is being constructed under a set-sum bond issue, there may not be any reserve funds. Most school systems, even under a set-sum bond, will establish a contingency fund of approximately 5 percent to cover such emergencies. When such financing is not possible, the scope of the project must be reduced.

There are two ways to reduce the scope of the project if more funding is not possible. One way is to reduce the size of the entire building either by reducing segments of the building or by reducing sizes of classrooms. In both instances, a less desirable building will result. The second way to reduce the scope of the project is to reduce the quality of materials that go into the building. In reality, this latter method of reducing costs simply shifts costs to a later time in the life of the building. Reduced quality of material will undoubtedly increase the maintenance costs of the building over its lifetime; therefore, it should be avoided at all costs.

UNIFORM BUILDING CODES

The design and construction of all public buildings are governed by the uniform building codes of the state. These codes are adopted to protect the health and safety of the occupants of the building. The codes govern the types and kinds of materials used in the building, the application of the materials, space allocations, sanitary provisions, and other legal matters. Buildings must conform to these codes before a building permit is issued. Administering the uniform building code occurs on the local level because that is where the permit to construct the building is issued.

Architects and engineers must be particularly aware and knowledgeable of all codes that govern school design and construction. Local building inspectors review the plans for conformity to codes and, when such is the case, issue a permit. Members of the Design Review Team do not have to be as familiar with these codes as the design professionals, but they should know the source of the codes, how they are administered, and where they can obtain authoritative information about code conformity. In cases where there may be a doubt as to the conformity of any design, school personnel can obtain assistance from the state as an impartial party. The first inquiry for assistance should be made at the office of the state fire marshal. In some states, the department of education can assist the local school system in applying building codes to specific designs.

STEPS OF APPROVAL

There are many approval steps in the design of a building. These can occur both inside and outside the school system. There are both formal and informal approval steps. The most important formal approval of a design is at the schematic stage, where the school board formally receives a presentation of the project and then approves the design for further development. Further approvals by the school board are not necessary, and in many instances would slow the architect's work. At the schematic stage, the building exterior is set and will not change; as a result, further approvals are redundant.

Informal approval steps occur at every design review meeting. At the end of each meeting, the documented approvals should be shared between architect and Design Review Team. This keeps the record straight and provides the architect with immediate feedback of decisions. These approval sessions continue throughout the design development stage of the project until the final working or construction documents are finished.

In some instances, local governmental offices or commissions may require approval of the project. It is not unusual for the local art commission to have approval supervision over public works projects. When this occurs, the architect or school staff person must apply for a presentation and seek approval at that time. The architect must know of and anticipate these regulations.

In many states, some state office or department may require approval of the building project. This is especially true if the state provides any funding for capital expenditures. Each state has specific requirements for the approval process and the architect should become familiar with the requirements. The school staff should make sure the architect is cognizant of these requirements so that the project is not delayed unnecessarily.

COMPUTER-AIDED DESIGN DEVELOPMENT

Before the computer came into general usage, architects had to produce all the drawings needed to complete a capita project by hand. Needless to say this consumed a great deal of time and effort. Numerous draftsmen were needed to produce the drawings. This was a costly effort on the part of the office of the architect. When the computer became a useful tool for the architect, the process of producing architectural drawings became much easier and complete. What took years to produce drawings by hand, took a matter of weeks and even days to produce with a computers. Computers greatly increased the productivity of an architectural firm and produced the building much more sooner for the local school system.

The computer has become a great assistance in the design of buildings. All architects use a computer in their work of designing a building. This process is called computer-aided design development (CADD). Use of the computer provides the architect with a great deal of power and speed in designing a building (Tanner and Lackey, 2005). The particular system that is used may require square-footage limits, preset relationships, circulation requirements, and many other conditions determined by the architect. Using CADD, a series of drawings are developed for consideration by the architect and owner. These drawings can be reproduced on hard copy for further study.

Using CADD can save the architect considerable time in just drawing alone. The computer can produce in a short period of time what would have taken a technician or architect several days to produce by hand. In addition, changes to any design can be made almost instantaneously and the results evaluated on the spot. Several variations of a drawing can be considered within a short period of time to allow for comparison. Needless to say, the rapidity of this kind of design development permits greater options for the architect and owner.

In addition to the capability of producing drawings at a high speed, the computer allows the architect to view the drawings from more than one dimension. Computers provide a three-dimensional display so that the architect can see through a design that is being developed. When designing a multistory building, relationships between different sections of the building are difficult to determine on a one-plane drawing. With CADD, two floors of a building can be juxtaposed and viewed from different angles. In this manner, creative design relationships can be produced that meet the requirements of the educational specifications.

Development of the construction documents, final drawings, and technical specifications can be completed with a higher degree of accuracy and speed with CADD. These documents are used in bidding the project and must reflect precisely the work to be done and the materials to be used in constructing the building. Cost estimates are also more readily available by using the computer (Means, 1996).

Despite the benefit with CADD of faster design work by the architect, there are some cautions that must be observed. The normal design review meetings should not be changed in any manner because of the rapidity in producing architectural drawings, except to have the review sessions closer together. Sometimes when a process is accelerated, approval points may tend to be eliminated or reduced, which would not be to the advantage of the school system. The increase in speed of obtaining design drawings from an architect should in no way eliminate the thoughtful and thorough review of each plan to ensure fidelity to the educational specifications.

SUMMARY

There are usually two teams to monitor the development of the building design. One team is from the architectural firm that does the actual design work. The other team is the Design Review Team and is composed of school system personnel to review the work of the architect. The basis of the review is to determine how closely the architectural design team is following the provisions in the Educational Specifications and to assist in keeping the project within budget. The process of design review incorporates many meetings between the two groups until the final design concept is completed. With the use of the computer to assist in the design of a capital project, the work of the architect is much faster. What used to take months to design, a major project now takes considerably less time. This is beneficiate to the school system because the proposed school can be put under construction sooner.

Chapter 13

Bidding the Construction Project

The bidding process for a construction project in the governmental sector is a complicated system of determining which firm or company will be able to complete the work at the best competitive price. This system of procurement is seen as an equitable way for all qualified firms to have a chance at being selected to provide services, and at the same time for the governmental agency to obtain work at the lowest possible price. It is a fair and advantageous system for procuring goods and services for all concerned. Not to use a bidding system in procuring goods and services is to invite practices that are not in the best interest of the school system and that may violate ethical and legal norms.

There are many misconceptions regarding the bidding process; therefore, anyone involved should be familiar with the legal requirements of both the state and local school system. Most states require the local school system to have some sort of procurement provision in the school board policies to govern the acquisition of goods and services. Whether or not the state mandates such a provision, the local school system should protect itself by establishing such procedures.

The school board policies regarding bidding procedures should address what goods and services are to be bid and the size of these projects or amounts. Usually a dollar figure is specified in these policies above which all projects must be publicly bid. The bidding procedure for items and projects below this set amount is usually handled differently, such as receiving telephone bids or some similar informal method. The procurement policies should also address advertising, opening, pricing, awarding, rejecting, and withdrawing bids. In addition, the policies must-have provisions for bonding and qualifying bidders.

Although most people generally assume all bids are sealed, such may not be the case. The policies should state which types of bids need to be sealed and which do not. Bids for small items usually do not need to be offered in a sealed container. Bidding on a project that involves a great deal of money, such as construction proceeds, needs the formality of being offered in a sealed envelope.

A quick review of the school board policies will indicate if these areas are covered. If, by some chance, they are not, the school board should enact such policies before any bid is publicly tendered. To avoid conflict, local school system personnel should also be familiar with state legal provisions governing the bidding procedure that might impinge upon local policy.

BIDDING DOCUMENTS

In the final stages of the design process, the architect produces bidding or contract documents, which are a set of architectural drawings and technical specifications.

The architectural drawings contain at least four different sets of plans of the building to be constructed. The different sets follow the usual disciplines involved in the design process. There is one set dealing with the structural and mechanical design of the building, another set details the electrical service in the building, another contains the plumbing and drainage systems, and the final set describes the heating, ventilation, and air conditioning system (HVAC).

These four sets of drawings are needed by the various engineering disciplines to determine the work to be done. There may be other sets of drawings, depending upon the complexity of the building. For instance, there may be a separate set of drawings detailing the communication and technology system in the building, or alternative structures, which might be bid separately. Additionally, there may be drawings for special areas in the structure such as a television studio, a stage area, or a locker area.

In any event, this set, or group of drawings, is called working drawings, final drawings, or contract drawings, and describe the same thing. The architect is responsible for preparing and signing all drawings to be used by the school system in the bidding process.

The architect is also responsible for preparing a document called the technical specifications, which describes all the materials to be used in the construction of the building and the amount needed. This description is quite detailed. The size and quantity of nails, bricks, and wood; the mix of concrete; the slope of the roof; and the quality of workmanship to be used in the building are all precisely described. This document is needed by the contractor to determine the bid price. From this document, accountants in the office of the contractor can accurately determine the price of materials.

The description of the building in this document also enables the estimator to determine the size and cost of the workforce for the project. All these documents provide specifications that form the basis of the submitted bid. Of course, the competitive nature of the bidding process means the estimator for the contractor must be precise to enable the contractor to have a good chance of being awarded the bid.

25 PREQUALIFICATION OF BIDDERS

A school system can request that potential bidders prequalify before they submit a bid on a construction project. This means that the school system desires firms to have certain qualifications before their bid is considered.

Although the surety bond is a way of prequalifying, that is the company has been appraised by a bonding company, usually prequalification means something more definitive. Prequalification can refer to any type of demand made by the school system. For instance, prequalification can refer to type and amount of experience, number and types of employees, financial security, and even location of offices.

Many years ago, the City of Philadelphia developed a prequalification based upon the number of minority persons employed by the firm. Firms wishing to conduct business with the city have to have a certain percentage of employees of a minority race on the payroll before they can successfully bid on projects. Potential bidders have to submit a list of their employees, with minorities identified, with their sealed bid. In this manner, firms qualify themselves prior to the bid opening. Firms that cannot qualify because they lack sufficient minority employees will not have their bid opened.

School systems may place prequalifications upon potential bidders so long as the prequalification has a relationship to the ability of the bidder to perform work and does not violate antidiscrimination laws. All firms submitting bids to federal, state, and local governmental agencies must agree before the bid to abide by the rules and regulations concerning affirmative action and equal employment opportunities. Agreement to the employment practices as derived from the Civil Rights Act of 1964 and subsequent revisions can be considered prequalification of potential bidders. All bid advertisements now carry the stipulation that successful bidders must agree to these practices.

PROCEDURE FOR BIDDING

The method of conducting bidding is rather simple and straightforward; however, it must be carried out in a manner that observes all legal requirements.

The first requirement is to advertise the bid publicly. The school system is responsible for placing a legal advertisement. This consists of placing an advertisement in the legal newspaper of the locality. Usually, a newspaper located within the jurisdiction of the school system or one that at least serves the general population of the school system is chosen by the school board as the legal outlet for advertising bids.

The advertisement must state in quite precise terms all the conditions relative to receiving bids. This includes when the bidding will take place, where materials for making a bid can be obtained, the deadline for when bids should be received, whom to contact for more information, and how a firm can be qualified. The advertisement must also specify how bidders should submit their pricing, such as lump sum, cost plus per Centrum, or fee basis. All three pricing arrangements are legal in school systems, but the method to be used must be stated in both the legal document, which is the technical specifications, and the advertisement.

School board policies governing the procurement of goods and services must be observed in this advertisement in as much as it is a legal notification of action by the school board. The box here shows a typical newspaper advertisement that a school system would place. Such an advertisement must be run in the newspaper for a certain number of days before the deadline for receiving bids.

The Fairfield School Board will receive sealed Bids for a new Kings Mill Elementary School, Kings Mill, Virginia, State Project 11-25A. One story, bearing wall, brick exterior, Elementary School, approximate area 55,850 sq. ft., includes associated site work, roads, grading, paving, bill-folds, etc. Kitchen equipment is in the Construction Contract. An early site work package has been awarded and work is under way.

Location: Kings Mill, Virginia
All bids must be on a lump sum basis, including specified allowances. Bids will be received until 2:00 p.m. local prevailing time, July 12, 2019, at Fairfield County School Board Room, 108 Main Street. All interested parties are invited to attend. Bids will be opened publicly and read aloud. Bidding documents (drawings and project manuals) may be obtained or examined at the architect's office: Smith and Smith, Inc., 86 Prospect Avenue, Fairfield, VA 24011. Other locations where bidding documents may be examined are: Dodge Plan Rooms at: Roanoke, VA; Richmond, VA; Dodge Scan.

1. One set of bidding documents consists of one project manual, and a complete set of drawings, plus all addenda issued prior to receipt of

bids. Addenda will automatically be issued to all parties on record of receiving bidding documents.

2. Bidding documents deposit will be $100 per set. The number of sets available with full deposit refund shall be limited to two sets for general contract bidders and one set for mechanical and electrical subcontract bidders. Additional sets and sets to other interested parties are available with a 50 percent deposit refund.

3. Deposits will be refunded as described above for complete sets of documents returned in good condition within ten days after bid opening.

A pre-bid conference will be held at the construction site on Tuesday, June 28, 2019, at 2:00 p.m. Each prime contract bidder must deposit, with his bid, security in the form of a bid bond, as described in the Instructions to Bidders. Withdrawal of bids due to error must conform to the provisions of Section 1 1-54A (a) of the Code of Virginia. The successful prime contract bidder will be required to furnish and pay for satisfactory performance and payment bonds as described in the Instructions to Bidders.

The attention of each bidder is directed to Title 54 of Chapter 7, Code of Virginia, pertaining to registration. All bids shall remain valid for a period of 60 days after the scheduled closing time for receipt of bids. Bid bonds will be forfeited for bids withdrawn prior to the end of this period. The owner intends to award a single lump sum contract to the lowest responsible bidder meeting the requirements of the Instructions to Bidders and this advertisement for bids providing the bid amount falls within the amount of funds available. If lowest bid exceeds available funds, the owner may enter negotiations with the lowest responsible bidder to lower the bid within the available funds, using the following procedure.

1. The owner and architect shall notify the first lowest responsible bidder, within 10 days following the bids opening, that negotiations will be entered. An itemized price and quantity break-down of the bid shall be furnished to the owner and architect by the bidder within 10 days.

2. The owner and architect shall prepare a revised scope of work that will be given to the first lowest responsible bidder for revision of his bid.

3. If the first lowest bidder's revised bid is within the available funds, a contract will be awarded.

4. If the first lowest bidder's revised bid is not within the available funds, negotiations will be entered into with the second lowest responsible bidder using the same procedures outlined above.

5. If the second lowest bidder's revised bid is not within available funds, negotiations may be continued with each subsequent lowest bidder until a satisfactory bid is obtained.

Bidders and subcontractors of this work will be required to comply with the provisions of Executive Orders 11246 and 11375, which prohibit discrimination in employment regarding race, creed, color, sex, or national origin. Bidders must certify that they do not and will not maintain or provide for their employees any facilities that are segregated based on race, color, creed, or national origin. The requirements for bidders and contractors under these executive orders are explained in the specifications. The owner reserves the right to reject any or all bids and to award contract to other than the lowest bidder, if, in his opinion, such action would ensure better performance and a higher level of function, quality, and value.

- Advertisement of the bid offer is not limited to the legal outlet of the school board.
- Advertisement of the bid is also made in various trade journals. These outlets may be architectural and construction industry journals such as F. W. Dodge and Cost Management Data Group publications. These publications notify their readership of opportunities for bidding on projects that may not be advertised in their local paper.

In small school systems located in rural or isolated areas, advertising in more widely circulated newspapers than the local legal newspaper is very likely. Legal requirements demand advertising in the official newspaper, but good administrative practices demand as wide a distribution of the advertisement as is possible to obtain a good number of bidders. In some circumstances, the architect may actually contact firms to encourage them to submit a bid. This may stimulate competition, resulting in better bids for the school system.

When the deadline for submitting bids arrives, the school system must conduct a public opening of all bids. This is done at the time and place stipulated in the bid advertisement. Usually, representatives of the purchasing department of the school system conduct the meeting and open the bids. Representatives of firms that have submitted bids usually attend.

As each bid is open, the submitted price is announced and put on a board for all to see. When all bids have been opened, the school system personnel must prepare a recommendation to the school board. The architect attends this meeting and advises the school personnel on the adequacy of the bids. This advice may be a recommendation for action on any and all bids, such as which to accept or reject. When all bid prices are over the budgeted amount, the architect may advise the school personnel on ways to reduce the project to come within the budgeted amount or to negotiate with the lowest bidder to reduce the bid price. The school system personnel must, of course, make the final recommendation to the school board, but the architect has direct input into that action.

The final recommendation by school system staff is presented at an official school board meeting. That body then considers the staff recommendation and takes appropriate action. Such action may be to vote to enter into a contract or to reject any and all bids.

LOWEST RESPONSIBLE AND RESPONSIVE BIDDER

Almost all procurement provisions of public governmental bodies stipulate that the lowest responsible and responsive bidder be awarded the contract. This is a common interpretation of the result of competitive bidding. Defining the lowest bidder is a very easy task that can be decided simply by looking at the offered prices. Defining the most responsible and responsive bidder is a little more difficult.

"Responsiveness" can generally be determined if the bidder submits a competitive bid, at least a bid that could be considered competitive with other bids. Responsiveness can also be defined as submitting a bid that meets the needs of the school system in the scope of the work and the established timeline. The important point is that the firm can be considered a viable company to do the work.

"Responsible bidder" may be more difficult to define in that it involves subjective judgment. A responsible bidder is a firm that can obtain the necessary bonding, such as the surety bond and subsequent performance bond. The quality of being responsible may also hinge on previous experience with either the school system or another public body. If the firm has a good history of completing projects on time and to the satisfaction of the owner, this is a good surrogate for that quality and can be judged accordingly. This is especially true if the previous employer is the school system.

Conversely, a history of poor performance might be a good indicator of irresponsible action. School systems can disqualify the lowest bidder if, in the judgment of the school staff and school board, previous performance was not adequate. There can be a great deal of latitude on the part of the school system in interpreting both responsible and responsive bidder, but it usually centers on financial stability and previous performance of the company in question.

REJECTION OF BIDS

One common misconception is that the school board may not reject the lowest bidder. This is not true for school systems, or any governmental unit. School boards may reject any and all bids depending upon the circumstances. If all bids are above the budgeted amount, the school board may reject all bids, even the lowest bid. If the school board does not identify a firm as responsible and responsive even if it is the lowest bidder, the offer can be rejected.

When all the bids are above the budget, the school system is obviously placed in the position of rejecting bids. Following this action, the school planners and architect need to downsize the project or find additional funding. Most often, the latter alternative is not available and the project must be reduced. This is regrettable because reductions made at this time often result in severe distortions of parts of the building or loss of space that is needed for the educational program. Reductions that take place at this point in time are desperation moves that often do not have the benefit of thoughtful examination. The reductions may in fact hinder the operation of the plant for a good many years in the future.

If a reduction in the scope of the project has to take place at the bid stage, there may have to be a redesign. Depending upon the reason the project came in above the budget, this redesign may incur additional design fees. If, however, the project was excessive because of architectural work, these fees would not be assessed against the school system. Most often projects draw bids over budget because of economic and inflationary factors, rather than anything the school staff or architect did or did not do. If the project adheres to the boundaries of square footage and cost of materials specified, excessive reductions at this stage usually do not have to be made.

During the design stage, the architect periodically estimates the cost of the project by applying the latest square foot costs to the school being designed. In this manner, the architect keeps the school system informed of the anticipated project cost. Once the budget is set for that project, it is incumbent upon the architect to keep the design within that price range.

Several things impinge upon that action. First, the programming of the project should be within the amount of funding set in the capital improvement budget. The school staff is responsible for determining the total square feet of space in the building on which the square foot cost is based. In other words, the building is budgeted for a certain amount based on the number of square feet in the building times the square foot costs for that space. Square foot costs are based on market conditions. If these factors are controlled, then the chance of the building costing above the budget is greatly reduced. But the quality of materials specified by the architect should also fit the budget.

If all are controlled, the building should fit within the budget. If any factor is not studiously controlled, the building may draw bids above the budgeted amount and force the school board and architect to take drastic action to reduce the cost of the project.

BIDDING FURNITURE AND EQUIPMENT

A new building or other major project will need desks, chairs, movable storage cabinets, physical education equipment, technology systems and equipment, and similar items. These are called "loose furniture and equipment" and are not considered a part of the building structure. Loose furniture and equipment are funded separately from construction and, in most cases, bid separately from the building. Technology systems and equipment are also included.

The task of writing specifications for the capital project usually falls to the school system staff. In medium and large school systems, there is an office or person responsible for writing specifications for all new furniture and equipment that will be used in the building. In these cases, the school system may also conduct the bidding procedure for these items.

In small school systems, the architect may be employed to write the specifications and include these items in the contract for the design of the building. This means an added fee to the architect, sometimes as much as 5–10 percent of the bid price of the furniture and equipment. Although this may seem like a small charge for this type of work, the school system could do the task itself at a savings to the school board. Of course, this task cannot be added to the daily tasks a person is already performing. A staff member must be released from current responsibilities. Even then, savings can accrue to the school system by taking responsibility for writing the specifications.

BONDING

When a contracting firm submits a bid to the school system, a good faith bond must also be submitted. This bond is called a surety bond because it guarantees that the bid is presented in good faith and is backed by a willingness to accept a contract if the bid is accepted. This surety bond tells the school system the bid price is a bona fide offer to do the work specified in the advertisement. The surety bond will serve to indemnify the school system in the unlikely case the successful contractor does not carry through to signing a contract to complete the work.

If this happened, the bond amount would be paid by the bonding company to the school system. The surety bond is usually 5 to 10 percent of the total bid price and the precise amount is stipulated in the bid advertisement. A bonding or insurance company issues the surety bond submitted by the contractor following an evaluation of the credit worthiness of the company.

Once a construction firm is offered a contract by the school system and signs the contract, the surety bond is returned. However, the successful bidder must produce, at the time of signing, a performance bond payable to the school system. The performance bond is equal to 100 percent of the contract price and guarantees the contractor will complete the work identified in the contract.

While the surety bond guarantees the earnestness of the bid, the performance bond guarantees the work will be completed by the contractor. There is a big difference in the relationship between bidder and school system and contractor and school system. In the former, the bidder indicates that the price is firm and the company stands behind the bid. In the latter, the performance bond guarantees completion of work and will indemnify the school system in case the work is not completed.

Caution must be exercised in interpreting what the performance bond will do. Some people might think the price of the construction will be paid to the school system if the contractor fails to complete the work. This is not exactly correct. The performance bond will indemnify the school system only to the extent of losses sustained in not getting the work completed because of failure of the contractor or in the event of demise of the company. The performance bond serves as a safety net for the school system only to the extent of losses.

THE CONTRACT

The contract signed by the successful bidder and the school board is a standard legal document that stipulates the work to be done. The contract makes direct reference to the contract documents that are the set of architectural drawings and technical specifications. In essence, the contract states that the contractor will build the facility detailed in these documents adhering to the quality and quantity specified in the documents.

Usually the school system's legal counsel prepares the contract in accordance with state law. Appendix F contains a sample copy of an agreement between a contractor and school board. There are general conditions that are in all contracts dealing with the construction of a building. Contract documents usually consist of the agreement, the conditions of the contract, the drawings, specifications, all addenda issued prior to, and all modifications issued after execution of the agreement. Specific sections in the agreement deal with the scope of the work, time of commencement and substantial completion, final payment, miscellaneous provisions, contract sum, and progress payments. Any special conditions that require additional work on the part of the contractor or that the contractor must be aware of are listed in the Special Section of the contract.

SUMMARY

Local school systems usually obtain goods and services outside the school system by the use of procurement. This means that when a school system builds a new school or needs renovation work done that competing public construction firms are asked to provide bids for the work to be done. The use of bidding in school systems is common. In the case of a major capital project the school system usually procures the services of a contractor through the bidding process. State legal constraints govern the process of bidding for any goods or services. The school system must follow these procedures. The only exception to this is when a capital project is contracted through a public/private partnership. In this case, the award of a contract to complete a capital project is through competitive responses to a request for proposals by the school system.

Chapter 14

Alternative Contracting
Plans and Commissioning of Schools

During the past few decades, several alternative contracting plans have evolved in the building industry. The motivation behind developing such plans is to provide the owner with better service, secure better coordination between the design and construction professionals, compress the time it takes to complete a project, and in doing so save precious funds and increase profits. These benefits would normally accrue to the owner and the professionals in the design and construction industries and result in a better product—a better school building, renovated building, or other capital improvement project that would make everyone proud.

Some of the alternative contracting plans are still new to school authorities and in some cases are not permitted because of state law relating to procurement practices. Nevertheless, many school systems across the country have participated in such agreements. As was noted in previous chapters, school systems can contract for goods and services in several ways: from the most restrictive to the most relaxed methods. In many instances, local school systems can contract with one firm to produce a complete building. This would be termed a turnkey operation, whereby the school system would contract all the processes leading to a new school building or renovation to one firm for one price.

On the other end of the scale, there is the contracting process whereby the school system secures the assistance of many firms to complete the processes of planning, designing, constructing, and equipping a new school. Each of these services would require a different contract. This is the most common method for school systems to build a new school or complete any major capital improvement project. The alternative contracting plans described in this chapter range from one end of the spectrum to the other.

PUBLIC/PRIVATE PARTNERSHIPS

A recent development in alternative contractual agreements for new facilities is the private/public partnership. Basically, such a partnership is an agreement between school systems and private firms to build a school facility. The school system prepares a Request for Proposals type of announcement stating that the school board would be interested in partnering with a private firm for the construction of a school building. This partnership, in essence, is an agreement for the private entity to plan, design, construct, and equip a new facility for the local school system.

When a private entity is selected based upon the criteria established by the local school system, a comprehensive agreement is entered into by each party. The agreement establishes in exact detail how the facility is to be built, what the school will contain, what it will look like, and the financial arrangement that will follow after the facility is constructed. For all intents and purposes, the private entity selected to do the work can then proceed to complete the project and construct the school building without any further input from the local school system. There are several important steps that a school system must take to affect a comprehensive agreement. The exact stipulations of the agreement may vary from state to state; the common stipulations are contained in the following sections.

Guidelines

Prior to requesting or concluding a qualifying project such as a new school building, the local school system must develop guidelines of the project. The guidelines must be reasonable, encourage competition, and guide the selection of projects. The local school system must encourage competition through notification and availability of representatives of the school system for private entities to reach.

The guidelines should include, in addition to a description of the educational program, financial procedures that would include a cost benefit analysis, an assessment of opportunity cost, and consideration of the results of all studies. The local school system must establish criteria for the selection of the firm, key decision spots, and approval process to insure the school system has considered the extent of competition before selecting the proposal from a private entity. All of this must be posted for public consumption before the proposal of the private entity is accepted.

Procurement Policies under PPP

In states that have legislation enabling school systems to enter into public-private partnerships for the construction of a new school building, the standard procurement policies of the state for the school system may be waived. This provision is in place to enable the school system to enter into an agreement with a private entity without the formal procedures of the bidding process. The very essence of this provision is crucial for the private entity to develop a successful proposal.

Although the benefit of the lowest bidder provision may not be in evidence, the exclusive nature of the agreement is maintained. That means that the school system is not bound to select the proposal with the lowest price, but can choose based upon other factors such as: (a) the general cost of the proposal, (b) the reputation of the private entity, (c) the financial strength of the private entity, (d) the benefit to the public, (e) the proposed design of the project, (f) the compliance of a minority business enterprise participating in the project, and (g) other criteria applicable to the project. Such terms and requirements are similar in nature to the prequalifications imposed upon possible bidders in the procurement policy of almost every state.

Comprehensive Agreement

The local school system enters into a comprehensive agreement with the chosen private entity. This agreement covers all aspects of the development of the project and eventually the operation of the school facility. The comprehensive agreement should contain provisions for the private entity to maintain performance and payment bonds and letters of credit in connection with the development of the project. The school system should also have authority to review the plans and specifications of the project to insure conformity of acceptable standards and the requirements for the educational program. This review does not, however, mean the private entity must have all design completed before the execution of the comprehensive agreement. The agreement should also make provision for the maintenance of the school facility by the private entity if it is eventually leased to the school system.

Further, the comprehensive agreement should stipulate that the school system should have the capability of monitoring the progress of the private entity by periodic meetings of representatives of both the school system and the private entity. The comprehensive agreement should also cover such major items as the payment of fees and lease payments, responsibility for default or termination of the agreement, filing of appropriate financial statements, and all other items deemed important to the project. In other words, the comprehensive agreement should cover all contingencies of a project that will produce an acceptable educational facility.

Financing the Project

In submitting a proposal, the private entity may use any financial scheme normally employed by private entities to engage in such a project as a new school building. In other words, a private entity is not restricted in how it plans to finance the project. Private entities may issue debt, equity, or other securities or obligations, enter into a leaseback agreement for secure financing by a pledge or security intent. In operating the project, which would be the school building, the private entity must be responsible to the school system in that the facility must be open for educational purposes.

Under most public/private partnerships, the private entity has the power of condemnation for the purpose of constructing an educational facility. In situations where the school system has already purchased a site upon which to construct the building, in these situations the private entity must have unlimited access to that site. Further, most legislation stipulates that should the school system maintain possession of the site upon which the school is located, the private entity has ownership and control of the building itself until other financial arrangements are concluded with the local school system.

Operations

When the facility is completed, the private entity must keep it open for intended usage at all times. The public entity and school system will enter into an agreement. The financial arrangement for operating the school building will be carefully stipulated in the comprehensive agreement.

There are a number of contractual arrangements that the school system can agree upon with the private entity. The school system may lease the school permanently or may complete a lease-purchase agreement whereby at the end of the agreement, title to the school building is transferred to the school system. The school system may also make periodic payments to the private entity, much like mortgage payments, until the entire cost of the school building is paid. The specific method of payment must be stated in the comprehensive agreement beforehand.

Benefits and Restrictions

The use of a private/public partnership might seem to be very advantageous to the school system. In the first place, the school system gets the use of a new facility without going into debt. This situation affects the credit rating of the school system in a positive manner. In addition, any such payments for use of the facility can come from the rental section of the school system budget and not from the debt service section.

A long-term of the school facility would be advantageous financially to the school system. The annual payment on such a lease would be much less than what the payments for a bond issue would be. A bond issue would have to be paid in twenty years with accrued interest. At the same time, the school system would be paying more for the use of the building over the long-term lease. Modification to the building to accommodate changing educational programs would be possible if included in the long-term lease.

A public/private partnership might look to the school system like the ideal solution to acquiring new facilities. There are no required funds up front by the school system, no interest to be paid, and the facility can be changed and modified to accommodate a changing educational program. Although this is true, there are some limitations to this method of procuring new facilities.

Basically, the public/private partnership is in all intents and purposes, a turnkey operation. The private entity designs and builds the facility for the school system and when finished gives the key to the school system with an agreement for payment. However, when the input from the school system personnel as to what the building will look like or to what the building contains is limited is when problems arise. This would be disastrous for the school system. The local schools would be permitting the private entity to determine what the school building will look like and what it will contain.

The private entity may or may not be knowledgeable about the educational enterprise and yet will have the final determination of what the school building will look like. This is a simply abrogation of the powers and authority of the local school system. The school system would be accepting what the private entity thinks a school should look like and what it should contain. This is nothing but disastrous for the school system.

If in the comprehensive agreement the school system can have provisions for their personnel to tell the private entity precisely what the school will contain and what kind of spaces are needed, there might be some reasons to believe that the school will resemble a facility in which the educational program can fit very well.

In addition, the comprehensive agreement should also contain a provision for school personnel to review the final architectural drawings before it is put out for bid to insure the building will fit the educational program and the manner in which student and teachers learn and teach in the facility. Unless these two provisions are in the comprehensive agreement, the school system might be accepting what the private entity believes is a school building.

No school system should be in a position to do that. There are too many school buildings in the country today where the educational program is compromised because the facility constrains it. Unless there is considerable school personnel input into the initial request and subsequent input into the design of the facility, the building may not fit the educational program.

JOB ORDER CONTRACTING

There are some school systems that have several capital improvement projects that need to be completed during a given year. These reoccurring projects can be, such as replacement of doors, or as extensive as completing a new addition to an existing building. An alternative method of contracting with a builder is Job Order Contracting (JOC). This is an alternative procurement method of securing services of a builder based upon contractor performance. Basically, the school system enters into a contract with a selected builder for a certain amount of money, representing selected construction projects.

The amounts to be paid can be determined from a number of uniform sources, such as those published by R. S. Means (1996), and are the basis of receiving proposals from prospective contractors. School systems can select from a number of contractors by issuing a Request for Proposals (RFP) stating a particular unit price book as the basis of the contract. Interested contractors respond by offering a price coefficient (multiplier) for the work and materials described. This is similar to a cost-plus-materials contract, except that the cost of the materials is agreed upon before the contract is signed by citing an established reference. This, in effect, eliminates some of the guesswork of how much the materials will cost after the contract is signed.

JOC is issued for a building program, not for separate building projects. In other words, JOC is designed to cover a number of projects. The entire capital improvement program for a school system is undoubtedly too large for JOC, but parts of the program could be amenable to it. As stated above, JOC is best used for small multiple projects that are repetitive in a capital improvement program. An example of how JOC works can be illustrated by the following example.

A school system may select a contractor, after close inspection of credentials and performance history, for a contract of $20 million over a three-to-five-year period. The average cost of the projects might range from $150,000 to $1,000,000, but without any obligation on the school system's part to exercise the contract. If the school system deems the projects under consideration not needed, there is no obligation on the part of the school system to put the projects under contract. This process simply means that the school system has a contractor on-call that will perform selected projects with a determined cost of materials and a determined cost to the contractor.

In essence, JOC is a process whereby the school system can have a contractor available and on hand for selected projects under a cost-plus-materials contract with the costs established before the contract is signed. This means that each project has a definition and perhaps a set of educational specifications established long before the project is assigned the contractor. JOC does not relieve the educator from the responsibility of establishing the need for and the details of the project. The educators must define what is to be done and how it is to be done. In addition, the school system must establish the budget and the time line for completion of the project. Supposedly, this process tends to reduce or eliminate change orders and claims. Needless to say, close supervision of any JOC project by school system employees is an absolute requirement.

Of course, contractors that are receptive to JOC can detail the benefits of such a contractual arrangement. Supposedly, JOC benefits small contractors because they can enjoy the stability of an established relationship over a period of years. In addition, small contractors can be motivated to deliver high-quality projects that are responsive to the needs of the school system. Under JOC, the contractor can also mentor and train small companies, especially in areas such as job-site safety and quality control.

Local school systems can benefit from JOC, provided the school board is judicious in selecting contractors to whom to issue JOC. The selection process can be selective and based upon predetermined criteria and a history of good performance in delivering a project. The school system is under no obligation to complete any or all of the capital projects put under JOC. This frees the school system from any legal contract to offer an established amount of projects. The need is controlled by the school system. The establishment of the cost of materials from a reputable national source also benefits the school system because the cost of materials is not subject to local commercial control. Rather, the cost of materials is determined before the work begins, based upon a set schedule of prices.

JOC may be a good investment for small school systems that have a limited maintenance crew and yet have enough maintenance jobs to demand a larger crew. JOC may be cost effective because the school system would not have to enlarge its maintenance crew to accommodate the work needed. JOC would in essence be outsourcing the maintenance projects to a contractor that has sufficient personnel to complete the projects.

Only those school systems that may have a backlog of capital projects can probably use JOC successfully. If such benefits, as outlined in the first paragraph of this chapter, can be obtained from different ways of contracting with firms in the design and construction industry, then it would be prudent for the school systems to engage in such agreements.

Like every process or product, the application is not always the way it is described. There may be trade-offs to engaging in such contractual agreements. In the interests of fast delivery of a building, there may be decisions made that might not be in the very best interests of the school system. Likewise, because of budget limitations, the quality of the materials going into the building may be a decision made not by educators, but by the design/construction industry in the interest of economy.

In every type of agreement for goods and services, regardless of the type, the school board and administration should jealously guard the decision-making authority vested in them. Decisions that are the prerogative of the educators and school board should prevail in every case to the betterment of the school system for the students. This means that educators must develop a set of educational specifications for every capital improvement project and adhere to these specifications tenaciously.

There have been too many instances where individuals other than educators make decisions that directly influence the educational program of the students and the instructional program of the teachers. Making decisions regarding the size of classrooms or any space in the building is the prerogative of educators only. Design and construction professionals can make suggestions, but decisions should be made only by educators and the school board.

DESIGN/BUILD CONTRACTING

The practice of one firm providing both design and construction services is termed design/build procurement. Under this arrangement, the school system contracts with the one firm to both do the design work and then construct the building. This process was discussed more fully in the previous chapter. Procuring both design and construction services from one firm is an alternative method of contracting for services. The school board and administration should thoroughly investigate these services before entering into a contract.

The problem of decision-making should be of vital concern for the school board and administration because, under such alternative contracting arrangements, the design professionals and construction agents might end up making rather basic decisions at certain critical times in the process that should be made by educators. So often, during the bid stage, decisions need to be made in a short period of time because of the necessity of reducing the project. The project may come in under budget because of these decisions, but the final results are not necessarily in the best interests of students and teachers.

The sovereignty of educators making vital decisions in every capital improvement project or new facility should never be compromised. When entering into such contractual arrangements, the school board and administrators should insist that they be part of all decision-making to ensure that the project will be what the students and teachers need.

PERFORMANCE CONTRACTING

Performance contracting is a method of delivery of a building or capital project where the owner defines the function of a building through a performance statement of work. The specifications of the performance statement dictate a special level of performance quality and a level of expectation of quality of workmanship. This is different from a description statement of work to be done, such as contained in a set of educational specifications. This means that the owners of the building, the school board and educators, would have to describe in sufficient detail the various functions that will go on in the building.

In other words, the educator must be able to describe in detail the function of the educational program in various locations in the building. An educator must be able to tell the architect or contractor the types of activities that will be carried on in the building. This would have to be done for each space in the building. This could entail quite a voluminous document.

Preparing a performance statement of work for a new building may sound rather ambiguous to educators who are normally accustomed to preparing statements that relate to the needs of students and teachers regarding specific types of spaces and certain sizes of areas. In addition, the state in which the school system is located normally has certain space requirements for various components of the school building that must be adhered to regardless of the size and complexity of the building.

In every school building there are various processes in which people engage in order to learn and work. The process of learning and teaching are two different activities or processes. There are certain activities in which students must engage during the course of the day to learn effectively whatever material is to be learned. Likewise, there are certain activities in which teachers must engage to teach effectively the material to be learned by the students. Where these two processes meet is the very heart of the educational program. As a result, under performance contracting, educators would have to spell out in detail how both the students and teachers would act in the learning process.

The reason given for using performance contracting is that the construction industry does not have a uniform standard of performance to apply to contractors. In other words, there is a lack of standards for the performance of contractors. This may seem rather strange to the educator and school board member who needs more of an explanation for using such a contractual arrangement rather than using the standard contract for the performance of work normally employed.

Additionally, this may not be a grounded justification for using performance contracting, because it makes no difference whether the industry does or does not have standards of performance. What the school board and educators want is a job well done, on time, and within budget that results in a new school building or a good renovation project.

In a way, performance contracting is a form of design/build contracting with a different twist. The firm wishes the school board to be able to describe more precisely the building in terms of how it performs or allows the users to perform. According to proponents of performance contracting, it is implemented through a statement of goals that the educators want for the building. This could also be a form of a statement of a problem educators are facing that needs to be solved. Further, the contractor sees the project as a challenge that must be met and at the same time identifies the constraints of the performance of the building. These constraints must be worked through by the architects and contractors because performance contracting focuses on the nature of the requirements of the owner and not the nature of the solution.

There are probably some drawbacks to this type of contracting for school systems. Firstly, school authorities need to set the limits for the planning process by specifying the numbers of different types of spaces, their properties, and relationships within the new facility. Further, the school board, and especially the educators, need to see in actuality the type of spaces in which students and teachers will learn and work. Only in this way will educators be able to evaluate how successful the building might be when finished.

The local school system authorities need to tell the architect and contractor exactly what they want in terms of kinds and amounts of spaces, relationships, and ancillary areas in the capital project before they contract for services. There is too much ambiguity in stating needs in terms of performance. The school authorities need to abide by certain state requirements regarding size of spaces and number of spaces in a school building. The amount of time spent in analyzing the performance needs of students, teachers, administrators, staff, and community members who might use the facility before any work on the design of the building can take place would delay the project beyond the immediate need of the school division.

Every educational facility is far too complicated to go through the process of identifying performance needs of individuals and groups. Identifying the performance needs for an office building or a factory might lend itself to such a way of contracting for services, but educators and school boards should probably thoroughly investigate this type of contracting for building services long before entering into such an arrangement.

COMMISSIONING OF SCHOOLS

Commissioning is a process of ensuring that what is installed is what was intended originally in the educational and technical specifications for the school facility. In other words, commissioning assures the educational authorities and school board that whatever building systems, such as heating and ventilation, lighting, technology, science equipment, and communication that were specified in the new or renovated building by the architect of record were actually installed, were installed correctly, and function as expected. In a way, the service of commissioning is a guarantee or insurance that the building systems and equipment that were specified in the building are what was actually installed and work effectively.

This service is usually accomplished by employing a firm, either an architectural or an engineering firm, to do the work of commissioning the building. This firm is called the commissioning agent and reports directly to the superintendent of schools and the school board. The commissioning agent provides oversight and inspection services of either all systems that are called for in a building or of specific systems that may be identified. These services are separate and in addition to the services of the architect of record for the project.

Naturally, these services cost the school board, and these costs are in addition to the fees of the architect of record, who is paid anywhere from 5 to 10 percent of the construction cost. The fees are always negotiable, but experience has shown that commissioning agent fees range from 1 to 3 percent of the construction contract price.

Commissioning seems to have paid for itself in many reported projects in that the school board is assured of getting the type of systems specified and the systems work when the school building is opened. In some cases, commissioning agents will specify that there is a three-year payback of the commissioning fees. Some architects state that on some projects the payback can be as short as one year. Such claims must be verified by the school board when discussing employment of a commissioning agent. Even at that, such guarantees must be weighed against actualities of performance.

Having said that, there are just as many architects who say that commissioning is not needed if a quality architectural firm is employed because that firm guarantees the systems being installed just as much as a commissioning agent. As a result, the educational authorities and school boards have to make a decision as to whether or not they want to commission a building project. The school board must decide if the extra funds to employ a commissioning agent are worth the price. The architect the school board employs will undoubtedly advise the board as to which alternative to pursue, but it is up to the school board to actually arrive at a decision, independent of the architect of record.

There are several modes of commissioning depending on the scope of the project. Commissioning may be employed for new buildings or any new structure. It can also be employed for renovating existing buildings. Any capital improvement project that is large enough to warrant a guarantee could use commissioning. Commissioning can also be contracted for specific building systems, and a commissioning agent can be employed for one or all of these systems. Such building systems as the HVAC, electrical controls, lighting, water, technology, and even the building envelope are amenable to commissioning.

The school board must decide if any or all of the systems in either a new facility or a renovated building should be subject to a commissioning process. Some architects recommend commissioning services for existing buildings because there is a tendency for all building systems to migrate to inefficiency over a period of years. There are good reasons behind this thinking, but again the school board must evaluate the cost effectiveness of employing a commissioning agent.

There are three basic documents that are created and used during a commissioning project. These documents are the Owner's Project Requirements (OPR), the Basis of Design, and the Systems Operation Manual. These three documents guide the professionals in completing their work of commissioning. The documents are in all likelihood written by the commissioning agent and the architect of record for the project.

The OPR is a document that specifies the functional requirements of the owner for the building and even each space within the structure. These are what the school system wants the various systems to do while in operation. One requirement, for example, would be the amount of air circulation desired within the classrooms. The requirement for the temperature range would be another criterion that would be included. Requirements for the lighting system might include the number of foot-candles that should fall on the desk of a student. All these requirements are listed in this document. Normally, the architect of record would be instrumental in helping the staff of the school system to compile this document.

The architect of record and the design team compile the Basis of Design document. This document details how the design team will implement the requirements found in the OPR. The document contains the important concepts, design assumptions, calculations, decisions, product selections, and rationale used to satisfy the OPR requirements. One important part of the document is how the various systems comply with the requirements and resources of the school staff.

SUMMARY

In the last few decades school systems have been provided an opportunity to contract in a different manner to complete a capital project. These alternative contracting methods are designed to provide better service to the school system, perhaps lower the cost of a project, insure quality construction, and provide better coordination between design and construction professionals. Perhaps the most important method is the public/private partnership. In this method the school system invites private design/construction firms to submit a proposal to plan, design, and construct a capital project under one contract. The private firm would finance the project and independently design and build the project. The amount of input from the school system for what the school building should contain would be in the initial request for proposals. The benefits from this method of contracting is that the private firm uses its own funds to do all the work, the project may be completed quicker, the school system does not have to have the staff to do some of the work in administering the project, and the school system does not have the debt of financing the project on its budget. The disadvantages are that the school system may not have as much input into the actual design of the structure and may not have final say about the quality of material used in the building.

Other methods of contracting for construction projects are the use of Job Ordering Commission, Design/Build, and Performance Contracting. These methods are more specific than general contracting for completion of the project. Some school systems use commissioning to obtain the services of an independent designer to insure the quality of the systems utilized in the building.

Chapter 15

Managing the Construction Phase

After the successful bidder is identified and the school board votes to accept the bid, a contract is executed with the winning firm to complete the building project. At this point, the school board returns the surety bond of not only the successful bidder, but also of the other firms that submitted bids. The successful bidder then must deposit a performance bond with the school board for 100 percent of the agreed-upon construction price. See Appendix F for a sample agreement between the owner and contractor.

In addition, the firm must also give the school board a payment bond, which guarantees all payments to workers, suppliers, and vendors so that liens cannot be placed against the completed building. Following this, the contractor mobilizes the workforce and proceeds with the construction, usually within ten days. All necessary building permits, applications for utilities on the site, and any easements are obtained before construction begins.

SUPERVISING THE PROJECT

A construction project is an expensive undertaking by the school system. In some cases, a new school building is the largest expenditure of funds over a short period of time a school makes. As such, supervising the expenditure of public funds is an important responsibility of the school system. Some school boards do not realize the importance of direct oversight in a construction project. The tremendous amount of public funds involved in such a project, and the responsibility for supervising all expenditure of funds should certainly demand close supervision of all construction projects by school personnel.

Every contract with an architect has a clause stipulating that the firm will provide some site supervision by the clerk-of-the-works. Careful reading of the clause, however, will reveal that the amount of supervision to be provided is marginal. The supervision of a construction project by an architectural firm is not intended to be a continuous process. The contract will probably call for only periodic supervision visits that could be once every week or once a month. Generally, the actual number of visits the employees of the architectural firm will make and their frequency are not stated. School boards should not rely, under any circumstances, solely upon the visits of the architectural firm to provide the necessary supervision the district should be giving to the project.

The difference in perception between the school board and the architectural firm on the amount of supervision the architect should give a construction project is often great and an area of constant dispute. Commonly, the school board thinks the architectural firm representative will supervise the construction project daily. The school board does not realize the architectural clerk-of-the-works has many projects that require supervision simultaneously; therefore, the project of the school board must await supervision until time is available, just as all other projects do.

Daily supervision is not only beyond the responsibility of the architect, it is beyond the scope of the contract. Architectural supervision serves more to provide the architectural firm with data on the progress of the project, rather than providing the school board with up-to-date progress reports. If the school board wishes the architectural firm to provide daily supervision, or supervision above what is normally given through the contract, the architectural firm will charge a fee in addition to that charged the school board to design the building. Purchasing such supervision is costly because overhead must be factored into the overall supervision fee charged the school board.

The school board is better advised to provide its own daily supervision for every construction project by employing someone to be the construction supervisor. This way, the school board has an employee at the site at all times, supervising the construction project. This school board employee should be charged with keeping the project on schedule and within the budget, and with ensuring good quality workmanship. The supervision provided by this employee should be in addition to the supervision by the architectural firm.

The school board can easily recoup the expense of this employee if their supervision keeps the project on schedule or allows proper administration of change orders necessitated by the project. The importance of having a school system employee on the site at all times cannot be overemphasized because judicious administration and prudent supervision of this very expensive project guarantees a quality product within available resources.

The person employed as the construction supervisor should be knowledgeable about all phases of construction and have experience in the field. The person should be able to discern quality workmanship and be able to show leadership in a group situation to protect the investment of the school board. A person with these qualities is not difficult to find, even in a small community.

In a large school system, the construction supervisor should report directly to the director of architectural and construction services, or, in smaller districts, to the person who is leading the school planning effort. In extremely small school systems, this may mean that the construction supervisor reports directly to the assistant superintendent for business or even to the superintendent of schools. Regardless of whom the construction supervisor reports to, there should be written monthly (or bimonthly) reports to the school board on the construction project's progress. The school administration may require other reporting times when the construction supervisor should submit reports.

As the representative of the school board, the construction supervisor usually conducts weekly job-site meetings between representatives of the architectural firm and the contractor to determine the project's progress. This is the time when schedule problems are settled. Questions regarding management of time by the contractor, types of materials used, substituted quality of workmanship, and other items may come up at these weekly meetings. Weekly meetings help keep a project on schedule more than infrequent meetings.

Regularly scheduled meetings also allow the construction supervisor to anticipate problems that could arise from specific work or as the contractor begins different phases of the building's construction. By anticipating such problems, many can be solved before they can occur. A complete job description for the construction supervisor is contained in Appendix G. Regardless of any other service provided by an outside firm, the school system should always employ a construction supervisor to guarantee that the interests of the school system are being protected.

CONSTRUCTION MANAGEMENT

Construction management (CM) services are offered by commercial firms to assist the school system in project delivery using modern management techniques. CM is defined by the industry as a comprehensive array of services spanning all phases of the design and construction process. The construction manager may be a member of the school system staff, or be selected on the basis of professional qualifications and experience from among firms and consultants offering services. CM services are compensated based on a negotiated fee for the scope of services rendered.

There are two basic contractual formats for delivering CM services from which all others are derived. One format is termed CM-Agency format. This arrangement is where the CM firm provides services to the school system, which holds the construction contracts for the work. The other format is called CM-GMP (construction manager-guaranteed maximum price), where the firm provides services to the owner and, prior to commencement of construction, guarantees the price of the project. Under this arrangement, the CM firm generally holds the construction contracts and assumes the risks and obligations of a general contractor.

Although this is a standard definition, there are many variations depending upon the firm and the situation. The CM may be simply overseeing the construction phase, like the employee of the school system, the construction supervisor, would do. The CM may also mean supervising and providing all services to the school system from the beginning of the design stage until the school building is occupied. Some firms even advertise they have the capacity to write educational specifications.

CM firms can provide supervision of many of the planning, designing, and supervising functions of a capital improvement project. At the same time, the firm can provide a certain amount of continuity over a large segment of the school system's planning process. However, there are some that feel that CM duplicates services the school system is or should be providing already. In addition, purchasing such services from an outside commercial firm might tend to divorce the planning process from the school staff, thus becoming something that others do for the school system. Needless to say, there is plenty written about the separation of planning efforts within the school system and the consequences of such action.

In spite of this fact, CM firms contend that they work in conjunction with school system efforts. In fact, most contracts ensure the independence of the planning and execution of the design and construction of the school building from the school staff.

There might be other problems that need to be addressed when using a CM firm to design and construct a school:

- legal constraints and requirements of the bid process
- lack of continuing school staff involvement in all phases of design and construction
- design changes made but not documented in final drawings
- design changes made but not approved by the school system
- additional supervision costs

State law requires every school system to ask publicly for sealed bids for major construction projects. The CM might be construed, by some educators, as a way of avoiding that process, because the management firm conducts the bidding effort. Depending on the locale, it may not be legal to do this. If a school system wants to use a commercial firm as CM, the school board should ask the state legal counsel for an opinion on the legality of the process.

Many decisions are made during both the design and construction processes. Unless the school staff is directly involved in these decisions, the resulting building may not be what was wanted, or needed. The propensity of this occurring is probably greater under a CM contract than if the school system directly supervises the project. Changes in the building are inherent in construction, and since design often proceeds simultaneously with construction, plan review is greatly complicated. This may be untenable for the school staff that needs to review plans.

Most school systems have neither the experience nor the staff needed to make the technical decisions to be resolved each day as the owner. Some educators feel the construction manager is, in essence, a general contractor relieved of all payment and performance-bonded responsibilities. Some school systems have found that, to preserve the time schedule, design decisions were made by the construction manager without involving the school system staff. This resulted in changed drawings, sometimes without proper documentation. If this happens, the school system could easily end up with drawings that are not necessarily accurate. If a CM firm is used, school systems should stipulate in the contract that "as-built" drawings be provided by the CM firm at the conclusion of the project.

Lastly, the school system must employ someone to provide an interface with the CM firm. If this person is in addition to the regular staff, the annual salary of this person is an added cost to the school system and must be factored into the total cost for construction management. Some school systems find they cannot save by employing a commercial firm to perform CM responsibilities when they can provide such supervision and management themselves by employing another staff member. If a CM firm is employed for any kind of services, the school system should also provide for construction site supervision by a school board employee to guarantee the success of the project. See Appendix G for job description for this position.

As with all kinds of professional services, the first task of the school system should be to decide, after careful examination, what services are needed and the cost of these services. Following that, a satisfactory contract can be executed.

MANAGING CHANGE ORDERS

Even with the best-developed architectural plans, changes in the project are inevitable. Such changes may occur during the construction phase and after the contract has been signed. For example, site conditions such as hidden rock may mandate changes in the design or certain materials may not be available ensuing different materials to be used. When changes are requested and processed, they are called "change orders," which are simply orders to change the contract between the school board and the contractor. When the change orders are approved, the contract with the contractor is modified.

Change orders may be initiated in two ways: from the owner (which is the school board) or from the contractor. When the school board originates a change, it is usually the result of omissions from either the educational specifications or the architectural drawings. Change orders originating with the contractor are usually the result of certain field conditions, such as difficulty with the site or changes in materials.

Once the request is identified, it passes to the architect to determine what modifications, if any, need to be made to the drawings given to the contractor. Once the contractor receives the request, it is priced and forwarded to the construction supervisor. After the construction supervisor reviews it, the order is forwarded to the proper superior and then to the school board for final approval.

Considerable negotiations can take place regarding the change order and its cost before it arrives at the school board meeting. It is during this process that the construction supervisor protects the interest of the school system. Following approval, the contractor is officially notified to complete the work.

Change orders require either the crediting or debiting of funds for the extra work involved. If something is deleted from the project, a credit is due to the school board from the contractor and the contract amount is reduced. If something is added, the contract cost is increased.

The work and materials called for in the change order are not publicly bid because the hired contractor is the firm that is doing the work and the change is in the contract in effect. Because the change order is not publicly bid, prices are often higher than on the open market. Thus, the fewer the change orders, the better it is for the school board.

A certain number of change orders are always needed, and some should be expected in the normal course of the project. If the number of change orders is excessive, the total price of the project may exceed the budget. Some school boards establish a contingency fund in the capital improvement budget to handle such cases.

Excessive change orders may indicate that the architectural drawings were not in sufficient detail or that the materials requested were not readily available. In either case, these problems are the responsibility of the architect. Excessive requests by school staff may mean that the educational specifications were not specific enough. In any event, the school staff should analyze the origin and reason for change orders and seek to remedy the situation for the next project. The number of change orders in a project may well be a criterion in determining the employment of an architect or contractor for another project.

SCHOOL BOARD-CONTRACTOR RELATIONSHIPS

There are many types and kinds of contractual relationships in which the school board and contractor can engage when a building is to be constructed. The usual method of securing construction services is to publicly bid a project and then sign a contract with one contractor to complete the work. There are variations in this method that school boards and administrators should know. Table 15.1 shows the continuum of contract types, ranging from a single contract to one firm to multiple contracts with several firms to design and construct a building.

State law and local policies govern all contractual relations between a school system and commercial firms. This often limits the type of relationships that school boards can legally enter. For example, some states mandate that four separate contracts be entered into for the different systems of a public building: one for the structure; one for the electrical system; one for the plumbing and sewer system; and one for the HVAC, or heating, ventilating, and air conditioning system. A single contract covering all construction disciplines is prohibited in these states.

In other states, a school system may employ a prime contractor that then subcontracts with electric, plumbing/sewer, and HVAC subcontractors. Under this arrangement, the prime contractor may supply the work on the structure of the building and coordination of the other three subcontractors.

Table 15.1. Continuum of Contract Types Available to School Boards

Number of Contracts

One>		*<Many*	
Turnkey	Design/Build	Design/Bid	Separate Materials

CONTRACT OPTIONS

Four different contractual relationships can be considered by the school board. Figure 15.1 shows the contract type and what the contractor is expected to do under the contract.

In a turnkey contract, the contractor does everything. The contractor writes the educational specifications, designs the building, constructs it, and equips it. After completion, the contractor gives the key to the owner. For office and apartment buildings, this might work out very nicely. For educational facilities where the educator is the one who writes the program for the building, this is not a very judicious way to go about building a school.

One such application of the turnkey application is the legislation that permits local school systems to enter into a public/private partnership. The state legislature enacts legislation to permit local school systems to enter into partnerships with private firms to plan, design, construct, and equip a new school building. The school system puts forth a notice they would like to partner with a private firm for the purpose of building a new school. The school system normally does not have to use the state procurement procedures to select a firm.

Once the firm has been selected, the school system enters into a comprehensive agreement that details the requirements of the school system in terms of an educational program. The private firm then proceeds to do all the necessary work to construct a new facility. When the building is complete, the school system and private firm exercise the financial arrangements that the comprehensive agreement stipulated. The school system can lease the building or purchase it in some fashion. At the completion of the building, the school system can use it for educational purposes. This practice is in essence a turnkey operation to produce a new facility.

Design/Build

In the design/build relationship, the school board enters into a contract with one company to provide both design and construction services. Under this contractual relationship, public bidding is not possible, so most school systems are prohibited by law from using this method. There is some caution and possible danger to a school system in this method, beyond the legal question. The amount of input by school personnel into the design development is very limited under this arrangement.

Design/Bid

The design/bid method is where the school board employs one company to do the design work and then publicly bids the project to secure a construction contract with a different company.

Separate Materials Purchase

On the other end of the scale from the turnkey option is a contract where separate materials and services are purchased under a series of contracts to different firms. The four-contract provision for different systems described above would fit into this contractual relationship. The school system would have to provide for the coordination of the project. Many school systems operate under this method of procurement of goods and services.

Design decisions must be reviewed by the school system staff regardless of the method used to contract for construction services. The design review process cannot be hurried or shortened without compromises that would not be beneficial to the educational program. Sometimes, to get the project under construction, architects from the firm contracted to design/build the school will make design decisions without school system input. This is not a good situation for the school system. Unless adequate time and safeguards are built into the contract with the design/build firm, there is a danger of short-circuiting the review process. This and the requirement for public bidding prevent many school systems from using this method of contracting.

CONTRACT PAYMENT OPTIONS

The contract payment continuum (Table 15.2) shows the different methods of making payment to a contractor.

Table 15.2. Continuum of Contract Payment Methods Available to School Boards

Firmness of Price

Most>			<Least
Bid	Negotiated Fixed Price	Target Price	Cost Plus Payment

Bid

This is the most common method that school systems use. A contractor makes a bid to complete the project, submitting one price. If this bid is accepted, the contractor is paid that amount over the course of the project. Some negotiating for price adjustments may occur when exceptional situations arise, such as rapid increases in prices of lumber or other building materials, but this is not expected over the life of the contract and the school system can hold to the original price.

Negotiated Fixed Price

There are some circumstances where it might be beneficial to the school system to negotiate with possible contractors for a set price. This is called competitive negotiations, but the final price is fixed for the life of the contract.

Target Price

This is where a contractor sets a target price that the school system will pay. The contractor tries to meet that target using whatever methods possible to keep the final price within a range. This method is very seldom used by school systems.

This method is where the contractor charges the school system for the cost of the materials and labor that go into the building plus a certain percentage for profit and overhead. This is used seldom by school systems, but when it is used, it is where public bidding is not demanded.

The last two methods of contract payment or fixing the price of the contract can be completed under a bidding arrangement. Potential contractors can submit a bid on each one, with the school system selecting the one it feels is the best and lowest and award a contract. In some states, this method may not be a legal arrangement for public school systems. Legal opinion should be secured to determine if these are feasible.

ACCEPTANCE OF THE BUILDING

When the school building is substantially complete, the builder notifies the school board in writing that the structure is completed and ready for occupancy. Upon receipt of this notice, the school board meets at the new building to complete an inspection tour. The school staff involved in this project, the architect, and representatives of the contracting firm officially tour the building to determine if the building is indeed substantially complete.

Upon finding the building substantially complete, the school board passes a resolution accepting the building. This is an important step for both the school board and the contractor because the liability for the building is then assumed by the school board and the contractor is relieved of liability. In addition, the utilities and associated costs of operating the building are transferred to the school board. The building is then officially added to the inventory of the school system and becomes the official responsibility of the school board.

Even though the school board has accepted the building as being substantially complete, many small items are undoubtedly missing or need repair or completion. All these items are put on a list called a "punch list." The punch list is an official listing of the things that need to be done before the building is complete. These items may be as insignificant as a missing switch plate or light bulb, or as major as air conditioning machinery. Nevertheless, the school board will permit the staff and students to occupy the new structure and use it accordingly.

The contractor usually has a year from the date of acceptance of the building to complete the items on the punch list. School boards usually withhold a small portion of the contract payment to ensure all the items are done. When all the items on the punch list are completed to the satisfaction of the school board and the architect, the school board makes the final payment to the contractor and the building is considered complete.

SUMMARY

The firm doing the construction work needs to be monitored so that the firm performs according to the contract and in a timely fashion. Normally, the school system would provide personnel to do the monitoring, however, in median or small school systems the personnel are not available. The school system can either employ an individual or can contract with a firm to do that monitoring. These firms are called construction management entities. One of the most bothersome parts of the construction phase is the management of the change orders. Change orders arise because of changes in conditions at the site or change of materials needed to complete the project. Successful management of change orders is very important to keep the project within budget and completed in a timely fashion.

There are several methods of contracting with a construction firm, but the most widely utilized is the lump sum bid, which sets the price of the project at the time of the bid. When the project is reasonably completed the school board inspects the project to determine completeness. Finally, the school board accepts the project. Normally, a punch list of items not completed is developed and completed within a year after building acceptance.

Chapter 16

Orientation and Evaluation

Following the acceptance of the building by the school board, the new staff and administration need to be oriented to the structure. Even if staff members were involved in planning the building, they need to be oriented as to how the building will work. They will want to find out how the architect interpreted their programming needs and how this is reflected in design features.

No matter how well designed, the success of the building depends to a great extent upon the perceptions of the teaching staff. If the architect has captured in brick and mortar the words used to describe the building features that are needed, the staff will be able to conduct the type of program desired. The architect may not have designed a specific feature the way some of the staff perceived it, but if the feature allows the staff to do the job, the building will not impede their work.

Thus, the specific features and their operation need to be identified and explained during the orientation. The specific purposes of the orientation process are the following:

- for the staff to become familiar with the building and how to use it to facilitate the educational program
- for students to find their way around the building and become familiar with the specific features they will use in learning
- for the custodial staff to become familiar with all of the systems of the building and how to operate them efficiently
- for the community to recognize and appreciate the building as a resource that can be used by all residents

An office or person within the school system should be placed in charge of the orientation for each new school building or major construction project. There should be a broad base of involvement by all school system departments.

In addition, the committee that plans the orientation should include a representative from the office of the architect, teaching staff, and the principal of the building. In some school systems, the principal of the new facility is the person placed in charge. In other settings, a person in the central administration heads the planning. The building principal should most certainly have a strong role in planning the orientation activities. Most of the orientation activities need to be completed before the entire student body occupies the building.

 ## ROLES IN THE ORIENTATION PROCESS

Even with just one building orientation, many roles must be fulfilled. The roles that different offices and individuals must play in an orientation are listed below.

School Board

- makes all policy decisions regarding the project
- approves the people involved
- determines and approves how much staff time will be freed for the orientation program
- authorizes reports
- decides the name of the building
- decides whether signs are in order and what they should contain
- establishes the wording of dedication plaques and programs
- accepts the building on behalf of their constituents and states the official words of thanks to those who participated
- approves expenses associated with the orientation program

Administrator

- helps get people involved
- sets up the communication system
- designates or recommends the person placed in charge of the orientation
- assists and arranges for continuing reporting
- arranges ways in which those unique needs discovered through the use of the building can be met

Teachers

- help to orient others
- visit the building under construction

- play an important role in the communication process as they receive and transmit information
- actively participate in the tasks of occupancy
- stay alert to new needs that may arise as the building is used

Students

- help explain the building and the program features to parents
- help write reports on what is going on
- aid the communication process by taking questions to the authorities and carrying the replies back
- help prepare simple floor plan maps and instructions
- serve as tour guides of the building

The Architect

- explains certain technical aspects of the construction to gain acceptance of certain features of the building
- plays a vital role during the occupancy of the building

The Public

- attends meetings, asks questions, gives opinions
- assists with the public dedication program

The form the orientation takes varies considerably, but the architect should have an opportunity to explain the building as designed. The architect should present drawings of the building to point out specific features and answer the questions that usually arise about the circulation patterns of both students and materials. Safety features need to be discussed with both the staff and the students. These features can be explained by the architect and engineering staff. The communication system of the building is usually complex enough to require explanation by the architect (CEFPI, 2004).

The presentation and question-and-answer period of the architect should take place at the first general meeting of the faculty and staff. This should be the kick-off activity of this group's orientation. Usually, the principal or person who is in charge of the orientation conducts the meeting and makes the necessary introductions to the faculty and staff. The superintendent might also wish to be present and speak to the group. Time should be left during the meeting for the architect to thoroughly explain the building and answer all questions.

After the general meeting, the architect should lead the staff on a tour of the entire building, pointing out selected design features. The tour should also include the outdoor spaces devoted to the school program. All unique features both inside and outside should be pointed out and explained. This tour also provides the staff with an opportunity to ask questions about features when the architect or engineer is available. By the end of the tour, the staff should have a good knowledge of the extent of the building and features in all parts of the structure.

These activities should enable the staff to conduct an orientation for the student body. Students will need to know circulation patterns and where certain sections of the building are located, such as the gym, cafeteria, library, and office. The teaching staff will have to explain the safety features of the building and assist the students in the first few fire, emergency, and evacuation drills. There will be many orientation sessions for the students during the first few weeks of occupancy. Some orientation activities may well extend through the first year. Of course, incoming students will have to be oriented in a similar fashion. In succeeding years, the orientation for new students may become a responsibility of the student organization.

COMMUNITY ORIENTATION

The completion of the building will probably be well-known throughout the community, but the orientation of the community is a very important part of the entire orientation process. After the building is in operation and staff members have become fairly familiar with its features, a public orientation should be held.

This should be an open meeting with all individuals in the community invited. This invitation should include people who do not have children in the school as well as students' parents. An invitation to attend should be communicated in every way possible, such as through radio, television, and the newspapers. Students can also deliver invitations to those who do not have direct contact with the school.

This event should be a large community celebration of the completion of a distinctive community resource. It should be advertised as a special event in the life of the community, regardless of the grade level of the school building. This event should also be a closure to a process of planning in which the entire community and school staff participated. Even if a person or segment of the community did not participate in the planning, this closure should be recognized.

The community orientation should be coupled with the formal dedication of the building and symbolic transfer of the keys of the building to the principal and a community representative. The dedication should not be a religious ceremony, but a public gathering where the school board dedicates the building to the community for its use. This symbolic gesture, along with the transfer of the keys, tells the community the building belongs to them, not only to the school system. Students should participate in the ceremony in a number of ways. Groups of students can sing songs, read poetry or other appropriate selections, play instruments, dance, or do other performances in celebration of the event.

Following this formal activity, the people attending should be taken on a building tour. Students, in particular, should assist in this activity, for by doing so, they gain pride in the building and enhance their feeling of ownership. Printed materials, such as programs, floor plans, fire escape routes, history of the school, and specifications of the building are usually made available during this event.

POST OCCUPANCY EVALUATION

Once the building is completed and occupied, it is time to evaluate the outcome of the entire planning effort. It is easy to overlook this evaluation because the building is occupied and working well. It must be remembered that some information can be obtained only at certain times. Post occupancy evaluation is one such time where certain data are needed and can be obtained in only a short period of time. The building will stand for many years and can be evaluated at any time, but people tend to forget the process that was used to plan the building.

Two things should be evaluated at the completion of a school building planning effort: the process that was used to plan the building and the product of the planning process, the building itself.

Product Evaluation

The product of the planning effort is the physical structure that was completed. The evaluation of the product covers the adequacy of the building for the type of program to be carried on, how the building operates, the cost of the building, and whether or not the school system acquired what it needs at the best price.

The cost of the facility can be determined in several ways with differing results, depending upon the measurement used. Typical measurements such as square foot rates, cost per square foot of space, costs per pupil, square feet of space per pupil, construction time, number and cost of change orders, cost-benefit ratios, and even life cycle costing are used in determining the cost of buildings. These are all very important cost comparisons when evaluating the building. Historical comparison between projects also produces excellent results. Comparing costs between school systems is rather difficult and limited because the quality of material used in the various buildings is never exactly known or specified. All these measurements will assist in making decisions on other projects, but the evaluation of the product should not be limited to cost comparisons.

The finished product should be evaluated using the educational specifications written for the project. The person who guided the program planning effort and wrote the educational specifications should do this evaluation. This is not an easy task and, if done properly, is time consuming. The evaluator should go through each room and space in the building and check off the items contained in the specifications to determine if the school system got what it needed.

The evaluator should also look at relationships of the various parts of the building to one another to see if what was asked in the educational specifications was observed. In this way, the educational specifications serve as a building appraisal instrument. Through this evaluation process, the school system can determine how effective the architect was in interpreting the educational specifications and also how successful the Design Review Team was in monitoring the architect's design.

The users of the facility should also be included in the data-gathering effort, for they have an important contribution to make regarding how well the facility works. Through interviews, successful design features in the building can be identified, as well as less successful ones. What one wants to find out here is how well the building is serving the people who are using it. Interviews or locally developed survey instruments can be developed for this purpose. An interview protocol can be developed to elicit the standardized information desired. Data obtained through this exercise should be used in future educational specifications developed for similar capital projects. Some of the data may well serve to correct deficiencies in the new building through the capital improvement program.

Process Evaluation

The effort exerted in planning a building is sufficiently important to be evaluated. The school staff and community representatives spent considerable time and effort in planning the school. As such, the school system should determine if the process was a success. Evaluating the process provides the school system administration with data to use to improve the process. The people involved in the process would also like to have a chance to tell the administration their ideas on the success of the effort.

The evaluation of the process should be done immediately after the school building is occupied while people can remember how they were involved and to what purpose. The longer this evaluation is put off, the less reliable the data will be. Individuals will be more ready to respond if they are surveyed while the new school is still an important item in the community and before other aspects of community life take their attention.

No predetermined, proven protocol exists for gathering this type of data, nor is there any standardized instrument. Rather, the school system should determine the purpose of the evaluation and develop a local evaluation instrument specifically for the school system and the planning process used. This evaluation should determine if the people involved in the planning process felt their contribution was significant and if the school system obtained the desired school building as a result of the planning.

Many items may be asked, but it is important to find out if the school building is what they believe it should be and if they believe it will work. The survey should also ask whether or not, as a result of their involvement, they would want to be involved in the planning process again. This type of question often shows how successful the individuals feel the process was.

Appendix H contains an evaluation instrument used by a school system to measure perceptions on just one part of the entire planning process: the development of educational specifications. This survey was administered to a committee of school staff and community representatives who assisted a consultant in writing a set of educational specifications for the school system. The results were given to the school board to appraise the planning process.

In this particular community, community involvement was particularly important and this survey enabled the school board to assess their success. If it is important to involve people, both community and school staff, then it is important to determine the success of the effort.

Another aspect of evaluation is the efficacy of the planning model. Many steps should be taken in the planning process to complete a capital improvement project, such as a new building, an addition, or a major renovation. These steps are the responsibility of the school staff, and it is important to determine how effective the organization was in completing all steps.

School systems that have a number of substantial capital improvement projects going on simultaneously need to monitor the work of a sizable staff charged with guiding the entire process. By using a checklist like the one shown in Appendix H, data on the effectiveness of the organization can be obtained. This is a very simple instrument, but it does cover important aspects of organizational planning.

DATA USE

The natural question is: *How do we use this data?* Evaluating the planning process will help determine organizational effectiveness in managing a process, in particular the facility planning process. The process evaluation will enable the school board and administration to streamline the process in future efforts and improve on effectiveness, or to maintain the effectiveness as measured. The other evaluation process deals with the product, namely, the school building. This provides information about the success of various architectural features that were program-driven, such as flexible walls between classrooms or certain area relationships desired.

The educational specifications are the basis of the evaluative instrument and, as such, the building should serve that program. Good or marginal architectural features of the building resulting from these educational specifications can be identified. This information should be worked back into the capital improvement program and into subsequent educational specifications.

If a mistake was made in a new building, that mistake should not be made in subsequent buildings; the school staff should learn from each building planned and constructed. Conversely, an architectural feature that works very nicely might well be incorporated in subsequent buildings. Only by evaluating the product of the planning process will the school system be able to make these kinds of judgments.

EVALUATION PERIODS

The purpose of the evaluation effort determines when and how often it is carried out. Obviously, the process evaluation should be conducted immediately after the building is occupied because it must occur within recent memory of the planning effort. This is a one-time evaluation and can be done only then.

The product evaluation should be conducted in several stages. The first evaluation should be conducted immediately after the building is occupied to determine the fidelity of the design to the educational specifications. In other words, how well did the Design Team and the Design Review Team adhere to what was contained in the educational specifications?

This is an important evaluation because not only is the building being evaluated, but so is the ability of the architectural firm to interpret educational specifications. This appraisal may well play a part in determining further employment of that particular firm. This evaluation also reflects how well the Design Review Team monitored the design phase. This evaluation will indicate if a finer-tuned design process is needed.

In addition to the immediate evaluation, an appraisal should be conducted within one year of the acceptance of the building by the school board. According to some, this evaluation should take place within eleven months—before the one-year warranties and guarantees expire. This would be a prudent evaluation to determine premature wearing of parts.

Following this evaluation, the building should be scheduled for periodic evaluations associated with the development of the long-range plan of the school system. These evaluations should occur regularly until the twentieth year of life of the building.

At that point a very substantial evaluation should take place. This twenty-year evaluation should include not only the adequacy of the building to accommodate the educational program offered, but also all of the building systems. Systems comprising the building's internal structure should be seriously examined by architects and engineers. Replacing certain parts of the building at this time would not be out of order.

Many times the roof has a twenty-year guarantee and would need to be evaluated, if this has not already been done. Other parts and systems of the building need to be critically examined and appropriate engineering tests conducted. Usually, a complete renovation is needed to bring the building up to the standards of the rest of the buildings in the school system.

In addition to these evaluations, the principal of the school should conduct an annual evaluation to determine maintenance needs that have occurred during the year. Although a formal evaluation instrument is probably not needed, the principal may develop a checklist to assist in appraising every part of the building. Data from these evaluations should be fed directly into the maintenance schedule of the school system for completion.

The school board needs to determine the evaluation program for school facilities in concert with its long-range planning effort. The purpose of evaluation, data-gathering instruments, responsible staff, and process all need to be determined and selected by the school board if adequate data are to be generated so that the school board can make decisions about housing students.

SUMMARY

Before the building is put to use, the faculty and staff need to be oriented to the features of the building. Normally, the architect should make an important contribution to this orientation. The architect should explain the features of the building and lead the faculty and staff on a tour of the structure. The principal should also play an important part in the program of orientation. Faculty and staff need to become familiar with the building and its features.

The community should be a part of the orientation as the building becomes a part of the community. An orientation night should be held for the community to explore the building and become familiar with the features of the structure. Finally, the process that brought forth a completed capital project and the product of that process should be evaluated by the school staff. These two evaluative processes should provide important data for the school board to be used in future projects.

Chapter 17

Planning for Technology

Technology became a driving force in the field of education with the miniaturization of various electronic devices and machines and the rapid development of educational software. Since that time, both the beneficial utility of
technology and the reduced cost of hardware and software have presented
the schools with an opportunity to expand educational opportunity for all students. At the same time, implementation of technology into all school buildings, new and renovated, has become a major item to consider on the part of
educators and school board members. The implementation of sophisticated
technology is no longer a haphazard proposition where the largest problem is
deciding which brand of computer to purchase.

A whole industry has been generated devoted solely to the application of
technology to the educational process and the subsequent impact upon school
buildings. Educators and other decision makers must now deal with the
problem of how to incorporate appropriate technology into the educational
program. Now the challenge is to define the technology skills students need
at each grade level and then how to assess them.

SCHOOL READINESS

A person might be tempted to think that implementing technology into school
buildings is a routine and commonplace activity because technology has been
in the public mind for quite some time. One could also be tempted to believe
that every student in the country is completely computer literate and has access to all of the latest electronic and digital devices and gadgets that are used
to support learning. Unfortunately, neither assumption is entirely correct for
two major reasons.

In the first place, the growing complexity, versatility, and speed of electronic communication have kept the industry in a constant state of tumultuous development. New advances in all aspects of electronic communication are being made almost daily. New sources of data become electronically available to students in rapid order. It is difficult for the average educator to keep current with the present state of development of the industry. For every new building that is constructed or an existing building renovated, the educator is faced with many decisions regarding the implementation of a system that will serve the student population not only now, but also in the future. Thus, the rapid change in the industry means that educators must continuously seek assistance in obtaining information to help in making decisions regarding technology implementation (ASBOI, 2001).

The second reason technology implementation is a continuing serious concern for educators is the poor state of condition of school buildings in the country. A report of the U.S. General Accounting Office (1995) in public school buildings indicated that 46 percent of the existing buildings did not have sufficient electrical service to adequately accommodate the new technology in the classrooms. In addition, 52 percent of the schools reported they did not have access to a computer network. Since that time, the percent of schools that do not have access has been reduced considerably as a result of the expansion of Wi-Fi capability. Nevertheless, there are places in the United States where network availability is limited. In these regions, teachers need to be sensitive when making student assignments to the fact that some students may not have internet access.

In today's world, lack of internet access is not acceptable. To administrators and school board members in these school systems, trying to implement a technology program is a very real issue that needs to be addressed. Even in those school systems that have a rather good level of technology implementation, continuous updating of hardware and software is a challenge because of financial constraints. Keeping technology up-to-date is still a challenge to all schools, because of rapid development.

✗ ℨ๒ EDUCATOR NEEDS

This book deals almost exclusively with the planning processes that educators and school board members must initiate, guide, supervise, and evaluate in order to complete any capital improvement project, whether it is a new school building or renovating an existing building. These identified processes all contribute to the completion of the total project. Each, in turn, must be completed to the satisfaction of all concerned before progress can be recorded. Each chapter in this book discusses and examines in detail the responsibility educators and school board members must exercise to make certain each process is completed satisfactorily.

In the matter of using technology to enhance and support the educational program, the type of guidance educators and school board members need is in identifying the right questions to ask and the right sources of expert information and assistance. This is the greatest benefit this chapter can impart to people engaged in planning a capital improvement project.

Because of this intent, this book does not necessarily deal with prescriptions as to what a school building could or should contain, how it should be configured, what kinds of spaces should be in the building, or even what type of hardware would best serve an educational program. Many books on school facilities show good examples of the latest trends in school construction, the most innovative approaches to a specialized area within the building such as technology, and the latest furniture and equipment.

These sources of information are excellent in permitting educators, school board members, and community members to expand their ideas of what the school they are planning should be like. The Educational Clearinghouse on School Facilities at The George Washington University, The National Clearinghouse for Educational Facilities in Washington, D.C., and the American Clearinghouse for Educational Facilities at Talton University in Texas, are very good sources for books and materials discussing these building needs and can be reached through the internet at www.edfacilities.org for NCEF, acefacilities.org for the ACEF, and edfacclearinghouse.com for the GWU Educational Facilities clearinghouse.

COMMUNICATION GROWTH

The growth and development of electronic communication systems within the last five years has been phenomenal. Today, through technological assistance, almost instantaneous communication with any person or data source in the world is possible. This has had a profound influence upon schools and how they operate. This development has also greatly influenced the school buildings in which the students are housed (Rollins, 2012).

The sophistication of technological equipment that is available today has generated a growing body of specific knowledge relating to application. This body of knowledge centers on the installation and proper use of both electronic hardware and software. Along with equipment expertise, there is also a growing body of knowledge relating to how students learn using all types of technology. The latter, however, has not proceeded as rapidly as the development of more sophisticated equipment.

The development of new hardware and of practical applications for existing equipment has outrun thoughtful consideration of how all the technology available on the market can be harnessed and used for effective and efficient learning by students. Part of this lag is the difficulty in conducting research involving human subjects, especially students in the public schools.

The development lag between hardware development and human application is not unique to electronic technology available for the public schools. The lag does present, however, some critical problems for those educators and school board members who are responsible for technology implementation in any capital improvement project. How the building will be configured and designed for new technology is not an easy decision to make.

⨉ 31   PRESSING QUESTIONS

What are some questions educators should initially raise and think about in considering technology application to a new building or a renovation of an existing building? Listed below are some major questions administrators, teachers, and school board members must address to successfully implement a program of technological assistance to the teaching and learning processes.

- What and how do students learn best with the use of electronic assistance?
- What kinds of hardware and software products are needed to implement the kind of teaching/learning strategy the school system desires?
- How will the technological systems in the new building, or newly renovated building, fit in with the rest of the school system? This includes internet accessibility throughout the school system.
- How can equity in technology application be assured for every student on a school system-wide basis?
- Does the school system have the expertise to plan and design an effective and efficient technology program that is as up-to-date as possible?
- If not, what kind of outside assistance is needed to ensure an effective technology installation, and where is this obtained?

All the above questions must be addressed before a sensible application of technology is implemented. The questions listed can be answered only through a self-appraisal and study of the needs of the school system done by the appropriate people in the local school system, with the assistance of whatever technological advice is available. This may mean an outside consultant is employed to assist the staff in delineating their needs. This appraisal or examination should take place long before any plans are developed for the building itself.

Such appraisal should answer questions such as:

- What learning activities can be enhanced by technology?
- Will some of the newer technologies permit the students to learn more effectively?
- What software now on the market will do this best?
- What kinds of hardware are necessary to permit use of this software?
- Are there peripherals, accessories, or complementary devices that are needed to implement this?

In addition to the above questions, some special issues and considerations must be accounted for in the implementation of technology.

SPECIAL ISSUES

Among the myriad questions and issues that surround the acquisition and implementation of a technology plan, four areas require the serious attention of school administrators and school board members. These four issues deal more with implementation than with the kinds and types of equipment that will eventually be acquired. Decisions need to be made and actions taken about these issues in plenty of time before the completion of a capital improvement project.

Staff Preparation

Regardless of the kinds of equipment and systems that are purchased for a new or renovated school building, the entire school staff need training in the proper use of the systems employed long before the school is ready for occupancy. The training should include not only explanations on how the equipment works, but also how the technology application fits into the overall educational program of the school. The training should include discussions on how technology influences student learning. It is important to have teacher input here to inform school authorities how the teachers plan to use the technology in their classroom.

In addition, such training might also be in the form of examination of recent theories on how children learn. All of this should take place long before the staff moves into the building. The technology consultant the school system employs to assist in the design of the technology system should have a part in the training program, as should experts in learning theory.

Technology Support

Along with proper training, each person in the school who will be working with the technology system should have the necessary technical support to maintain the equipment in working order. Occasionally school boards may not understand the need for such a staff to keep the system functional at all times. Equipment that is not functional at all times does not represent prudent management of resources. Sometimes these staff support personnel can be located within a school building, which is the ideal situation. Every local school system with more than one building, however, will probably need to have a system-wide cadre on call to the staff in each building.

The size of the technology support staff will largely be determined by the sophistication of the system employed and the number of buildings to be served. The consultant who advises the school system on the technology system should also advise on the size and complexity of the support staff.

Equal Availability

This issue deals with the equal treatment of all students in the school system. Each student needs to have the same accessibility to hardware and software as every other student. This includes the number and kinds of equipment as well as the types of programs and activities utilized. The central administration needs to assure that every student in the system has equal access to technology equipment and programs that are in the school system. When a new school building is opened with rather sophisticated equipment and programs, these same kinds of programs and equipment need to be available to students attending school in older buildings, even if this means a special renewal program of upgrading for all existing school buildings.

Uniformity of Technology Application

The technology application of a local school system should be uniform for the most efficient use of equipment and programs. The school system should develop technical specifications regarding the kinds and types of electronic equipment that will be used in every school in the system. These specifications should assist the staff in individual school buildings relative to the kinds of systems that can be purchased.

Many times the parent-teacher association provides funds for the purchase of personal computers, cameras, laptops, and other finite equipment. The equipment purchased through such plans and schemes needs to be compatible with what the school system purchases. This is especially true if the equipment and programs in the school system are networked for more efficient use of programs.

In addition to the compatibility of equipment, a system wide approach to technology implementation also enhances and simplifies the warehousing of computer parts for repair purposes. Compatibility of equipment also allows better repair expertise to be developed in the technical support team. This permits the support staff to develop a great deal of expertise in keeping all equipment functional because they do not have to repair and maintain a variety of equipment (CEFPI, 2004).

BASIC CONSIDERATIONS

There are some basic considerations that educators need to address before any technology system can be designed for implementation. These considerations deal with some decisions that need to be made early in the project.

Computer Displacement

Some school systems with older school buildings are still using personal computers in the classroom rather than the newer versions of the computer. In these locations the school authorities must account for the displacement of space for the computers in the classroom. A single desktop computer in the classroom requires the same amount of space as one student. Because of placement of one computer in the classroom, the student capacity of the classroom is diminished by one student space. In the past, computer displacement has been a serious problem for the classroom teacher. The teacher had to contend with a full complement of students, including special needs students, plus an additional teacher in some cases. In the past, this has caused some space problems. However, with the development and use of laptop computers, IPad, and Chromebooks this has ceased to be a problem

With the introduction of wireless mobile labs, computer displacement is not much of a problem. Mobile computer labs permit much more flexibility for the use of computers and free up needed classroom space. With such labs, the need for hard-wired computers in every classroom no longer exists. Laptop computers can be located on a cart and shared among classrooms, thus posing fewer space issues than the more traditional approach.

Nonetheless, the die seems to be cast that computers of some sort are needed in every classroom. In new buildings, there is a reasonable possibility of having wireless computers in throughout in the building. When an existing building is renovated or renewed, the opportunity to use wireless mobile computer labs is even more important because of the limitations on the structure of the building.

Rudimentary Classroom Needs

Every classroom, laboratory, and instructional space in the building needs to have the basic provisions of receiving and sending voice, video, and data signals throughout the interior and exterior of the building. This means that all these spaces will have appropriate wireless capability for all types of communication. This applies even if the school system does not plan to purchase sufficient hardware for full implementation in the immediate future.

Students need to be able to access the internet, receive and send voice and electronic mail, electronically obtain and analyze data, participate in closed-circuit television activities and programs, and use programs such as Skype and Web 2.0 tools to obtain an adequate education. Without these capabilities, students cannot be adequately prepared for a world of technology use. The knowledge boundaries of the classroom extend far beyond the four walls of the school building, and the physical means for extending it need to be made available to all students.

In addition to the electronic means for communication, the proper-sized student furniture should be available at all locations. Sometimes little thought is given to the sizes of students who will use equipment while seated. Research findings regarding the proper height for a computer keyboard and monitor, the distance a person should be from the screen, and the types of desks for productive work should be used in designing all electronic stations (Loveless, 1996).

Each classroom should have a presentation device such as an ActivBoard or a Clear Touch Interactive TV. The teachers should also have a document camera and laptop for use with the presentation device. Teachers also need a laptop/computer with which to access the student database to record attendance.

COMPUTER LABORATORIES

Many school systems still make a point of having at least one computer laboratory in every school building. In a new building a desktop computer lab is not necessary because of the portability of laptops, Chromebooks, and IPads. Nevertheless, in some older buildings the computer lab is a normal application. The usual application is for approximately twenty-five to thirty individual computers to be located in one dedicated room to be used as a laboratory for instructional purposes. Both computer literacy and keyboarding can be effectively taught in such a laboratory setting. These are the basic skills and knowledge for which a large number of computers are needed.

Other instructional activities can normally take place in a laboratory under the supervision of a teacher. In some cases, students are permitted to use the computer laboratory on an individual basis when it is not being used by a class.

Some educators argue that if computers are located in the classroom there is little or no need for computer labs. Further, most school systems are purchasing laptop computers for every student. This practice could well negate the need for computer labs and even the desk computers in the classroom. With individual laptop computers, students can learn keyboarding and other applications in the classroom under the direction of the classroom teacher.

Of course, the very reason for using electronic equipment to support an educational program should be the basis for decisions regarding how many to purchase, how they should be deployed, and where to locate them. A school system should purchase as much equipment and software as possible, as well as the most modern applications.

TECHNOLOGY FUTURES

At one time, a great deal of the electronic communication available in schools required some sort of wiring. At the present time wireless communication through a satellite is available everywhere. Almost every new school building that was built within the last decade is now serviced by wireless communication systems. Wireless communication, of course, greatly facilitates updating older, existing buildings that are not currently wired for modern technology applications and where rewiring is a severe problem.

The personal computer has given way to the laptop computer and Chromebook for significant student use. The laptop computer can be carried around by a student and used to access data throughout the school building. In fact, some newer schools have electrical service in all areas of the building, especially in such areas as the student commons and the library, for specific recharging use by students. In fact, most electronic equipment does not need external sources of energy with better batteries available. Several schools have provided every student with a laptop computer as a means of enhancing their studying. In this way, students can study on an individual basis.

Most school systems are now looking toward research to determine (1) whether or not the school system should actually provide laptops or some similar device to individual students, (2) what the device should be like, and (3) the affect technology has upon the physical and mental health of students. Personal phones and similar devices might well be something the schools should provide, or it could be something not yet invented because development in personal communication is rapidly expanding. Many school systems permit students to keep their cell phones in class to do research, make electronic flashcards, text or communicate with experts in the field, or take quick formative assessments like Kahoot or Quizlet.

The example of a school system providing individual laptops to students illustrates the argument made by some educators that every student should have access to an individual laptop or similar device. As desirable as this may be, the local school system must weigh the cost-benefit of this expenditure of funds with other applications for enhancing the educational opportunities for all students. The school board also needs to establish policies governing theft, loss, or inappropriate use of equipment. The laptop computer has already made an important appearance in today's schools and this presence will continue to increase. The impact technology has upon the learning process of students will increase as new and better electronic hardware and software become available in the future. The size of technology hardware is increasingly becoming smaller with Chromebook and Surface Pro as examples. Miniaturization of hardware is the key to new equipment.

Educators all over the country are experiencing the frequent use of cell phones, iPads, Chromebooks, Kindles, Nooks, tablet PCs, and other individual electronic devices within the school building. How these devices will be put to use in the educational program in the future is still in the exploration stage. Nevertheless, these devices will be put to use in the future as new educational software is developed. The use of such devices will not influence the configuration of the school classroom as far as can be seen.

SUMMARY

Technology needs in the schools are changing constantly, especially as new applications and programs are developed. However, the basic need to properly evaluate the application and relate that to the educational needs of students is ever important. The technology industry develops applications and programs as needed, however, the industry is not responsible for determining the fit of these programs or applications for student needs. This is where the educator must properly evaluate every program and application to determine the appropriateness for students. There is a growing awareness of the dangers of the amount and appropriateness of technology in the normal development of students. Nevertheless, educators must be aware of the benefits of technology and plan for the incorporation of appropriate and necessary technology applications and programs. The planning for technology use in a new building entails a complete evaluation of the physical needs of technology. With the widespread and universal use of Wi-Fi rather than cable means that the educator has more flexibility in meeting the needs of the students and educational program.

Chapter 18

Critical Issues in School Facility Planning

A Look to the Future

Today, public school systems in the United States have perhaps reached their highest levels of efficiency and effectiveness in the history of the country. That said, however, one must also realize that public schools do not always meet the expectations of the various client groups who interact with the educational establishment. Public school systems have a long way to go before most citizens feel comfortable with how schools work.

In addition, public schools struggle to educate properly a varied and polyglot population of students. Nevertheless, considering the purpose of the public schools and the numbers of children and youth who are enrolled, the country is well served by the system of public schools currently in existence. This does not mean, however, that public schools do not face challenges in the future.

In the early 1990s, President George H. W. Bush and the National Governors Association adopted a set of goals toward which the schools should work leading to the next century. These goals were eventually cast into the Goals 2000: Educate America Act (1994). These were a set of rather modest, but important, goals dealing with the performance of public schools.

In December 1998, the National Education Goals panel presented a report on the accomplishment of the states toward meeting these goals. They gave public schools a marginal success score. According to the commission, public schools had made valiant efforts toward these goals, and in the process made considerable headway in improving their performance. Yet the panel stated, "The nation as a whole is not likely to meet the ambitious education goals set for 2000" (Associated Press 1998, A9).

Public education in this country apparently still has a way to go to meet these goals. In the process, schools face many challenges. In this chapter several critical issues are presented that the public schools of this country are

237

facing and that will undoubtedly intensify over the years. These issues are not necessarily new, and some of the issues are not really problems so much as movements, conditions, or issues that can and do influence how the public schools operate, which in turn have an influence upon the capital improvement efforts of the school system.

ECONOMIC TURMOIL

The United States has a strong economy, yet even at that, experiences difficulties. The nation suffered through the Great Depression of 1929, lived through the exuberance of the technology stock explosion and its subsequent decline, and even saw the Dow Jones Industrial Average exceed 14,000 points. In 2009, the economy went through a crisis in the lending industry, which negatively affected the entire economy, with the result of depressing the stock market at a rapid pace. The economy since has showed a steady, and in some periods, exuberant growth. Since 2016, the economy has enjoyed a rapid growth, yet within the past few months of 2018 the stock market has seen severe declines. This simply indicates that in the future the economy will be strong, but may experience some periodic down drafts.

Regardless of the length of the most recent market action, public schools are affected by these fluctuations. The ability to raise taxes to pay for bonded indebtedness is influenced by the state of the economy (Holt, 2002). In a declining economy, citizens are more reluctant to vote increases in bonded indebtedness than when the economy is advancing. This presents a problem for the school board that needs to complete capital improvement projects. In addition, the cost of building material increases must be shouldered by the local school system when constructing new buildings or renovating existing buildings, making it more difficult to complete capital improvement projects.

On the other hand, when the economy is advancing rapidly, the wages of workers increase, as does the cost of building materials. School systems oftentimes find themselves in competition with the other segments of the economy for workers and building materials. This type of competition, although healthy for the total economy, makes the school system search for ways to stretch limited capital dollars to cover more projects. School systems all over the country are legally limited as to the resources available for either new construction or renovations to existing buildings. By prudent administration of the school systems and the capital improvement programs, educators and school boards are able to work through these economic changes and still house student populations efficiently.

POLITICAL DECISION-MAKING

Many problems relating to the planning, construction, and maintenance of school buildings suitable for students have a political aspect to them. What individuals believe is important in life usually governs the decisions they make, and in some instances these decisions may fly in the face of empirical evidence.

Empirical evidence must first pass political and philosophical muster before it is used to arrive at a decision. This has been the case in the field of education since the inception of the country. Political and philosophical beliefs of individuals in authority influence public decisions regarding all aspects of how schools operate. This is especially true regarding capital expenditures for any major building project.

The intensity of politicization of decisions has increased over the past decade as resources have become more limited. It is expected that political and philosophical beliefs will increasingly influence decisions regarding when and where schools are constructed, as well as how much funding will be available. School administrators will want to use strong empirical evidence as to the benefits of good school buildings for the education of students to mount an effective case for building needs.

Public schools and the individuals who are associated with them are not necessarily included in the power structure of the community. Nevertheless, there are ways that both the individuals who work in the schools and the members of the community that support them can influence the politicization of the public schools and the decisions that result. Collective actions on the part of both the teachers and their unions have indeed influenced political decisions made for and within the public schools. Because these groups have their own political agendas, these decisions can be either for their own betterment or for the betterment of the school system. Likewise, parents can influence decisions and thereby negate political agendas that are not always in the best interest of the schoolchildren.

SCHOOL FACILITY EQUITY

One very pressing problem relating to school buildings is that of providing equitable buildings throughout the local school system, as well as the state at large. Everyone knows that equitable school facilities should be provided to all students by the state and local school boards, yet this has not happened in a large majority of the states in the nation. The idea that students in one part of a local school system should have the same access to safe and modern facilities as students in every other part of the school system is indeed a vital part of American educational philosophy.

The most poignant example of inequity of school facilities, however, can be found in some large cities, where students in the inner city attend school in buildings that are not even safe to inhabit, while at the same time, students in the outer portions of the city or in the suburbs attend school in safe and modern buildings. A similar inequity scenario is duly played out in some of the rural and isolated regions of each state.

Perhaps the absence of an application of providing equitable educational facilities in every part of the school system or country relates more to the political process inherent in the allocation of funds than anything else. The reason for such political inaction may be as mundane as the desire on the part of the governing body to keep taxes at a low level. Such inaction might also relate to decisions regarding priorities of spending public funds for various projects besides school buildings.

Sometimes educators find that decision makers firmly believe a good education can be obtained in any kind of a physical environment, regardless of condition. This is patently false because there is a large body of empirical research dealing with the condition of school facilities and student achievement. In study after study, the findings have been rather significant. Students in modern and safe school buildings outperform students in unsatisfactory buildings on achievement tests.

STATE LITIGATION

There has not been significant legal action to force states or local jurisdictions to equalize school facilities, even though the principle of equal treatment is fundamental to public education in the United States. Many states have experienced litigation to rectify inequitable operational funding plans. Approximately forty states have experienced litigation because of inequities in funding to local school systems, or have changed their funding system because of court orders (Young 2003).

Most of these suits and subsequent court decisions have not directly affected the equity of educational facilities. A number of states (Arizona, Alaska, California, South Carolina, Texas, and West Virginia) have had to address this issue through the force of a judicial decision rendering the state funding program for school facilities unconstitutional (*Pauley v. Bailey*; *Roosevelt Elementary School District No. 66 v. Bishop*; *Williams v. Los Angeles School District*). These court decisions are promising and more, undoubtedly, will occur in the future.

TECHNOLOGY

Another critical issue school systems are facing relating to school buildings is the provision for access to the latest technology. Everyone agrees each student in the public schools should have such access to the most advanced technology applications, yet many schools do not have even have the most basic or elementary parts of a good technology system in operation (DeJong, 2008). To prove this assertion, one has only to visit school buildings to witness the lack of decent technology applications.

The difference between technology availability in the commercial sector and actual application of technology in the classroom is wide and constitutes a critical issue. How can the schools adequately prepare users of technology or workers for the new technology world, unless the most advanced applications of hardware and software are available to every student in public schools? Almost all new school buildings have access to the most up-to-date technology applications, but this does not apply uniformly to existing buildings. Schools will have to invest more funds for technology to keep abreast of the developments in this field.

The phenomenal proliferation of personal devices for communication has presented the schools with a problem of how to control the use of such devices during school hours and at the same time not infringe upon the rights of free speech. This problem has not been satisfactorily resolved throughout the country, but some local school systems have taken action to put the matter to rest in the interest of protecting the instructional program. Whether or not these actions infringe upon student rights is yet to be decided by the courts.

The other side of the coin regarding personal devices for communication is the possibility of developing devices that can be used in the education of students. Several companies have developed devices that incorporate learning activities that benefit students. Such applications have not yet reached a sophisticated level that can be used in the schools and have not been universally adopted by educators. As the application of these devices increase and the educational offerings become more relevant, these devices may play an important part in the educational program of students.

SCHOOL PLANNING PROCESS

Within the past decade, many school systems throughout the country have implemented strategic planning efforts as a process to give direction to the school system. There has been considerable success with this process in both addressing community needs and involving the community. And yet strategic planning in the public school sector has not always achieved the intended re-sults and perhaps needs to be expanded to provide for a more comprehensive internal planning effort. Local school systems are complicated and complex organisms, and there are a great number of planning efforts that proceed con-currently within the organization of the school systems that are not integrated into total planning efforts, such as strategic plans.

For instance, the planning for capital improvement projects often is not directly related to the overall strategic planning efforts of the school system. In many cases local school systems plan for a new building, or the renovation of an existing building, to accommodate growth without that process having any relationship to the strategic planning of the rest of the school system. Planning for a new school or a renovation in that case becomes an isolated event in the history of the school system.

The planning for any capital improvement project, whether a new building or a renovation project, must result directly from the major school system planning effort that determines how the educational program will evolve and develop over the next segment of time. How else can the building fit the needs of the educational programs and students unless the planning for the building goes hand-in-hand within the overall planning of the school system?

Planning of this nature can be termed "integrated planning." Such com-prehensive planning of the school system incorporates the needs of housing students based upon an examination of: (1) the educational program, (2) the number of students to be served, (3) the condition of the school building in-ventory, and (4) financial costs. Lack of clear identification of school system goals, the complexity of the organization, and communication that is often-times fragmented all hinders the implementation of a planning process that should be integrated and comprehensive. Each local school system must work to marry the individual planning efforts within the organization to the overall strategic planning effort of the school system in order to achieve stated goals with the limited resources available.

DEVOLUTION OF DECISION-MAKING

With the advent of different contractual arrangements between the school board and design and construction professionals, there has arisen devolution of the decision-making process toward the design/construction profession-als and away from the school board and educators. These new contract ar-rangements often remove some of the decision-making ability of the school system in the interests of speeding up the completion of the project, keeping the project on schedule, or keeping the project within the budget. This means that, instead of the educators making the decisions regarding what will be in the building and the arrangement of spaces, the design professionals make these decisions in the expediency of keeping the project within the budget constraints.

Such situations do not bode well for the school system in getting the type of educational facility that is needed by teachers and students. Budgetary limitations and the need for project completion seem to be the prime motivation for these contractual arrangements. Alternative contractual arrangements can work to the advantage of the school system only if the decision-making process regarding what is in the building is left solely in the hands of educators and the school board. The supremacy of the decision-making process in the hands of the educators and school board is essential, regardless of the contractual arrangement for design and construction services.

EXISTING BUILDINGS

Perhaps the most pressing problem or critical issue facing each local school system is the inability to keep the present inventory of school buildings in safe and usable condition. This is not a recent occurrence or a new problem, but is probably the most crucial in that it affects so many school children. Upwards of fourteen million students, according to a GAO (1995) report, attend school in buildings that are below standards or even considered dangerous. Educators and governmental officials have known for a long time of the need to save and upgrade the infrastructure of local governments.

For over one-quarter of a century, reports on the poor condition of public schools have been made by the U.S. government and various professional organizations. The American Association of School Administrators (1983) completed one of the first such reports, indicating the need for infrastructure repairs in schools in all parts of local jurisdictions. In a subsequent report, the Educational Writers Association (EWA, 1989) identified the need for public school building repair and maintenance to be $41 billion. This figure has since increased due to greater need and inflation for the intervening period.

In a study on building needs, GAO (1996) projected the monetary need to bring all public school buildings up to standard at $112 billion. Of this amount, more than $11 billion was needed in the next three years to bring the buildings into compliance with federal mandates to make all programs accessible to students and to remove certain hazardous materials. The continuing litany of reports shows that the total need for construction funds has increased to more than $322 billion, which was estimated at the turn of the century by the National Educational Association (2000). Obviously, the need will continue to grow because of political decisions not to properly fund the maintenance needs of the local school systems and because of the continued aging of existing school buildings.

As staggering as this reported amount of public funds might be, it is only an estimate of the total amount, based upon a survey of ten thousand school buildings out of a possible population of more than eighty thousand individual school buildings. The actual cost is undoubtedly higher than that stated in the report. Later reports by professional organizations used larger samples of the local school systems and reported a larger amount of funds needed. The amount of funds needed to update the existing facilities will continue to grow because of inflationary pressures and because of the continued aging of the inventory of school buildings in every locality (AASA, 1992).

The EWA reported that more than 50 percent of all school buildings in use today were built during the 1950s and 1960s, a time of rapid growth of the student population. Many of these schools were constructed rapidly and made of inferior materials because quality building materials were not in great supply during the decades immediately following World War II. School buildings constructed at that time had a life expectancy of approximately thirty years at the most.

As a result, these school buildings have not stood the test of student use over the years. As these structures approach the fifty-year period of life, school boards across the country will be faced with the decision of what to do with these aging buildings, some of which may not be worthwhile to renovate. Consequently, the critical issue of keeping the school building inventory in good condition is a growing problem.

BUILDING CONDITION AND STUDENT ACHIEVEMENT

The almost overwhelming need for upgrading existing school buildings and the extremely limited resources available make it even more important to ensure that any funds spent on school buildings are spent wisely. Although there are a variety of criteria used by the various states and communities to determine priorities, perhaps educators and school board members should look at the findings of research to determine where the funds should be spent for the greatest good of the students.

School board members and educators have a responsibility to make certain all students are housed in safe and modern facilities because of their custodial responsibility and moral accountability for students. These professional burdens extend beyond the letter of the law. Educators and school board members must create the best possible environment for the most productive learning of students. This implies that every student will be in a school building that will promote good learning.

The literature is replete with studies that show that air conditioned classrooms are a large factor in facilitating effective student learning. Likewise, research findings convincingly argue that classrooms where there is ample daylight and sufficient windows, where the roof does not leak, heat is controlled, educational and scientific equipment is available and working, the non-educational sounds are controlled, the building is invitingly painted and kept clean, and where students are not overcrowded goes a long way to improve learning on the part of the students (Earthman, 2004).

Recent research findings have shed some light on the relationship between student learning and the condition of the physical environment in which the student is located. Research completed by Edwards (1992); Cash (1993); Hines (1996); Earthman, Cash, and Van Berkum (1996); Phillips (1997); Lanham (1999); Thornton (2006); Crook (2006); O'Sullivan (2006); Bullock (2007); Fusilier (2008); and Hewitt (2017) has explored the relationship between the variables of student achievement, student behavior, and building condition.

All these researchers found there was a positive relationship between the condition of school buildings and the achievement of students. In each study, the researchers found from five to seventeen percentile rank differences between the achievement scores of students in buildings in poor condition and students in buildings that are in good condition. In other words, students in buildings in good condition had higher mean scores on achievement tests than students in buildings in poor condition.

The findings of these twelve researchers, and others, corroborate previous studies as described by McGuffey (1982) in his review of research. The percentile rank differences found in the above studies represent the variance school buildings can account for in the learning of students. The total amount of variance accounted for by all school-related factors, at best, is small compared with the influence parents, the home, and community have on the student, therefore, whatever the variance accounted for by the building takes on increased importance. A five to seventeen percentile rank difference in student scores may seem at first rather insignificant, but it can mean a great deal to the administrator who is trying to raise all student achievement scores.

Additional research by Uline and Tschannen-Moran (2006) has explored the relationship between building condition, school climate, and student achievement. Their research indicates that there is a relationship between school climate and building condition. These findings would indicate that when students and teachers are in marginal buildings they do not perform as well as they could in better buildings.

These research findings could well mean that the expenditure of funds to improve the condition of the building might result in increased student learning. The suggested relationship between the two variables might be tenuous, but it is rather significant to every educator. A building principal or administrator would be remiss not to take advantage of any possibility to improve the learning of students; improving the building condition is one such way to directly influence student learning.

FEDERAL FINANCIAL ASSISTANCE

These researchers become even more important when one considers the urgency the federal government has recently placed upon improving the condition of school buildings throughout the country. During the last decade of the twentieth century, and even into this century, there were several efforts to make federal funds available for local school building construction. None of the proposals were funded and, as a result, today there are virtually no federal funds for the construction of local school buildings. The federal government does provide, however, funds through various laws to provide construction funds for buildings in specialized areas of study such as science, mathematics, and other essential areas. Some efforts in the past provided limited funding, but as of now are nonexistent. Considering the present economic situation, federal funding for facilities is low on the priority list.

In 1994, the U.S. Congress passed the Improving America's Schools Act (P.L. 103-382) that provided federal funds to improve the condition of public school buildings. In a later budget request to fund the act, $100 million was allocated. However, this budget request was not funded and, as a result, no federal relief was provided to local school systems.

Then again, in 1997, President Bill Clinton sent to Congress proposed legislation to help communities and states rebuild public schools. This proposed legislation, entitled "Partnership to Rebuild America's Schools Act of 1997" (S. 456), requested $5 billion in federal funds over the next four years to help upgrade old schools and build new schools. The proposed act called initially for $2.45 billion in federal tax credits to help the states fund increased school construction and renovation. This would have been accomplished by permitting the leveraging of additional local and state spending on school construction and renovation. The legislation would have focused on incremental spending by local school systems.

In this manner, the federal funds could have been leveraged so that the total amount spent on school construction in the states would increase. In addition, the state and local governmental units would have had the flexibility to determine which construction activities would be deemed the highest priority and thereby funded by federal funds. Of course, this proposed bill was not passed.

There have been several interesting measures put forth to provide federal monies for construction of school buildings at the local school system level. For the most part, these measures have not been funded if the measure was passed or else the measure was never passed into law. The reason for this, especially in light of the pressing need for more funds to be injected into the building programs of the local school systems, is that many lawmakers feel the funding need is beyond the level of funding that the federal government can afford.

Further, some lawmakers feel that the federal government should not be in the business of providing capital funds to the local school systems because education is not a function of the federal government, according to the U.S. Constitution. In any event, it seems that the majority of the elected lawmakers do not want to enter into that stream of thought to provide federal funds to the local school system for construction of facilities.

EDUCATIONAL PROGRAM LOCATION

Many decades ago, Alvin Tofler (1980) made the prediction that in the future, more and more students would be educated at home rather than in the school building. The implication was that, because of the availability of computers, students would no longer need a school building in which to learn. He predicted this statement on the supposition that technology would make a dramatic change in how and where students would learn. He specifically thought the computer would become readily available to all students and that there would be suitable educational programs available through varied technological sources to provide a complete education without having to go to a school building.

Obviously, this prediction has not come about yet, in spite of vast improvements in the computer and in the availability of computers to almost everyone. Perhaps the biggest flaw in the prediction was in ignoring both the nature of children and youth and the tenets of many reputable learning theories. Even recently, several sources have argued that the school as we know it will disappear (Northwest Educational Technology Consortium, 2002). This thinking suggests that in the near future the brick-and-mortar structure known as the school will no longer be on the scene.

The socialization of students would have to take place in a different environment. Such thinking seems to be based upon the idea that electronic learning can supplant the educational program that the schools offer. There seems to be little evidence to support such contentions other than the availability of technology and the interest students have in many of the devices available. Such thinking is extremely limited and with little evidence to support it.

Even if all students, regardless of age, could have a computer and iPhone at their disposal, the prediction would not come about because of the social nature of children. Students of all ages want and need to be together for social purposes. Even if the opportunity were given to students to be out of school, they would find it necessary to congregate for these purposes.

Equally important, however, is the fact that technology cannot fill all the educational needs of students. There are some things students can learn very efficiently and effectively by means of technology. Other, more esoteric, concepts and meanings can be taught better through the aid of a teacher and the group process.

The idea that students would not have to go to a school building to receive their education gave rise to the idea that the country would not have to build or maintain school buildings in the future. As with most generalized predictions, this idea was short-lived. Local communities still need to maintain school buildings for their students and will for the near future.

The alternative school program has grown considerably over the past three decades, so much so, that almost every school system has at least one such program. In the beginning of this movement, students were many times housed in buildings that might be termed marginal. Most of the early high school alternative programs served students who were either in trouble with the authorities or had difficulty being in the regular education program. Existing commercial structures and older school buildings were almost routinely converted for these programs. As a result, the building sometimes did not exactly fit the type of program.

Now that alternative programs are accepted by the educational establishment, new buildings are being planned and constructed to house these programs. The stigma of alternative programs has been removed because the benefit of alternative educational programs for various ages of students has been recognized. Alternative educational programs and the buildings that house the students are seen as a viable means for meeting the needs of more students. More consideration and attention is now given to the type of building these programs and students need. This change has resulted in some exemplary school buildings to house students in alternative education programs.

Another ramification of the idea that students do not need to be in the school building can be seen in the various programs designed to have the students use more community resources to supplement their education. These practices have been used in vocational programs for many decades, but the recent growth of the internship and similar outreach programs has allowed students great opportunity to use community resources, even outside of vocational education preparatory programs, to augment their education.

GROWTH OF CHARTER SCHOOLS

The growth of charter schools has accelerated since the first one opened in the Minneapolis Public Schools in 1991. This charter school, named City Academy, was developed as an alternative school, but under the auspices of a charter from the state. City Academy enrolls about 150 students in a high school program designed for students who want an alternative to the regular public schools. Charter schools have grown in every state. The state of Minnesota has the largest number, but these schools are common to every part of the country.

The basic premise of the charter school is to develop a school that will meet the particular needs of the students and be free of the normal regulations of the state-supported schools. Being free of these regulations, the charter school supposedly will be able to develop a unique educational program and devote more energy and resources to it, according to experts in the field. Each charter school has a special-interest curriculum in addition to the regular subjects students are required to take in state-regulated schools. In fact, almost all students in charter schools must take the same assessment tests that the state requires of all other students.

In some states any group of individuals can establish a charter school, whether they live within the school system boundaries or not. Other states place more regulation on charter schools. Some states even require the permission of the local school board before a group can establish a school. Regardless of the manner in which charter schools are established, there seems to be a growing interest in such schools.

Charter schools receive their funding from the local school system. They are paid the amount of funds that the public schools expend in educating students there. There are some instances where private funds are available to the charter schools, but for the most part the charter schools educate their students with the same amount of funds the public schools expend for such purposes.

Charter schools are housed in a great variety of facilities. Some are fortunate enough to find an old school building, or they locate in a church or other facility that can house the students. It is incumbent upon the directors of the charter school to locate the place where the school will be housed and, in many instances, both limited funds and a lack of knowledge concerning the adequacy of the facility place the school population in a less-than-desirable facility. Charter schools are not noted for having the latest in school facilities. Students in charter schools are housed in both adequate and inadequate facilities throughout the country.

The impact charter schools have upon the local school system is probably dependent upon the number of such schools in existence. Where there are a goodly number of charter schools, certain students may be drained off from the public school student population, but this is exceptional. When a charter school attracts the upper level of students, the public schools then have a larger number of low-achieving students to educate. Such situations are indeed rare; however, in very small school systems the drain of students can have repercussions upon the educational program of the public schools. This has been the criticism of charter schools.

The possibility of the number of charter schools continuing to grow is probable. Charter schools do not seem to be an educational fad that will diminish in a few years. Almost three decades of growth indicates charter schools are here to stay. Further impact upon the public schools in the future should be minimal, or at least no different from what has been in the past.

SIZE OF SCHOOL BUILDINGS

All the above-mentioned ideas and extensions of the educational program have not resulted in the need for fewer educational buildings. Quite the contrary, school systems have felt the need to expand their building inventory to meet a growing need for more space within which to educate students. The increase in size of buildings has resulted in many cases from educational program changes.

The most important impact upon the size of school buildings in the past four decades has been felt from implementation of special education programs to serve a larger population of students. Even with a program of complete inclusion of special education students in regular education classrooms, there is need for certain spaces in a building for special functions. School buildings need to contain specialized laboratories, small classrooms, diagnostic areas, training rooms, conference rooms, and a variety of offices for specialists to serve adequately the special education program needs. These areas, of course, increase the overall gross square footage of a school building. This increase must be factored into the total per-pupil square footage allocation for a building (Stevenson, 2007).

A different ramification of the space issue revolves around the increasing number of adults who are now housed in all levels of school buildings. Most school systems have implemented a program of employing aides to teachers, whether or not they service special education or regular education students. It is not unusual to find two adults working with students in a single classroom designed for a specified number of students. Many classrooms are simply not designed to accommodate the activity of two adults working with various groups of students or with individual students.

Most school systems employ some form of inclusion for students of special needs. Such a scheme places students with special needs into the regular education classrooms. Most times the teacher assigned to these students also helps them while in the general education classroom, working alongside the regular teacher.

Most existing school buildings are not sized to accommodate two adult teachers. What is needed in the classroom is a space that can be devoted to private small-group or individual instruction, where the noise of the other students will not interfere with their learning. Obviously, most existing classrooms do not have such a space, whereas in new buildings alcoves can be designed for such purposes.

A great number of schools also conduct a strong volunteer program where adults from the community come into the schools to assist with various aspects of the educational program. Whether these activities include supervising students in the cafeteria, on the playgrounds, or in the library, space is needed for these individuals. Most volunteer programs include adults working in the classroom in a tutoring or assisting role. It is very unusual to find space in the building during the school day to allow these adult volunteers to have a place to relax or sit when not on duty. Although schools do not see it as their responsibility to provide a space for volunteers to either complete some paperwork or meet with a student outside of the classroom, the need is there for the most beneficial use of the time of the volunteer.

The increased emphasis on the physical well-being and development of students has influenced the size of space devoted to physical education. This, plus the desire of the adult community to have a space in the school to conduct wellness and physical exercise programs, has placed a new demand for additional space for these activities. A typical elementary school physical education program needs a space of only about four thousand to five thousand square feet, yet the community desires a regulation sized gymnasium of more than ten thousand square feet for their programs.

With the demand for more community use of the physical education space, school systems are constructing regulation-sized gymnasia in all elementary schools. The size of a regulation gym ranges from ten thousand to twelve thousand square feet of space, thus increasing the overall per-pupil square feet allocation and subsequent total cost of the building. This application, however, is a good example of shared use of facilities between school system needs and community desires.

All these programs are beneficial to the work of the school organization; yet, each program requires space for the people to function efficiently and effectively. These requirements have all increased the need for space in the building and have increased the overall square footage of buildings. As the demand for more services increases and the number of individuals involved in the educational process expands, school buildings will increase in size.

STANDARDIZATION OF SCHOOL BUILDINGS

The use of the computer and the computer assisted design (CAD) system has greatly aided the architect in the design of new school buildings. All architectural work now employs the use of the CAD system. With this use the architect is able to speed up the work of designing a school building, often times reducing the time to a matter of weeks or months.

At the same time, there can be a tendency to standardize components of a school building. For instance if the size of the classroom space mandated by the state department of education is set as at certain amount, such as 850 square foot of space, the architect can then produce a prototype of classroom with all of the component parts. These components might be cabinet space, sinks, entrances, and even windows. Thus, the architect can duplicate these prototypes for any number of classrooms, depending upon the number contained in the educational specifications.

Duplication of prototypical spaces can be applied to almost every component of a school building. The office suite can be reduced to a prototype office. Even the kitchen and cafeteria space can be made into a certain prototype of space with the flow of materials and students configured in a certain manner.

With all the speed in which a design drawing can be produced reduces the manpower needed to physically draw such designs. In effect, the cost of producing all the drawings needed for a new building or a renovation project can be reduced. There is a cost of the computers and the software to actually produce such drawings. This is not to suggest that the cost of architectural services will be reduced, because such is not the case. Rather the total cost for architectural services is simply redirected within the firm.

Like everything else in life, when mechanical or computer services are available in place of human efforts, there is a certain standardization that takes place. Standardization of school building plans is not new to education. Such standardization has occurred long before computers were available.

Such plans, however, have been rather limited in use and often time used successfully only in a local school system.

The kind of standardization of building components enabled by the use of computer driven CADD systems might produce a different kind of standardization of buildings. It might well be that the individualization of school buildings that an architect can bring to a project might be diminished because of the availability of computer building components. For instance the configuration of the classroom units might take on a standardized look such as a linear effect rather than a more imaginative configuration. Of course the imaginative architect will work to make certain this does not happen. The educator also needs to review any architectural plans for configuring the general purpose classroom units to fit the educational programs.

GENDER RELATED ISSUES

The recent ascendency of identification of transgender students and their need for restroom facilities has caused many school boards to consider what their policy should be. Whether or not to provide restroom facilities to students who identify with either their birth gender or a different gender has been extremely vexing. Whatever the decision of the school board, restroom facilities need to be provided for students who identify themselves as transgender. Whether or not to permit students to use the restroom of their identified gender or their birth gender is a serious question and could have implications for the building. Policy decisions can in all probability solve this problem; however, building changes to accommodate an identified sex may involve additional funding in a newly planned school building. Decisions of the local school board will determine whether or not building changes will be needed.

SUMMARY

Several of the issues discussed in the sections above revolve around the availability of sufficient funds to either complete new construction or upgrade existing buildings. Part of the dilemma stems from the political decision-making of all three levels of government—local, state, and federal. In years past, there was a push for federal funding of local school capital projects. The political environment seemed receptive to the idea and the federal government was in a little better financial shape than it is today. The political climate has changed and this feeling is not evident on the federal level of government.

Nevertheless, the condition of school facilities throughout the country and the need for new construction has placed local school systems in a situation where the need cannot be matched because of the limitation of local funding. Most local school systems do not have the financial ability to go into debt to fund such improvement projects. In some states, the bonding capacity of the local school system is constitutionally set and results in fiscal ability too low to produce the needed revenues to upgrade the facilities. In other states, local school systems are already to the debt limit. In addition, certain debt-limit measures apply in some states so that the needed upgrades are legally impossible to fund.

Some agency other than the local school system must assist with the massive upgrade of school facilities, and that agency must be either the state or federal government. Most federal legislators, however, now think that the federal government is not the level of government that should provide any substantial assistance to the local school system for capital expenditures. Further inquiry into this aspect of federal funding will have to await future elections.

Some states have the ability to provide assistance to the locality, but do not have the mechanism to do it. Other states feel that the localities should shoulder this responsibility. This difference in philosophy then places a heavy financial burden on the locality to address the need. In the absence of a response to a public need on the part of either the locality or state, the federal government must then step in to resolve the need.

However, this raises the specter of too much federal government influence and possible control of the local school system. This is a legitimate stance because of the nature of the educational system in the country. The alternative is to let the need stand as is or use makeshift alternatives for housing students. This, of course, is not the wise decision for the future of the country or its citizens.

Many of the critical issues relating to school facilities identified above revolve around the question of how we should fund public education. The real issue is not that we do not have the financial ability to fund the needs so much as to whether or not there is the will to fund them. This may sound rather fatalistic, but it is a truism that we invest our money in things or efforts we consider important. The nation does have the means to provide an appropriate and healthy learning environment for all children in every location in the country.

In spite of the fact that the country as a whole and every level of government is in dire financial straits at the present, the country does have the means to upgrade all school facilities by making the hard decisions to fund both the maintenance and operations and the debt services sections of the school budgets. The country, however, does need to consider what is the most important thing in which we wish to invest our time and resources. There is not a better way to influence the future of our country than to invest in our students and thereby positively influence the next generation.

Chapter 19

Green Schools

Up until the latter part of the twentieth century, almost all school buildings were constructed with a minimum of concern for the impact the building would have upon the environment. Further, the actual construction costs of the building were of great concern to the school board and community. In fact, many school boards had the idea that controlling the initial cost was of high importance. Keeping the initial cost of the building within a certain range was very important in decisions regarding what went into the school building.

The reasoning behind that idea was probably a multitude of concerns. In some communities, the rapid increase in student enrollments forced school boards to maintain a constant building program to properly house the growing student population. Capital funds were limited, yet the student body still increased. As a result, the school board thought that if the initial cost of a building could be controlled to within the budget, more schools could be built. Some school boards also thought that the tax burden for building schools should not become a strain on the community, and they believed that by keeping initial costs low, the tax burden could be kept at a minimum.

Regardless of the reasoning, up until this point in time school buildings were constructed without much thought as to the environmental impact the building would make upon the surrounding community, initially, or in the future. Further, the use of standard building materials was not thought to have any negative influence upon the environment. Over the past five years, the acceptance of incorporating green measures into new school buildings has been such that almost every new building can be classified as a green building.

GREEN SCHOOLS DEFINITION

A green school is defined as a building that is designed to conserve energy and water and is constructed from environmentally friendly building materials. The U.S. Green Building Council (2000) defines a green school as a building that creates a healthy environment that is conducive to learning while saving energy, resources, and money. Not only are green schools supposed to have a small carbon imprint on the environment, but they are also to be used as teaching instruments.

These two general criteria serve as the basis of determining if a school building can be called a green school or a conventional school. Under these definitions, other criteria and regulations exist to govern the definition of green. Green schools can also be called high-performance schools or sustainable schools. All these terms have been used to describe schools that could be called environmentally friendly.

Even in the construction of a green school, care is used to maintain an environmentally friendly building site through such measures as reducing the creation of waste material, and even using material that would be considered waste in the construction of the structure. A successful construction project would greatly reduce or eliminate building waste materials that would normally go to the landfill. Reduction of landfill material is an important part of constructing a green school.

The Massachusetts Technology Collaborative (National Research Council, 2007) defines a "high-performance green" school as having three distinct attributes: (1) it is less costly to operate than a conventional school building; (2) it is designed to enhance the learning and working environment for students and teachers; (3) it conserves important resources such as energy and water. Guidelines for "green" or "high-performance" schools have been issued by California, Washington State, and Massachusetts. Other states are currently in the developmental stages for this type of construction.

Guidelines for high-performance green schools typically move well beyond design and engineering criteria for school buildings. The guidelines address land use, processes for construction and equipment installation, and operation and maintenance practices in an effort to ensure the long-term health and performance of students and teachers as well as the durability of school buildings. Guidelines may include such design and engineering goals such as:

- locating schools near public transportation to reduce pollution and land development impacts

- placing a building on a site to minimize its environmental impact and optimize daylight and solar gain
- designing irrigation systems and indoor plumbing systems to conserve water designing energy and lighting systems to conserve fossil fuels and maximize the use of renewable resources
- selecting materials that are healthy, biodegradable, easily recycled, minimize the impacts on landfills, and otherwise reduce waste
- creating an indoor environmental quality that provides occupants with thermal comfort, and acoustic, visual, and air quality

Guidelines for high-performance green schools also include construction and commissioning goals such as:

- the appropriate storage of materials on construction sites to avoid water damage
- the reduction of waste materials and appropriate disposal to reduce resource depletion
- the introduction of commissioning practices to ensure the performance of integrated building systems

To address the life cycle performance of schools, guidelines for operation and maintenance practices are also included, such as: changes in cleaning products and practices, the systematic replacement of air filters in ventilation systems, and a long-term indoor environmental management plan.

#34 LEADERSHIP IN ENERGY AND ENVIRONMENTAL DESIGN

The U.S. Green Building Council (2000) has developed a set of guidelines for judging buildings that are classified as green or high performance. The guidelines are termed Leadership in Energy and Environmental Design (LEED). These guidelines are used in designating how environmentally friendly a building is. The original criteria were used for all types of buildings.

In 2007, the U.S. Green Building Council developed a set of guidelines suitable for school systems specifically. There are six categories of credits for which a school building is judged. These categories are Sustainable Sites, Water Efficiency, Energy and Atmosphere, Materials and Resources, Indoor Environment Quality, and Innovation and Design Process.

Buildings can be rated on a score from 29 to 79 points, depending upon how many credits the building design meets. Judgment of the building is made by the U.S. Green Building Council based upon documentation furnished by the architect of record and the school board. The highest rating is Platinum status, and a building must score from 58 to 79 points. The other two major designations are Gold and Silver. There is a certain amount of prestige associated with these designations.

GREEN SCHOOLS COSTS

One of the first things a school board and educators ask about green schools is the possibility of the increase in building costs. For the most part, green schools do cost more than a conventionally built school building. Some estimates of the increase in costs range up to 5 percent of the total construction costs. The U.S. Green Building Council (2000) estimates the average increase in construction costs for building a green school to be 2 percent.

There are some architects who state that a green school does not cost any more to build than a conventionally built school building. With this extreme variation in estimated costs, a superintendent and school board should be extremely cautious about any claims of increased cost. When the school board is planning for a new school that may cost upward of $50 million, an increase of 5 percent is rather daunting. Regardless of the percent of increase in construction costs, the school board must be able to justify accepting a design that will increase the total cost of the project.

Even with that said, most experts in the field agree there is a payback for incorporating green measures and material into a school building through the resulting lowered operating costs. Depending upon the materials used and the processes for using less energy and water, the payback may be as short as two years or as long as five years. These are short periods of time to receive a payback on a tremendous expenditure for a school building.

As with many claims of savings or payback, the superintendent and school board must be cautious in their decision on any "green" design agreement. There are several methods of estimating the possible savings or payback to the school system that can be employed by the architect and builder. School boards should insist upon an independent estimate of payback if the expenditure of the capital project is increased because of possible green design. Nevertheless, the superintendent and school board must ascertain the payback period before accepting a green school designed school building. Nevertheless, the school board and superintendent must ascertain the possible payback before accepting a green designed school building.

RENOVATING FOR
GREEN SCHOOLS DEFINITION

The renovation of an existing building should be a time when green materials, improved energy-saving systems, and environmentally friendly designs are incorporated into the process of upgrading the building. Incorporating such features in an existing building is difficult, but not impossible. Good architects are able to use recycled materials in the structural renovation of the building.

In addition, new energy-efficient systems should be placed in the building. Such things as low-water-usage bathroom fixtures, highly efficient HVAC systems, improved lighting systems, and modern technology can be installed in any renovation project. Again, the total increase in cost and the possible payback should be examined by the school board long before the project begins. The school board needs to ask for such reports at the very outset of the renovation.

SCHOOL AS A LEARNING TOOL

As stated above, one important part of a green school is the educational program that is to be carried on in the building after completion. LEED guidelines require curricular studies to inform the users of the building more about how the building was constructed, the socially accepted impact the building has upon the community, and how users can do their part in living an environmentally friendly life. This means that teachers will actually carry on lessons demonstrating how the building was constructed so that students will better appreciate it.

BENEFITS OF GREEN SCHOOLS

There can be many benefits of a green school. Some of these benefits can be in the improved appearance of the structure in the community. Green schools are naturally new structures and this fact enhances the entire community. One aspect of a green school is the control of runoff water from the school site. Control of this runoff is an important contribution to the community, especially the neighboring property.

Green schools are designed and built to minimize the environmental impact they might have upon the surrounding area. Further, these schools are built of durable materials that require less maintenance. Green schools are placed on the site to help protect the surrounding land and other buildings. The waste from the construction process is oftentimes used in the construction of the school, thus reducing or eliminating the amount of landfill. All these conditions enhance the community.

Almost every green school or high-performance school has an educational component attached to its designation. The school building itself is to be a learning tool for students, teachers, and the community. Further, educational lessons on conservation are normally incorporated into the curriculum in every grade level. It is important to prepare a citizenry to cope with the significant problems facing our environment, which will require action on their part.

Properly designed green schools provide a better indoor environment as far as air quality is concerned than do conventionally designed buildings. These buildings are designed to minimize indoor air quality problems and thereby reduce mold, dust mites, and dust particles. Such surroundings should then produce a healthy atmosphere and reduce the incidents of illness. The result is a better environment for students, teachers, and other persons who use the building. Absenteeism should then be reduced.

The introduction of daylighting into classrooms has also helped produce a healthy environment for the school. In addition, daylighting seems to be related to student performance. The findings of a Heschong Mahone Group (1999) research study support the claim that classroom daylighting influences student achievement. According to the report, students in the study population who were in classrooms with daylighting scored higher on math and reading tests than students in classrooms without daylighting. The differences in scores of students in day-lighted classrooms were 20 percent higher than students in non-daylighted classrooms.

The study concluded that daylighting has a consistently positive and highly significant effect in classrooms. Like all research studies involving human subjects, the reader needs to use caution in accepting the results. This study is no different. Nevertheless, initial studies involving green schools, or high-performance schools, indicate the positive influence these buildings have upon student performance.

RESEARCH ON GREEN SCHOOLS

With the advent of high performance and sustainable school buildings, a movement called Green Schools has become current. The definition of Green Schools varies from locality to locality, but there are certain commonalities that can be associated with schools that have high performance and sustainable components designed and constructed into the structure.

With the high expectations of an environmentally friendly school building comes the suggestion that perhaps these buildings could also be more beneficial to students and teachers than conventionally built buildings. That proposition is enticing for researchers and for those involved in designing Green Schools. As a result, the proposition becomes more of a question of, Do students perform better in Green Schools than in conventionally built schools or do Green Schools influence student and teacher performance and health? That was the question put before the National Research Council of the National Academies of Science.

In 2005, the National Research Council, through the Board on Infrastructure and the Constructed Environment appointed a committee of researchers and scholars to "review, assess, and synthesize the results of available studies on green schools and determine the theoretical and methodological basis for the effects of green schools on student learning and teacher productivity" (National Research Council, 2007, p. 1).

The result of this request was a funded study of the available research on Green Schools and the influence this body of research has upon student and teacher health and productivity. A group of fourteen individuals, from several universities, was enlisted to complete the work of the study, which required fifteen months to accomplish. The members of the committee represented a variety of academic disciplines.

With this kind of expertise represented, the committee was able to investigate a wide range of disciplines for any possible research studies that would be germane to the task of the committee. Committee members from each of the disciplines represented brought to the committee the results of their individual search for relevant research studies and presented the findings for consideration. The committee weighed the relevance, rigor, and applicability of the findings of these studies based upon the National Academies of Science criteria.

Charge to the Committee

The committee was originally charged with the following tasks:

1. Review and assess existing empirical and theoretical studies regarding the possible relationships between the characteristics of "Green Schools" and the health and productivity of students and teachers.
2. Develop an evaluation framework for assessing the relevance and validity of individual reports that considers the possible influence of such factors as error, bias, confounding, or chance on the reported results and that integrates the overall evidence within and between diverse types of studies.

3. Report the results of this effort in a manner that will facilitate the identification of causal relationships and the subsequent implementation of
   beneficial practices.
4. Identify avenues of research that represent potentially valuable opportunities to leverage existing knowledge into a better understanding of
   the relationships between green building technologies in schools and the
   performance of students and teachers (National Research Council, 2007).

The task of identifying studies was not easy for several reasons. Firstly,
there was a paucity of research studies dealing with green schools as such,
because of the definition of what a green school happens to be. There are
many definitions of what a Green School should look like and some variations on the exact components the building should have to be considered
a Green School. There is not a common definition of the components of a
Green School. Even with those programs that have a definition, there is not
complete agreement. As a result, lack of a definition of what a Green School
happens to be resulted in the lack of identifying of research studies.

Secondly, the term Green School is of recent extraction and this also means
that there would be few if any research studies because of a lack of adequate
population of buildings. Even those school buildings identified as Green
Schools by some governmental agencies is limited in number, which means
that a respectable population of Green Schools are not available for research
purposes.

For these reasons, the committee was left with the situation of not being
able to find any evidence-based research studies using Green Schools as the
population of the research study. Nevertheless, the committee decided to look
at existing research studies in the various disciplines that a Green School would
normally exhibit. For instance, all Green School programs list control of the
thermal environment as being necessary to achieve Green status. Likewise, good
lighting and even daylighting are components of Green Schools. The list went
on to include acoustical control, proper ventilation, and building conditions.

The committee then evaluated the research in these areas to determine the
rigor and relevance of the research for the task. Each committee member presented research in a corresponding discipline determined to be part of what a
Green School would possess. In this way the committee was able to review
systematically relevant research presented by an expert. In addition, some
researchers who were investigating components of Green Schools, such as
good air quality, made presentations to the committee. As a result, the committee reviewed research that would complement what a Green School would
look like upon completion. This was in the absence of identifying research
that used Green Schools as a population basis.

Findings of the Study

The committee began with a charge to review and assess existing empirical and theoretical studies regarding the possible relationships between characteristics of green or high-performance schools and the performance and health of students and teachers. Because of the paucity of research directly related to Green Schools, relevant research on disciplines corresponding to components of a Green School were identified and analyzed. From that series of analyses, the committee developed forty-five major findings and twenty-three recommendations. Naturally, this is a large number of findings for any research study, but careful analysis reveals that many of the findings stem not from research studies directly related to Green Schools, but rather from a body of research that deals with various building components that would be considered appropriate for Green Schools.

But the findings from this body of research do not directly relate to Green Schools as such. Nevertheless, the findings do reinforce the findings of other researchers who have been investigating the relationship between the physical environment and student and teacher health and productivity. Whether the school is rated as a green building or not, researchers need to continue to conduct such research studies.

Eventually, all new school buildings will be classified as either Green Schools or they will be constructed in such a manner that many green components will be incorporated into the school building. Researchers then will be confronted with the prospect of researching the influence that new buildings have upon student and teachers. This is basically the same type of research that was conducted over forty years ago with substantial results. Research on the influence old and new school buildings have upon student achievement has been conducted for quite some time and the findings of these studies have been rather consistent. Students enrolled in buildings that are old and inefficient perform lower on achievement tests than students in new and efficient school buildings.

FUTURE OF GREEN SCHOOLS

Although incorporating all green school components into new school buildings may increase the total cost of the buildings, the benefits may well outweigh the initial costs. With the anticipated payback in a relatively short period of time, incorporating all components of a green or high-performance school may prove prudent. The school board should not hesitate to go forward in building a school that is environmentally friendly.

Of course, the benefits of a green school go beyond the immediate surroundings of the school system and extend to the entire community. As such, it seems reasonable to conclude that, in the not too distant future, all new buildings and renovated existing buildings will be classified as green schools or high-performance schools. The trend toward constructing these types of buildings has gained considerable momentum in the field of education. This trend will increase as more school boards realize the benefits not only to the students and teachers, but also to the entire community. This is a case in which the benefits of a high-performance school building prove the worthiness of incorporating these components in every school building.

SOURCES OF ASSISTANCE
FOR GREEN SCHOOLS

Sources of assistance for green schools include governmental agencies, state agencies, and even local architectural firms. Listed below are some of the more prevalent sources:

- American Clearinghouse on Educational Facilities—www.acefacilities.org
- Educational Facilities Clearinghouse—www.efc.GWU.edu
- National Clearinghouse for Educational Facilities—www.edfacilities.org
- U.S. Green Building Council—www.USGBC.org; www.buildgreen schools.org
- Sustainable Buildings Industry Council—www.SBICouncil.org
- EnergySmart Schools Program—http://www1.eere.energy.gov/buildings/ energysmartschools
- U.S. Environmental Protection Agency—www.epa.gov/iaq/schools

SUMMARY

Green Schools have been a recent phenomenon in the building industry. A Green School is a building that is designed to conserve energy and water and is constructed from environmentally friendly building materials. The benefits from constructing a Green School as compared to a so-called regular building can be measurable. The benefits of Green Schools have so infiltrated the building industry that it is almost impossible to find a school building that does not incorporate most, if not all, the features of a Green School. Research on the benefits of a Green School in terms of the influence upon student learning has been inconsequential. This is largely the result of the difficulty in finding a school building population to compare with a non-Green School. Most Green Schools are new buildings and it is difficult to isolate the Green building features that might have an influence upon student learning from the usual building elements that do actually influence student learning. Nevertheless, the physical and financial benefits of Green School construction will continue to increase in the school building construction industry.

Chapter 20

Planning Schools for Safety

For the most part, humans are born into, live in, and die in a relatively safe physical environment. The only danger for the vast majority of humans comes from human inattention or carelessness. Humans have for the most part adapted to the vagueness of climate and weather and have learned to deal with acts of inhumanity. Yet there are times when unusual or unnatural things happen to cause danger. Regardless of the source, humans need to try to anticipate such dangers and plan for the eventuality of a dangerous situation.

The events of the past few years have certainly indicated that the environment of the world is changing and that such change can and does cause disasters of various sorts. In the United States, schools have been subject to tornadoes, hurricanes, floods, raging fires, and earthquakes of untold proportions. Educators have had to react to such events in trying to protect students and staff from danger and to continue the educational process. Such efforts are far beyond the normal training or experience of most educators.

In addition to the disasters that have occurred in the natural environment, there have been repeated acts of violence against students and teachers by other humans. Such acts are not normal or common and cannot be predicted. Yet, for the most unsuspecting location such occurrences happen with deadly force causing untold sorrow and suffering. Educators, students, and community members must react to such happenings.

Preparation programs for school administrators do not necessarily contain elements to prepare them for horrific occurrences. That would be almost impossible to do because every event is separate and individual in nature. How would a preparation program prepare administrators for some of the most terrible crimes perpetrated against school students that have happened in recent years or against the loss of a school building? Nevertheless, school authorities

267

must have plans for the basic survival of the school systems in case any such natural or human disasters happen.

The present text is based upon the planning processes required to be performed to bring about a new school building. How educators respond to disasters of either kind is not within the purview of this text. That is a separate body of knowledge that educators need to access to become informed as to recovery procedures that are effective. There are also numerous plans of personnel deployment in schools that increase the safety of the building. Such plans also are not within the purview of this text. On the other hand, educators should know what kinds of planning for building design should take place for the protection of students, faculty, and staff and should try to implement such measures. Research on needed safety design features, as articulated by both school principals and architects, is an important source of information about what school authorities should require for safe buildings.

RESEARCH ON DESIGN
FEATURES FOR SAFE SCHOOLS

Educators are aware of the need for safe school buildings. The possibility of an accident caused by a faulty structural environment is very much in the mind of every school administrator. Because students are in a custodian position to educators, their safety is paramount. Educators continually protect students from any possibility of harm. With this mind-set, educators are aware of features in a building that could be a potential hazard to students.

Principals of school buildings are responsible for the upkeep and safety of the building they administer. They are required to report any kind of hazard or potential hazard in their building to the proper authorities for correction or elimination. As a result of such responsibilities and experience, principals are observant of areas in a school building that can be dangerous to students and teachers. Principals are experts in safety features of a building and are knowledgeable of potential dangerous areas for students.

Several recent research studies used the expertise of principals to identify features in a building that promote safety. Two studies used the results of interviews of principals regarding safety features and compared their thinking to that of architects who design school buildings. The results of both sets of interviews were compared to determine if there were similarities. As might be expected, the responses of the principals were like those of architects (Walton, 2010; Trosper, 2017). The overarching safety feature identified was visibility; the ability to see and be seen was the most important feature in the interior of school buildings. This ability could be manifest in such design elements as wide hallways, interior windows into classrooms, and open areas for student gathering. The ability to see from the outside, however, was a concern of principals because of the possibility of unwanted intrusion by outsiders. Principals preferred limited outside observation of the inside of the school.

Both principals and architects stated that stairways were a potential safety concern because most interior stairways are fire towers that need to be enclosed for safe exiting. These stairways must be fire resistant, which means limited glass exposure thus limiting visual supervision. Within the stairways, however, there should not be any hidden areas or areas where students cannot be seen by an adult. Designing such areas requires skillful thinking as well as the expertise of a principal in reviewing the drawings. In addition to the stairwells, there are other areas of the school that can present safety concerns for educators. Restrooms and locker areas were identified by both principals and architects as being potential safety concerns. These areas normally have limited visibility and there are usually quite a few students using such facilities at one time.

One solution suggested by the architects was to design a two-way entry system whereby visitors must pass visual observation before entrance to the building is permitted. Another feature they identified was to eliminate doors on the restrooms. This provides a way of hearing unacceptable actions and provides ease of exiting in case of trouble. Locker rooms present a different problem because of the necessity of having banks of lockers. One solution suggested was to install low-rise lockers so that there is some visibility evident. Most locker rooms have at least two entries and in most cases some visibility for the office of the coach.

Principals identified doors leading to the outside as a potential safety concern. They stated that students as well as teachers prop open the doors for various reasons. Doors that are ajar are a perfect invitation for someone from the outside to enter the building without being noticed or identified. Of course no design can be perfectly safe in deterring this practice, but architects have been able to place electronic devices on outside doors that indicate to those in the office that they are open or being opened. Such surveillance is necessary for the safekeeping of students and teachers.

Both principals and architects state that the main entrance to the school building is a matter of concern. They stressed the fact that again visibility and control is necessary for anyone entering the school building. First, the location of the main office of the school should be in the front of the building and highly visible from anyone desiring to enter. In addition, control of the entrance needs to be provided by a secure vestibule and by devices such as a card reader or some means of identification for individuals wishing to enter the school. Some architects even suggest that the entrance should have large glass areas for visibility and should have bulletproof glass. The principals suggested the use of cameras to provide surveillance and also to record who is entering the building.

The use of cameras inside the school building was also suggested by both groups as a way of maintaining proper surveillance in the halls. The use of 360 degree cameras that can record images in all directions are very useful. Informational technology based internet protocol cameras should be used according to principals (Walton, 2010). Using cameras in the school does bring up the issue of privacy, but prudent use of such cameras does not cause litigation.

All of the above indicate that principals need to be involved in reviewing the original designs of the school building. Experienced principals have encountered enough problems caused by the design of the building to be expert in locating such potential problem areas. Principals are able, based upon experience, to identify possible areas that might cause educators some concern.

Other individuals who should be involved in the review of designs should be the school security officers, teachers, custodians, maintenance personnel, and representatives of the local law enforcement and fire marshals. These same individuals should be involved in the annual safety audit of the school conducted by the principal. These audits should identify any potential safety concerns of the building. These concerns should then be presented to the proper authorities for remedy.

HUMAN FACTOR IN SAFETY

Although it is necessary to have the best designed buildings for safety concerns, there is the human factor that also needs attention to prevent unnecessary happenings. It is the combination of a well-designed facility that enhances user safety and the practice of good behavior on the part of the users that can produce a building that is as safe as any building can be.

One such approach is by using the program called Crime Prevention through Environmental Design (CPTED; Carter and Carter, 2001). CPTED is based upon strategies and actions designed to result in safe and orderly school facilities. These strategies may help to militate against the perception of students, teachers, and community as a prison-like environment. These design strategies may also help improve the aesthetic qualities of the building and in doing so, may improve the pride users of the building have about the school. The strategies consist of design factors that should be implemented in a school building and individual and group behaviors and perceptions that need to be either promoted or diminished through actions.

The National Crime Prevention Council (NCPC) offers training in CPTED strategies for any school that wishes to participate (Carter and

Carter, 2001). The training sessions should include a wide array of individuals who have a relationship to the school building. Those who should be included are teachers, students, principals, facility personnel, designers, school security personnel, local law enforcement officers, and parents. The training includes sessions on design elements that make the building safer and sessions on behavioral aspects. The latter are predicated on the belief that the building can influence how an individual reacts to design elements within a building as well as the cumulative influence the building can produce upon individuals.

Some of the design elements stressed in the training sessions deal with the following:

- Reduce dim or dark areas
- Proper use of all areas of the school
- Properly secured entrances and exits
- Wide hallways to avoid congestion
- Eliminate hidden views
- Maintain all school yards and fields
- Provide good lighting
- Adequate sightlines
- Clear orientation in the building
- Appropriate landscaping to avoid hidden places

Some of the behavioral strategies emphasized in the training sessions involve the following:

- Eliminate inappropriate behavior
- Take action on illegal activities
- Provide a system of assistance to individuals in need
- Provide for consistent enforcement of standards and rules (Carter and Carter, 2001)

CPTED endeavors to reduce conditions that would lead to unsafe conditions and increase the perception of safe facilities. There are six strategies that are emphasized in this program: natural surveillance, access management, territoriality, physical maintenance, order maintenance, and activity support.

- *Natural Surveillance.* This design feature deals with providing maximum visibility. These features might include wide hallways, open stairs, windows, good lighting. The main objective is to see and be seen to increase the presence of humans.

- *Access Management.* This design feature deals with the manner in which users of the building get around the building safely. Design elements might include secure entrances, proper signage, lighting, color, fencing, and landscaping. The objective of these features is to provide safe access to the school building and within the building.
- *Territoriality.* This design element attempts to delineate space and show ownership. They can be expressed through art displays, signage, fencing, landscaping, and pavement treatments. The elements serve to increase the sense of pride and ownership of the users of the building. Important components of territoriality are the student's choice of displays and other features, and the physical representation of all students in the building.
- *Physical Maintenance.* This feature deals with the proper maintenance of the facilities of the school system. The element includes proper repair and upkeep of the buildings. Unkempt buildings give the users of the building a perception that the school authorities do not care for the physical facilities. Any sign of decay and neglect is to be avoided so as not to create such perceptions.
- *Order Maintenance.* This feature deals with the maintenance of good behavior on the part of all users of the building. Good behavior should always be stressed and respect for the building inculcated into all who are interested in the school. Conversely, inappropriate behavior of any sort should be dealt with promptly.
- *Activity Support.* This feature deals with the planning and development of activities that promote the presence of users of the building. This aspect supports the idea of casual surveillance and access to management. It also addresses the need for proper facilities to enhance the human element such as: staff parking, teacher's lounges, administrative suites, resource officer spaces, and physical education facilities (Carter and Carter, 2001).

SECURITY MEASURERS

School systems employ certain measures to insure the safety of students and teachers while in the school building. Most of these measures result from the work of the National Crime Prevention Council. In a recent survey of school systems conducted by the National Center for Educational Statistics, results indicated an increase in the implementation of all the security practices, except one. The exception was the use of random metal detector checks. Results of the survey are found in Table 20.1.

As can be seen, all the major measurers or practices have increased over the years. The security practices most widely used are the ones that have the

Table 20.1. Security Measures Used in Schools

	1999–2000	*2013–2014*	*2015–2016*
Controlled access to buildings during school hours	74.6%	93.3%	94.1%
Security cameras used to monitor the school building	19.4%	75.1%	80.6%
Required faculty & staff to wear badges or picture ID	25.4%	68.0%	67.9%
Enforced a strict dress code	47.4%	58.5%	53.1%
Random dog sniffs to check for drugs	20.6%	24.1%	24.6%
Required students to wear uniforms	11.8%	20.4%	21.5%
Required students to wear badges or picture IDs	3.9%	8.9%	7.0%
Random metal detector checks	7.2%	4.2%	4.5%

Source: *Education Week* Vol. 37, No. 26 (April 11, 2018), p. 7.

most impact upon school buildings: controlled access to the building and security camera to monitor the school building. Controlling the access to the school building is the most implemented building element with 94.1 percent of all school buildings having some sort of control feature.

The measure of control may be as sophisticated as having double doors with a window for a security officer to check identification or it may be simply a single door with a control device. Nevertheless, most school authorities feel that some type of control is necessary for the safety of students and teachers.

The next most popular building feature is the use of security cameras throughout the building so that the halls and larger spaces can be monitored. This feature was mentioned by both principals and architects in the above mentioned research studies.

One other practice not listed in Table 20.1 is the employment of resource officers or law enforcement officers in the schools. The same survey that produced the above data also showed that for elementary schools, 21 percent employed law enforcement officers in 2005–2006. That figure rose to 35.8 percent in 2016. For high schools, 57.8 percent employed law enforcement officers in 2005–2006, whereas in 2015–2016 the figure was 64.8 percent. Employing law enforcement officers in the schools has proven to be effective in helping to create a sense of well-being among students and teaches.

CASE STUDY: PLANNING FOLLOWING A CRISIS

In the late winter, heavy snow accumulation on the roof of the gym in the local high school building resulted in the collapse of the roof, causing considerable damage. Luckily, the girls' basketball team that was practicing in the gym at the time heard the rumble of the roof and saw cracks in the wall appearing and were able to exit the building safely. Fortunately, no one was hurt. However, this was not good timing as it was the middle of the school year and school was in session. The damaged roof would prevent students from using the building for some time.

The problem of where to house the high school students for the remainder of the school year was solved by placing the nearby middle school on double sessions. School authorities placed the middle school on a half day morning session and put the high school students on an afternoon session. This school organization sufficed for the rest of the school year, even though the move created schedule adjustments in the schools, inappropriate lunch schedules, parental scheduling problems, and a severe traffic problem at the middle school.

Subsequent investigations revealed that some of the roof structure in the remaining building was not installed properly. Local building inspectors ruled that the building was not safe for use. This presented the school authorities with a dilemma of where to put the high school student population until adequate facilities could be found. Agitation by parents and other community members motivated the school board to decide to build a new high school. Planning for the new high school began, but the problem of high school student placement for the next two to three years also needed planning attention.

Planning Alternatives

A plan had to be devised to place the high school student body numbering some 1,100 individuals in suitable facilities. At the June 15, 2009, work session of the school board, the superintendent suggested five options that could be implemented for the coming year. The following alternatives were suggested:

1. Use the middle school building to house grades 9–12
2. Use the middle school building to house the high school students and use the old middle school in a neighboring town to house grades 6–8
3. Use the middle school to house grades 8–12 and locate grades 6 and 7 at a neighboring middle school and run as one school
4. Use the middle school building to house grades 8–12 or 9–12, establish the neighboring middle school as the site for both student bodies on a split schedule operating as separate schools
5. Use the middle school to house grades 9–12; establish a neighboring middle school as a location for grades 6–8 students, and for both student

bodies to operate on a unified schedule with 1705 students (Montgomery County School Board, June 15, 2009, p. 7)

As can be seen, not all the alternatives were educationally sound, and every option assumed that the high school students would be housed in the middle school building. The quality of these options left much to be desired because it would mean that in every case, students would be placed in inappropriate buildings or merged into another middle school student body.

Moreover, assessment of the alternatives would indicate that one option was always paramount and that was having the high school students occupy the present middle school building. These alternatives would insure that two student bodies would be housed in buildings not appropriate for the type of educational program to be offered. Such type of planning indicates that both the school authorities and school board were unduly influenced by outside pressures or that the school personnel did not want to open the planning process to a rational process. Nevertheless, the five options were seriously discussed and the school board decided that they should be presented to the community.

According to one school board member, there were several plans suggested by the superintendent and some by the school board. One such plan was to move the displaced middle school students into an operating middle school in a neighboring town. Another plan discussed was to move the high school student body into the operating high school building in a neighboring town on an alternating day schedule. For instance one student body would attend school on a Monday, Wednesday, Friday schedule and the displaced high school student body would attend school on the alternative dates. Although such plans were highly questionable educationally, the plans were actually discussed as viable possibilities.

Involvement in the Planning

School authorities presented the above five alternatives to the community in a series of meetings to seek comment and possible input. Although highly desirable to bring the community along, presenting several alternatives to a group of parents and community members would only serve to divide the community as to which option was best.

Following these meetings, the school board decided to put the high school students in the middle school building, which was only seven years old, and put the displaced middle school students in an old school building in a neighboring town ten miles away. The building in which the displaced middle school students were placed was built in the late 1950s and had been abandoned because of building obsolescence. The building was a campus-style structure with separate buildings. In addition, several mobile classrooms had to be placed on the site to accommodate the student body of 1,200 students. This would necessitate students moving from one building to another in all kinds of weather for different subjects.

Sentiment about the eventual solution to the problem of housing the high school and middle school students varied greatly. The high school students and their parents thought the decision was suitable. The middle school students and their parents were not necessarily satisfied with the decision and thought that they were suffering the brunt of displacement into an old building. Teachers in the high school were satisfied that they were in a building where they could effectively teach. Naturally, the middle school teachers felt the same as that of the students and parents. They felt displaced and put into facilities that would not suit the educational program of a modern middle school. The finality of the decision moderated these sentiments after a year of placement.

Consequences of the Plan

The consequences of the adopted plan were that two student bodies were moved to buildings that were not designed to accommodate the type of educational program that would be carried on in the building.

The result of this decision was that both the middle school and high school students were in buildings that did not fit the educational program offered. The middle school building did not have the necessary facilities to support a high school program that included chemistry, physics, music, vocational technology, and interscholastic sports. Even the library was sized for middle school students.

The middle school students fared even worse. They were housed in a 1950s-style building where the newer exploratory laboratories were not in existence and where the buildings had none of the necessary components that new buildings have for a modern middle school program. These structures did not have thermal control, proper lighting, good acoustical control, modern science equipment, nor proper physical education facilities. All the physical facilities they enjoyed in the middle school building were lacking in the building in which they were housed.

There is considerable research available to inform school authorities on the influence school buildings have upon student and teacher health and performance. Studies have repeatedly found that students housed in inadequate facilities underperform than students in modern facilities. Such findings have been produced by researchers in several different states. To purposefully place students in old buildings that have been abandoned because of inadequacy is not in keeping with available research, especially when other alternatives for housing were available.

Lessons to Be Learned

What lessons can be learned from this scenario? Everyone can learn from the experiences of others. This is a much honored form of learning, even when the experience is not necessarily the best. The unfortunate experiences of some can be a learning situation for others. Such is the case with this planning process.

Expediency Rules Planning. Planning during a crisis is much different from the normal planning modes of schools. Usually, there is a set schedule for planning to which all participants adhere to during the planning phase. In many cases, planning must follow legal timelines to accommodate public hearings and involvement. The normality of the planning process in the schools is not in evidence during a crisis. The time frame for planning is much encapsulated into much shorter periods of time. Plans must be developed and implemented in matters of hours or minutes, rather than in days or weeks. Decisions resulting from an accelerated planning process must be implemented immediately. This means that whoever is in charge of planning must initiate the planning process as soon as possible and involve whoever is available to help plan. In extreme cases the planning process has to be done by an individual with no assistance from others.

For the most part, planning in a crisis is completed on a much-accelerated schedule and is initiated on the question of, What do we have to plan for? In the case of the loss of a school building, the immediate concern is where to place the students and how to begin the educative process as soon as possible.

Quality Planning Is a Necessity. Quality planning steps must be taken even in the most accelerated time frame for planning. This means that every alternative must be up for discussion and evaluation. Quality planning also means that everyone possible who has a responsibility should be involved. To abandon quality planning is to invite later regret of decision.

Well-being of Students Is Paramount. The well-being of the students must be in the forefront of any planning and eventual decisions. Whether it is the safety of students or the correct placement of students, this concern must be in the thinking of all school authorities from the very start. Decisions of student placement must be judged on the basis of how the students will be safe and perform normally. Research can give guidance to school authorities on where best to place students for effective learning. In the case above, school authorities did not examine all the possible alternatives for housing both student bodies. As a result, both student bodies were disrupted and placed in facilities that did not fit the type of educational program that was to be offered to the students.

Community Involvement. There is considerable research available on effective community involvement and communication. School authorities should learn from and utilize the results of effective communication and how to involve the community in school issues. A school in crisis is an issue in which the community should be involved but in an effective manner.

Community involvement should not arouse the anxieties of people in the community. Rather, a research-based systematic and justified method of communication and involvement should be employed. This was not necessarily the case in the situation above where a set of alternatives, that were flawed, were offered to the community for comment. Such actions invite distrust and anxiety about the planning process utilized by the school authorities.

Political Considerations. Every school board, and the educators within the school system, are subject to a certain amount of outside influence in planning and decision-making, whether it is political or community generated. In some instances, political influence can be substantial, even to the point of influencing what can be taught in the classroom. Parental influence, for the most part, is supportive of the efforts of the educators in the school system but it is not necessarily so in every situation.

In the case above, it is evident that the parents and politicians of the town in which the damaged high school was located did not want the students to move from the town. The school authorities and school board acquiesced to political and community influence of where to place the high school students. The only defense from undue influence is transparency, and even this has its limitations.

Rational planning is also useful in mitigating against undue, outside pressure on decision-making. School authorities should stand up against any outside pressure if the solution requested is not in the best interests of the students. That said, however, school authorities must be aware of what constitutes the best well-being for students and articulate that forcefully. Such was not the case in the above situation.

School safety has become an important consideration for school buildings following several tragic events, both natural and human initiated, in the past few decades. Of course, the safety and well-being of students and teachers have always been a vital concern of educators, but recent events have proven to be seminal in their impact upon the life of schools.

School buildings should be considered a safe haven for all users of the building, and a prime consideration in the design in all school buildings. Architects are aware of this factor and design buildings to insure the safety and well-being of the users of the facility. In addition, school administrators must do all within their power to insure the safety of students and teachers by holding safety drills, insuring the building is as safe as possible, and by providing and practicing safe behavior.

That said, no one can foretell or prevent disasters. But if the school building is designed properly and kept safe and secure by the administrators, there should be a great degree of confidence that the building will in fact be a safe haven for all concerned.

SUMMARY

Students and teachers expect to be in a safe environment when in the confines of a school building. This is especially true for the parents of students. Despite the fact that many deadly events have taken place in schools recently, that expectation is still in the minds of all individuals. Nevertheless, school authorities need to take every precaution to protect the lives of students and teachers. This can be done by properly designing new school buildings or retrofitting existing buildings to provide school authorities with a building that help authorities to maintain proper control of the building at all times. This could mean restricted entrance doors, wider hallways, no dead-end hallways, no spaces for a person to hide, and proper supervision at all points in the building. In the design stage for a new building, school authorities, especially principals, must examine the architect's plans to identify any possible dangerous place and ensure the existence of proper controls. This is also true for any renovation of existing buildings. A careful examination of the building should be made to insure that proper controls are in existence. Recent research has identified necessary control measures for a secure school building. These findings should be incorporated into new and existing buildings to help provide a safe environment.

Chapter 21

Problem-Based Learning

Planning for new capital improvement projects, regardless of the size or complexity, always lends itself to problems that must be solved in some fashion or the other. In some cases, the problems are straightforward and can be resolved by the application of relevant data. In other circumstances, the problems are nebulous and have no real solution based upon data. In these cases, the application of relevant data does not produce an exact answer and the problem is resolved based upon the considered thinking or feeling of school authorities.

Oftentimes, the resolution of the problem is based upon the power structure of the community. Resolutions can be based upon some political or ideological belief. School board members bring to the decision-making process the same beliefs that guide their lives. These beliefs may or may not always reflect the majority of beliefs in the community.

For example, many decades ago an upper Midwestern community was planning a new high school, which was the first school building planned in more than twenty-five years. The educational consultant employed by the school board drew up a set of educational specifications that detailed the normal school administrative suite necessary for a modern high school. The board reviewed them and responded with what they wanted for the new school. In the consultant's specifications, a small nurses' clinic was included next to the administrative suite. Nurses' clinics are normally included in all new school buildings. However, there was one school board member who happened to be a dentist and objected to putting a clinic in the school. He convinced the rest of the board to remove it from consideration because, he stated, it "smacked of socialized medicine." Therefore, the school was built without the clinic, but eventually subsequent modifications produced a clinic.

Such extremes as this case are rare, but similar incidents have occurred in the past all over the country and will continue to happen in the future.

The planning process for schools presents some problems that lend themselves to informative discussion in the process of resolution. There may not be any resolution based upon hard data, but nevertheless, the problem must be resolved. When a great number of individuals are involved in a planning process there are as many sets of beliefs and wishes as there are individuals. In the resolution of the problem, all these sets of beliefs and wishes have to be heard, and the resolution must reflect at least the majority.

A set of problems that have been encountered in the public-school scene is included in this section of the book. These problems come from actual situations where public school educators have had to confront certain issues. Some of the problems may seem easy to solve, but because there are considerations on both sides, the problems must be analyzed first before resolution or recommendations are made.

Today, the problem of consolidation in public schools is still evident. These problems are not often solvable by the application of hard data because they deal with the very lives of students and parents. Nevertheless, such problems need full discussion and should be based upon a rational application of data and beliefs. Students are asked to look beyond the superficial emotional aspects of the problem.

The programming of a new school can present a problem. In an effort to involve as many people as possible, school boards can find themselves with the task of people asking for too much. Resolving this problem is the subject of one case in this chapter.

Renovation projects can be messy, especially when school is in session. Of course, the hoped for end result of the renovation is a nice project with everyone happy. What should the school board consider when thinking about a renovation project besides the initial cost of the project?

Employing an architect is an important part of planning for a new school building. If a school system has several new schools to design, who should design them? Should one firm be employed to do all projects, or should the projects be divided up among several firms? This question presents some interesting aspects for the school authorities to consider.

The seemingly age-old problem of whether to build one or two schools to accommodate a growing population is always present in some school systems. How can the superintendent properly advise the school board on what to consider rationally and without allowing bias to influence their decision? This is a serious question for any superintendent, and one that so often comes up for resolution.

Educational theorists, educational planners, government officials, architects, and others, have at various times explained to practicing educators and members of school boards that the process of education is changing and that these changes will impact how the school building is planned and designed in the future. Some of the changes, innovations, reforms, new teaching strategies, and organizational changes have had some impact upon how the school building is shaped.

Many such changes have had little influence. Nevertheless, it is interesting to speculate on the future of the school building. One exercise below asks student to look into the future and predict changes in the school building of the future. Several sets of critical issues from the 1960s to 2012 have been given as a review of past issues that the schools have had to or will encounter.

Public schools have not necessarily changed much as a result of these past critical issues because one look at the new school buildings of today indicates that there has been little substantial change in the buildings themselves. There may be more total space in schools than in earlier buildings, and perhaps more specialized areas, but the schools built today look very similar on the interior to schools that are thirty years old, except for the newness of the building materials. Nevertheless, this exercise gives students an opportunity to think about the future and define what they think will be critical issues. Needless to say, there is no right answer to this exercise.

1. BRAMWELL HIGH SCHOOL CLOSURE

A medium-size school system of approximately 10,000 pupils has a high school located in a small, unincorporated area of the school system called Bramwell. The community is close-knit and value their high school as a community asset. Further, the students at Bramwell High School perform very well on standardized academic tests administered by the state. The high school building is located approximately twenty minutes away, via good highways, from a neighboring newer high school, Braddock High School, within the same school system. The newer high school building has a capacity of 1,000 students and a current enrollment of 700 students. Eight years ago, Bramwell High School had an enrollment of 450 students. Currently, there are 190 students enrolled in grades 9 to12. The Bramwell High School curriculum currently lists thirty-five separate courses; the neighboring high school curriculum has seventy-five courses listed.

Although the building is approximately forty-five years old, it is in fairly good condition and there appears to be no major physical defect or major maintenance needs. The building, however, does have the features of a thirty-five-year-old school, which means that things such as wooden floors in most parts of the building, a small gymnasium, a kitchen with old equipment, and a small library are evident.

Because of the rapid and consistent drop in enrollment at Bramwell High School, the school board is considering closing the building and transporting the students to the neighboring high school building. The school board is divided on the issue of closure and has asked you to prepare a report to give them guidance. You, as superintendent, have been asked to provide the school board with sufficient reasons and explanation to either:

1. close the building and to justify this action to the parents, or
2. keep the building open and identify the ways to improve the educational opportunities while keeping the per-pupil costs to what they are now

What *factors* should the school board take into consideration in making the decision? As superintendent you have been asked to prepare a written report to the school board that incorporates justification for *both* positions so that they can be informed when they make the decision.

2. MADISON COUNTY HIGH SCHOOL
Space Requests Problem

Madison County School System is planning for a new high school to accommodate future growth in the county. The school board has reviewed the growth pattern of the student population over the past ten years and the projections for the next ten years. This data indicate a continued growth in students over the next decade. The existing high school is extremely crowded and needs relief. The school board decided, based upon the student projections for the future and the functional capacity of the existing high school, that a new high school with a capacity of 1,200 students should be built.

The school board and administration employed an outside educational consultant to help develop a capital budget for the new school to determine what the impact of this project might be on the taxpayers of the community. The consultant came up with the following figures based upon current data from the state department of education:

1,200 students $\times$ 155 square feet (state average) = 186,000 square feet
186,000 square feet @ \$250/square foot = \$46,500,000
Instructional space @ 75% = 139,500 square feet
Non-instructional space @ 25% = 46,500 square feet

The 75/25 division of allocated space is the difference between the space the educational program (75%) needs, and the other spaces, such as halls, toilets, mechanical equipment, and kitchen (25%), that need to be dedicated to non-instructional space.

The consultant determined that to implement the educational program adequately in the new building would require at least 139,500 square feet of space for instruction purposes, with an additional 46,500 square feet of space for such services as circulation, restrooms, kitchen, mechanical rooms, and storage. The cost of the new school would be within the financial limitations of the school system but could not exceed that square footage.

The school board also asked the consultant to initiate a planning process for the new school that would include input from many sectors of shareholders—teachers, principals, central office personnel, M & O personnel, and the community. The school board felt that it was important that these groups have a say in the planning of the building. The consultant met with all the above groups over a period of several months from January to April and developed a composite of requests from all the groups. Because of these meetings and input from the groups, the consultant reported to the school board the requests of these groups.

When the consultant aggregated the total requests from the various groups, the following analysis was made. The groups had requested additional instructional spaces, special education classrooms, laboratories, shops, studios, auditoriums, gymnasia, auxiliary spaces, offices, libraries, and miscellaneous spaces that were above what the educational consultant recommended to the school board. These additions amounted to a grand total of 207,600 square feet of space for the 1,200 students that would be housed in the new high school. This amount was approximately 21,600 square feet above what the consultant recommended and the school board approved.

Based upon that situation, the school board asked the consultant to make recommendations so that the requested amount of space could be reconciled with the adopted amount of space and funds.

Requested Space from the Various Groups

This is a summary of the amount of space the various groups requested in their meetings with the consultant, along with what it would cost the school division:

1,200 students $\times$ 173 square feet = 207,600 square feet
207,600 square feet @ $250/square foot = $51,900,000
Instructional space @ 75% = 155,700 square feet
Non-instructional space @ 25% = 51,900 square feet

The consultant to the school division, in compliance with the school board, suggested the following reductions (Table 21.1). These reductions are for the elimination of *selected spaces* in the proposed high school building. These

Table 21.1. Reduction of SPACES

Reductions—Elimination of SPACES	Space Savings/Sq. Ft.
12 GP classrooms @ 720	8,640
12 faculty offices @ 100	1,200
1 computer lab @ 1,500	1,500
1 science lab @ 1,200	1,200
1 math lab @ 800	800
1 math office @ 100	100
1 health ed room @ 700	700
1 business lab @ 900	900
1 AgEd classroom @ 700	700
1 AgEd office @ 100	100
Total	**15,840 Square Feet**

reductions would reduce the number of *total spaces* in the building from what the various groups requested.

In addition to the above reductions by eliminating SPACES, the consultant suggested further reductions by reducing the *SIZE of certain spaces* (Table 21.2).

Table 21.2. Reductions of SIZE of SPACES

Reduction of SIZE of SPACES	Space Savings/Sq. Ft.
Reduce the size of spaces of the following areas to:	
Science Labs (6) from 1,200 to 1,000 square feet each	1,200
GP classrooms (26) from 720 to 700 square feet each	520
Math Labs (6) from 800 to 720 square feet each	480
Art Labs (3) from 1,200 to 1,000 square feet each	600
Choral Music (1) from 1,200 to 1,000 square feet	200
Music Office (1) from 300 to 200 square feet	100
Auditorium from 5,500 to 5,000 square feet	500
Stage/dressing from 2,500 to 2,000 square feet	500
Driver education from 3 @ 1,200 to 3 @ 1,000 square feet	600
Exercise room (1) from 2,000 to 1,200 square feet	800
Administrative Systems lab (1) from 1,200 to 1,000 square feet	200
Information Technology (1) from 1,200 to 1,000 square feet	200
Multipurpose lab—eliminate	1,000
Control Technology lab from 2,800 to 2,000 square feet	800
Production Technology lab from 2,800 to 2,000	800
Communication Technology lab from 3,000 to 2,000 square feet	1,000
Marketing Education lab from 1,200 to 800 square feet	400
Agriculture Education lab from 3,000 to 2,500 square feet	500
Total	**10,400**

Recapitulation

Budget—What the consultant originally recommended, and the school board approved.
1,200 students × 155 square feet (state average) = 186,000 square feet
186,000 square feet @ $250/square foot = $46,500,000
Instructional space @ 75% = 139,500 square feet
Non-instructional space @ 25% = 46,500 square feet

Requested space from meetings with various groups:
1,200 students x 173 square feet = 207,600 square feet
207,600 square feet @ $250/square foot = $51,900,000
Instructional space @ 75% = 155,700 square feet
Non-instructional space @ 25% = 51,900 square feet

The consultant offered three alternatives to help reduce the size of the proposed high school. These are listed as Alternatives A, B, and C.
A. *Alternative (Reductions I and II)*
Original square feet request = 207,600 square feet
Reduction in square feet = 21,600 square feet (difference between 21,600 and 207,600)
New instructional square foot allocation = 186,000 square feet
Net cost of building = $45,340,000
B. *Alternative (Reduction I)*
Original square feet request = 207,600 square feet
Reduction in square feet = 15,840 square feet (difference between 15,840 and 207,600)
New instructional square foot allocation = 191,760 square feet
Net cost of building = $47,940,000
C. *Alternative (Reduction II)*
Original square feet request = 207,600 square feet
Reduction in square feet = 10,400 square feet
New instructional square foot allocation = 197,200 square feet
Net cost of building = $49,300,000

How can the requests of the staff and community be reduced to comply with the budgetary constraints imposed by the school board? Which alternative in space reduction offered by the consultant would you be more comfortable with and why? Which alternative would fit your educational program best? Or, if none of the alternatives suit your needs, are there better alternatives to reducing the requests by various groups? As the superintendent, you are requested by the school board to make a recommendation to them for reducing the total scope of the project, and to justify your decision.

3. MONROE COUNTY HIGH SCHOOL RENOVATION
A Case Study in Renovation of Space
School Description:

Monroe County is a suburban area of a major city and has a population that exceeds many major cities. It is unincorporated and has many subdevelopments that produce a sizable student population. There are eight high schools in the county, one of which is Monroe County High School. The high school was constructed in 1984. The building is situated on a site containing forty-four acres in the northern part of the county.

The school is in a residential area, and because of shifts of population in the general area, the attendance zone has been changed several times in the thirty-five years the school has been in operation. The original building was constructed for $11 million. The cost of the site, equipment, and fees raised the total cost of the high school by another $1.4 million for a total of $12.4 million.

The original school capacity was 2,200 students, but the enrollment is now 1,800, reflecting some shifts in population. The professional staff number 172, including the principal and three assistant principals.

Renovation/Renewal Project

The Monroe County Public Schools has a program of renewing or modernizing all schools when buildings reach twenty-five to thirty-five years old. The Renewal Program identifies all school buildings in the county that fall within that age group each year. These buildings are then selected for renewal. The intent of the program is to bring all school buildings up to the standard of the most recently constructed building. In this way, the county can ensure some type of equity in educational facilities between the various sections of the county.

The Renewal Program also identifies the type and extent of work that is to be done in the renewal/renovation process. In addition to the general scope of work, each school building is evaluated to determine other segments of the renewal/renovation. In the case of the Monroe County High School building, additions were scheduled because of program needs.

The Monroe County High School building was identified for funding during the 2020–2021 school year to the extent of $30 million. Replacement cost of this high school was estimated at $50 million, plus equipment and fees, or a total of $55.5 million. This did not include the cost of a new site. In as much as the school system needs to have a high school in the area to accommodate the student population and to address the facilities equity issue, the decision was made to renovate/renew the building.

The general scope of work includes items for the four major systems of the building—architectural/structural, mechanical, plumbing, and electrical—plus the site. The funds budgeted for the renovation were distributed as follows:

Construction contract—including renovation of existing building and site: $24 million

Furniture and moveable equipment: $1.35 million

An addition of 10,000 square feet of new construction: $4.65 million

Total Contract: $30 million

In addition to the items contained in the general scope of work, specific items needed attention to improve the school and provide the types of spaces a modern educational program needs. These items follow:

Hall Congestion. Part of the library is used for circulation in the front hall.

The library has an open space on one side to permit students to circulate from one part of the building to another. To prevent loss of books, a security system was installed. This security system slowed student traffic and considerable congestion occurred before and after school, as well as during every change of class throughout the day. A better definition of the circulation pattern is needed to prevent congestion.

Library. The library was designed on an open space plan with one side open to the hall. Students use this area to move from one area of the building to another. This movement causes considerable disruption in the quiet areas of the library. In addition, the open area permits students to have free access to the library; consequently, considerable loss results.

What is needed is to have a secure area for the library function and at the same time permit access to the library holdings. Also, the existing library is not capable of handling the improvements in technology in the access and use of information.

Lecture Hall. The large group lecture hall is simply two classes joined together. The floor is flat and has four parallel walls. There are electrical service outlets on only two walls, the front and back. Lighting is fixed and of poor quality and level. Moveable student arm chair desks are in use. The room is not very functional for large group lectures.

Classroom Space. Over the years, many classrooms have been converted to computer labs. This has reduced the capacity of the school sufficiently to cause the school staff concern in light of recent community growth. Additional general-purpose classroom space is needed to accommodate the growth of the student population.

Technology. The school building was designed during a period of time when technology was not a great concern. As a result, the building lacks sufficient electrical power and outlets to accommodate the increase in equipment. In addition, there is a lack of visual and audio communication between the classrooms and various other areas, such as the library, within the building, and also among this school and other schools in the county. The cooling system is incapable of keeping the technology instructional areas at a workable and/or comfortable temperature level.

Parking. Because of the growth in automobile usage by students and teachers over the years, the existing parking area has become overcrowded and inadequate and needs expansion.

Besides these major items, the total scope of the project includes some requests from the staff of the school:

Guidance—more offices and conference rooms
Music—additional space for orchestra program
Drama—dressing rooms, better lighting in theater
Business—requested additional labs
PhysEd—new gymnasium and supporting facilities

These requests were evaluated for need considering limited resources. The requests of the guidance staff, music department, drama department, and physical education department were included in the renovation project. Some of the requests were included in the new construction, and other needs were incorporated in the renovation of the existing space. The following items were included in the new construction:

Open Court Infill. A two-story addition was constructed in one of the open courtyards. This addition housed a lecture hall and nine new instructional areas—four classrooms, two mathematics computer labs, one business computer lab, and two special education classrooms.
Music Storage. An area of 1,200 square feet was added to the building for instrument and uniform storage.
Auditorium Lobby Extension. The music storage addition permitted the lobby of the auditorium to be expanded.
Arcade Infills. There were two arcades or breezeways in the academic portion of the building. These were enclosed to form lobbies. Additional offices and storage areas were also gained through this enclosure.

Renovation/Renewal Results

The architects worked with the staff of the high school and the central office in designing the new spaces and the renovation of the existing space. The results of the design phase were put out for bid and a contract was awarded to a successful bidder who was a local contractor.

In a complete renovation project, the Monroe County Public Schools allows renovation work by a contractor while school is in session. Some school systems are able to move the entire student body to a different building for the time of the renovation project, but in this case the educational program for the students at the high school was not interrupted. The county obtained five temporary classrooms and placed them on the site of the high school. The plan was that five classes would be moved out of the building and into the temporary classrooms while work was being done on the vacated classrooms.

When the contractor was finished with those five classrooms, another five classrooms would be vacated and moved to the temporary classroom units. In the case of Monroe County High School, the social studies team of teachers volunteered to stay in the temporary classrooms for the entire period of the renovation project. The rotation of the vacant classrooms still continued with various subject departments moving out of their classrooms into finished classrooms and then back into the original classrooms. This rotation continued for the entire two years of the renovation project.

What was completed during the renovation and new construction was the following:

Hall Congestion. A new front hallway was constructed to allow students to go from the academic units to the administrative suite without going through the library.

Library. The existing library was enclosed and expanded into the existing multipurpose room, which enlarged the area for the library function. The library now has a central entrance with a new circulation desk. An electronic classroom was created and new equipment installed.

Technology. A new and increased electrical service to the building was installed—existing wiring was replaced with new wiring. Electrical wall molding was installed in almost every instructional area to provide electrical and telecommunication service. Electrical poles were used in many classrooms and computer labs to bring electrical service where needed. Special four-pipe heating and cooling was installed in all computer sites to ensure even temperature in those areas. The school was equipped with a telecommunication infrastructure, which included fiber-optic wiring. Two outlets of four-pair shielded twisted pair cable ran from the fiber-optic backbone to each classroom unit.

Open Court Infill. The courtyard infill provided the additional classrooms and a lecture hall seating two hundred students. The lecture hall was equipped with sophisticated sound and telecommunication equipment to become a top-light lecture area.

Parking. The parking area was resurfaced, and different parking widths used to increase the parking by one hundred additional spaces.

Renovation Problems
As in every construction project, the renovation/renewal project of Monroe County High School generated some problems for the school staff. Classes were interrupted daily for any number of reasons. Several times there was an interruption of electrical service to a wing of the building or the entire building. The local fire marshal became a frequent visitor to the school for either problems with the construction operation or because of false alarms. The movement of classes and teachers from classroom to classroom to vacate their rooms caused considerable confusion; however, the educational program was not seriously interrupted during the two-year period of the renovation project.

Project Outcome
The high school building does contain the numbers and types of educational spaces a modern high school needs to function effectively. The building is presently able to handle the technology requirements the county educators perceived as being implemented in the next few years. Further, the building has been expanded in those areas that were constrained.

The renovated Monroe County High School will be able to serve the youth of the county for another twenty-five years in an effective manner, and the project cost less than constructing a new building on the existing site. Although financial considerations entered the decision-making process, the fact that the building was in good condition at the time of renovation and that there was a need for a school building in this area were contributing factors in deciding to renovate the building.

a. How can a school board evaluate a renovation project when it is completed? By what means and what data does a school board have and need to do this?
b. How can the renovation project be evaluated by the users? Can you develop an evaluation instrument to measure the success of the project?
c. What does research have to say about renovation projects that would be useful to a school board and educators? What effect does a renovation project have upon student and teacher health and productivity?
d. Did the renovation comply with various formulae about the ratio of new to renovated space?

4. EMPLOYING THE ARCHITECT
You are the superintendent of a 20,000-student school division in a state where the local school division is fiscally independent and can raise tax revenue on its own. The school system is located within the boundaries of a city.

The community has recently passed an $180 million bond issue to construct a new high school that will accommodate 1,200 pupils, a new 1,000-pupil middle school, and two new 500-pupil elementary schools. The bonds have been sold and the funds are available to the school board to construct these schools.

One of the school board members suggested that the school division hire one architect that has been employed before to do all of the design work for all four buildings. You have been asked to advise the school board on the feasibility of having either one architectural firm do all the above projects under one contract or to split up the projects and award them to multiple architectural firms. Your board is split on this issue and you need to help them resolve this issue.

Your assignment is to develop two recommendations regarding the number of firms to be used and develop a rationale to support your recommendation, detailing the pros and cons of either approach. One recommendation should support the idea of employing one architect, and the other recommendation should support multiple architects. You should approach it from both sides of the question so that you can support either position.

What should you, as superintendent, consider when making these two recommendations?

5. ONE OR TWO HIGH SCHOOL BUILDINGS

Renovating Sun Prairie's existing high school would be a Band-Aid approach to growing enrollments. This was the recommendation of consultants to the school board. The school board took the advice of the consultant and decided to build new facilities to accommodate the growing student population of the school system. A high school facility task force was organized to discuss the prospects of either building one high school or two. One high school would be planned for 2,200 students. If, however, the school board decides to build two high schools, each school would be planned to house 1,100 students. In either alternative, the present high school would be remoled into a middle school for 750 students. This would leave the school system with three middle schools.

The first option on the table involves building a new high school for 2,200 students on an eighty-to-ninety-acre site, at a cost ranging from $87 million to $95 million. It has been estimated this project would cause an increase in property taxes of up to $1.36 per $1,000 of assessed value, or an extra $204 in taxes for the owner of a $150,000 house.

The second option would involve building two new high schools for 1,100 students each on two seventy-to-eighty-acre sites. This option would cost between $94 and $109 million and involve an estimated tax rate increase of up to $1.85 per $1,000 of assessed value. This would mean a $277 maximum increase for the above homeowner.

Both new high schools would be expandable to 1,400 students in the future. A consultant to the school board indicated there are about five or six sites around the school system that would be available for $20,000 to $60,000 per acre. The consultant said that both options would necessitate purchase of land.

As superintendent, you have been asked by the school board to provide some data to the task force regarding the feasibility of both options. The task force will present the school board with a recommendation as to which option to choose.

What kinds of data will you provide the task force to help them make their decision? What kind of information is important for them to consider? What problems would the school system encounter in the future for either option chosen? What does research say about school size, and can those findings be adequately used in discussions of the options? What will be the impact of additional taxes on property owners and the economy of the school system? Can you present data so that the task force will not allow bias to enter their decision?

Please prepare a report on the factors that the task force should consider.

6. CRITICAL ISSUES IN EDUCATION THAT INFLUENCE SCHOOL BUILDINGS

Below is a series of lists of critical issues in education that have been thought to influence the design of new school buildings. Most of the items in the various lists are self-explanatory and are derived from conference programs, presentations of futurists, or publications of various sorts. The lists are not comprehensive, but are rather representative of the time at which the statements were made.

The lists give the reader an idea of the teaching strategies, organizational patterns, differentiated programs, technologies, and curricular adjustments that were important at the time they were promulgated.

1960s: The Progressive Stage

During the 1960s, considerable change took place in the educational setting, which resulted in changes in the school building. Some of the more significant educational changes:

1. Introduction of team teaching in the high school—J. Lloyd Trump
2. Computer-assisted instruction programs
3. Open space education and buildings
4. Downward extension of the curriculum—especially math and science

5. Introduction of the middle school organization—first middle school buildings
6. Head Start and Follow-Through programs become available
7. Development of the Instructional Materials Center—IMC (Old Library)
8. Introduction of special education classes in each school building (PCA Decision)
9. Introduction of School-within-the-School Organization—house concept

1980s: Alvin Toffler—The Third Wave
Toffler predicted more learning would occur outside, rather than inside, the classroom. He argued that, despite the pressure from unions, the years of compulsory schooling would grow shorter, not longer. Instead of rigid age segregation, young and old would mingle in the educational scene. Education would become more interspersed and interwoven with work, and more spread out over a lifetime. We would not have to build any more school buildings because students would learn at home using a computer.

1991: Educational Reform—The National Governor's Conference
1. Choice in where students will attend school—vouchers, open enrollment, charters
2. Education of three- and-four-year-old children by public schools
3. Increased programs for at-risk students in the schools
4. Initiate and expand to full-day kindergarten classes
5. Daycare programs and services in the schools
6. Increase in remedial and compensatory programs (SpEd)
7. Increase in technology in public schools
8. Reduced class size in kindergarten and primary grades
9. Expansion of alternative education programs for all grades
10. Expansion of magnet school programs
11. Expansion of year-round education programs
12. Increased graduation requirements

1995: Six Agents for Change That Will Influence School Buildings
Meeting of the Southeastern Region Council of Educational Facility Planners, International

1. Implementation of technology in the classroom
2. Public/private partnership in planning/designing/building new schools
3. Environmental issues
4. Extended time and use of buildings
5. Program-driven schools—magnet schools, schools of choice
6. Participatory design

Technology so far has not changed design of schools. Schools are still using industrial-age learning strategies—teacher centered information-age characteristics—geodesic, cooperative learning, learner centered.

2000: Critical Issues in School Facility Planning for the Twenty-First Century

1. Political decision-making influences how schools operate and what they teach
2. School facility equity—California, Texas, Wyoming, Alaska, South Carolina
3. State litigation—legal suits against the state for funding purposes
4. Technology needs in the schools
5. Planning process—who makes decisions in planning schools—encroachment of architects on planning decisions
6. Condition of existing school buildings
7. Research on building condition and student achievement—continued efforts
8. Possible federal funding for school buildings
9. Educational program location—where students go to learn
10. Size of school buildings—small vs. large question

2008: Educational Issues That Will Affect School Facilities

Virginia Educational Facilities Planners Conference—March 2008

1. Blurring and Blending—face-to-face instruction vs. online instruction
2. Mobility Galore—people moving around the country more today than in past
3. Gaming—video games can aid instruction—see seriousgames.org
4. Social Networking—more online networking of individuals—Facebook. com
5. High-Impact Presentations/Engagement Technology—greater use of computer
6. Analysis, Diagnosis, Evidence-Based Education—different instruction strategy
7. Human Touch—facilities and technology are important, but need human touch

Are there similarities in these critical issues from year to year? Write your critique of the similarities of the critical issues.

2030: What Are the New Critical Issues in Education That Will Influence the School Building Tomorrow?

Your school board is in the process of planning a new high school building and has asked you, the superintendent, to advise them of the latest developments that will influence the design of the building. Please develop a list of the issues you think will influence school buildings in the future. Please refer to the chapter in the book devoted to issues of importance to educators.

7. THOUGHT PROBLEMS

Complying with federal government regulations and the Green School movement are two of many so-called hot topics for educators to understand. How do these seemingly different topics affect how a school is planned and designed? Please write a report to the superintendent explaining the impact each topic has for educators.

The length of the report will depend upon how many resources you uncover and use, but the report should give the superintendent and school board sufficient knowledge that they can take action. In the next building project they will want to know what federal government regulations they must comply with to meet standards. As far as the green school, they want to decide if the architect should design a green school based upon your findings.

Complying with Federal Regulations

The federal government has certain regulations dealing with the accessibility of school buildings. All students are guaranteed access to all educational programs, regardless of disability. The question arises, then, Is every part of the school building to be accessible to every student regardless of ability? What is the basis for deciding how far accessibility to all areas of the building is to go?

- Do existing school buildings have to conform to these regulations?
- Where do these regulations come from in the first place?
- What should educators know about the law to make certain the school building complies with every federal government regulation regarding accessibility?

Please prepare a paper detailing the laws and regulations educators should be knowledgeable about and how they play out in either a new building or an existing school building.

Green, High-Performance, and Sustainable Schools

We have heard a great deal about the Green School movement being environmentally correct. The terms *green schools*, *high-performance schools*, and *sustainable schools* have all been used to describe certain types of buildings that are environmentally friendly and leave a small carbon footprint. In addition, the U.S. Green Building Council has developed the Leadership in Environmental Education Design system to rate buildings according to how closely they conform to the regulations for an environmentally friendly building.

These regulations encompass not only how the building is constructed, but also the types of materials used in the building and the follow-up education program for students. The U.S. Green Building Council also has a program of criteria to which school buildings should adhere if they are to be rated as green schools. All of these green school applications and additions to new and existing buildings increase the cost of construction. Even though these increases may be small, they do add to the total cost of the school building.

Please write a description of what these terms mean and what educators should know about them. What should a superintendent advise the school board to consider on this matter when a new school is to be built or an existing school renovated? Please list the issues to be considered.

8. A PROBLEM OF EQUITABLE SCHOOL FACILITIES FOR ALL STUDENTS
The British Columbia Experience: How Equity of School Facilities is Determined

Introduction
1. Canadian citizens whose native language is French are guaranteed that their children can attend a French language school financed by the BC government.
2. Under Clause 23 of the Canadian Clause of Rights and Freedom, French Language schools will be maintained and financed by the Ministry of Education just as all other government sponsored schools are funded.
3. The Conseil Scolaire Francophone (CSF) has served as the governing body of the French Language schools in British Columbia.
4. The CSF has had the responsibility of finding suitable housing for Francophone students. This has not been an easy task because of the manner in which Francophone schools have come into existence after Anglophone schools have already been established.
5. This fact causes the CSF to obtain school housing that may not be in the best interests of the school children.
6. Capital funding of the province is structured in such a manner that the capital projects of the CSF are prioritized along with all other capital requests from all of the school districts in the entire providence.
7. As a result the CSF has had to obtain facilities by either purchasing abandoned school buildings or renting facilities. Neither method of securing facilities has been successful according to the parents of students attending these schools.

Initiating a Legal Complaint

8. The parents and the CSF initiated legal action claiming their students were located in inadequate school buildings. The resolution of the legal action according to the parents and CSF is for the Ministry of Education to provide more than $286 million in funding for new schools claiming inequity in facilities housing students.

9. To bolster their case, the CSF sought an expert's report on the influence educational facilities have upon student educational outcomes. The intent was to secure their position that school buildings do have an influence upon student learning. The CSF secured the services of Lance Roberts at the University of Manitoba to prepare a report on the available research on the relationship between the condition of educational facilities and student educational outcomes.

10. The report Roberts (2013) prepared reviewed available research on the subject and concluded that the condition of the school building did in fact influence student achievement.

11. The most important building elements or components that do influence is: complete control of the thermal environment, proper lighting, control of the acoustical environment, presence or absence of graffiti, proper furniture and equipment, and a sound building structure (Earthman, 2004).

12. The Roberts report was presented to the court and became part of the judiciary evidence to support the claims of the CSF and Francophone parents that the school building does influence student learning.

Judgment

13. In the initial trial of this legal action, the courts sided with the parents and CSF claiming inequity and ruled that relief should be given to the parents and CSF. The judge indicated that the facilities were inferior to English Language Schools.

14. The Ministry of Education appealed the case to the British Columbia Supreme Court.

15. The Ministry of Education secured an expert witness to reply to the claims of the Francophone parents and CSF.

16. The Ministry of Education asked the expert witness to develop a report detailing the research related to a relationship between school building condition and student achievement and to then determine if the complaints of the parents had any basis of research to back up their complaint. This methodology entailed the review of numerous data sources to determine if there were any research findings that related to the subject of the complaint. Data sources such as the three clearinghouses related to school facilities—National Clearinghouse for Educational Facilities, the American Clearinghouse for Educational Facilities, and the Educational

Facility Clearinghouse, plus Google, EBSCO, and the Virginia Tech library were all explored to find relevant research findings. When no research findings were available, the researchers provided an explanation as to this fact. Thus, the individual complaint was judged not to have a negative influence upon student educational outcomes.

17. A report was developed on related research and then the individual complaints of the parents (284 complaints) were analyzed to determine if there was a research basis.

Parental Complaints

18. There was always the question of whether or not the parental complaints had any relationship to the educational outcomes of students. Of the total complaints (284) only 16 could conceivably be related to student educational outcomes. Close examination of these sixteen complaints, however, indicated that none of the complaints were even remotely associated with research findings that related to student educational outcomes.

19. For instance, one such complaint stated that the school site had an animal smell that was very distasteful. The school was located on a site next to a working farm and apparently fumes from manure and animals were carried onto the school site by wind.

20. Several other complaints were that the school building was not located centrally to the student population, which resulted in long bus rides for students. With the Francophone student population spread over a large catchment area it would be natural for some students to have to ride the bus for a long period of time.

21. Parents also complained that the school facility housing the student body was a rented building and as a result parents and administration could not plan for future expansion of the Francophone program. Apparently, the lease agreements were not long term, which prevented the faculty and administration from formulating long-term plans. Granted that short-term leases do not facilitate long-term educational program plans, there is no research to indicate that students housed in rented or leased facilities perform less well than if they were housed in facilities owned by the administration.

22. Parents further complained that the school was not large enough to fully implement the curriculum. Other complaints were that there was no library and cafeteria in the school. The school is unattractive was another complaint with several schools.

23. The nature of all the complaints was rather personal and dealt with how the school looked and did not apply to educational attainment of students. The complaints were what parents had knowledge about, but did not

address what should probably have been the main complaint about the buildings and student achievement.

24. The methodology used in determining if the parental complaint had standing and if the complaints were research based was a normative comparison to available research. On all complaints the experts looked for a research base to determine if the complaint had merit.

Questions for the Court

25. The question the courts had to address was the seriousness of the parent's complaints and the equity of the school facilities. But the real question seems to be the equity of the process of formulating a new school district. How does one go about providing adequate school facilities for a new school district within an existing school district? The question of how to house a new student body in an adequate building when none is available is the problem the Ministry of Education has to face.

26. Several questions are still not resolved. These questions center around the equity of the system used to provide the CSF with funds to adequately house the students. To try to establish a new school organization and then house it properly in any neighborhood is an extremely difficult task. Normally, established neighborhoods do not have large tracts of land available upon which to place a new school building. Neither are there vacant school buildings that are available to the CSF, unless the school building has been abandoned because the building is obsolete. Further, buildings with a large square footage that could be converted to a school building are not readily available in neighborhoods where students are located.

27. The problem is further complicated by the scarcity of students who would benefit from a Francophone school. The scarcity of French-speaking students causes these students to travel long distances to the local school. In some cases students ride a school bus for an hour.

28. The first question concerns the suitability of the facilities that are currently utilized by CSF to house the student population. None of the complaints stated that the school building was unsuitable for the education of students because of lack of thermal control, poor lighting, uncontrolled acoustical environment, unsuitable furniture and equipment, the presence of graffiti in the building, and a structure that was not sound, which are essential building elements necessary for successful student progress (Earthman, 2004). The complaints were of the nature of superficial complaints related to the parents being unsatisfied with the housing arrangement. Complaints about rental facilities speak to the desire of parents and CSF to own their school. Somehow renting a school facility is deemed less desirable than owning the building in which the students are housed. There may be something to that argument, but the complaints

do not relate to student educational outcomes. In fact, the CSF states on their website that the Francophone student performs better on the provincial academic assessment than do students in the English Language schools. This fact cannot be used as evidence that the facilities utilized to house the Francophone students are not suitable for them. Apparently the facilities in which the students are housed do not hinder them in their educational outcomes.

29. Although there are alternatives ways to housing student populations, none seemed to be employed by the CSF for whatever reason. Conversion of existing commercial buildings to school use is one such alternative. This alternative has been quite successful in other localities, such as the school district of Philadelphia (Philadelphia Public Schools, 1970). There also may not have been any suitable buildings for educational conversion in the fourteen catchment areas of the Francophone Schools when they were initially established. Some of the Francophone schools in the fourteen catchment areas were located in rural areas and there were no facilities that could be converted satisfactorily to educational purposes. In one catchment area the Francophone school had to rent facilities in an operating English language school. The school rented six classrooms and jointly used the support facilities. This arrangement proved unsatisfactory for both the Francophone school and the Anglophone School.

Questions for the Reader

How does a governmental organization establish equity policies?

What are the rules for establishing a new school system?

What should be the basis of equitable treatment for starting a new school system?

How could the Ministry of Education provide equality to both the Francophone and Anglophone Schools in this situation?

Appendix A
Sample School Building Appraisal Form

Lexington Public Schools

Middle School Appraisal Form

School Location

Grades

Number of Teachers: Regular _____ Special Education _____

Itinerant _____ Special Programs _____

Stated Building Capacity _____

Enrollment _____ as of _____ / _____ / _____

Number of Instructional Spaces

GP Classrooms ____ SpecEd Resource ____ SpecEd ____ Self-Contained ____

Music Room _____ Gym _____ Technology Room _____

Computer Lab_____ Art Room _____ Home Arts Lab _____

Exploratory Lab _____ Auditorium (seating) _____ Conference Rooms _____

Cafeteria (seating) _____ Male Toilet _____ Female Toilet _____

Other Instructional Spaces _____

Building Configuration and Organization (room configuration, size, adequacy for program)

General Condition of Building (inside upkeep, maintenance needs)

Building Appearance (general upkeep, outside maintenance)

Site (size, general appearance, fields, equipment, parking, traffic)

Potential for Continued Use (suggested building changes to improve instruction, changes to convert to other use)

Appendix B

Checklist for Development of Educational Specifications

Data Collection	*Time Elapse-Days*
___ Budget Approval for Design to Begin	
___ Project Assigned to Educational Planner	
	5
___ Confer with Site Specialist	3
___ Confer with District Superintendent and Principal	5
___ Confer with School Staff	5
___ Meet with Community Groups	5
___ Confer with Curriculum Department	1
___ Development of Rough Draft of Educational Specifications	5

Program Confirmation	
___ Review by School Planning Director	1
___ Review by District Superintendent and Principal	2
___ Meet with the Staff	5
___ Meet with Community Groups	5
___ Revision of Educational Specifications	3
___ Final Approval by Director of School Planning	2

Production and Distribution	
___ Confer with School Planning Draftsman	1
___ Graphics Completed	10
___ Type Educational Specifications for Printer	8
___ Send Document to Printer	10
___ Distribution of Educational Specifications	1

Appendix C

Letters to the Architect

INITIAL LETTER TO REQUEST PROPOSALS

Washington County Schools   May 1, 2019
100 Elm Street
Washington City, VA 22031-2045

William Jones, AIA
Jones and Jones Architects, Inc.
303 Elm Street
Washington City, VA 22031

Dear Mr. Jones,

    The Washington County school system is planning to construct a new elementary school building to serve 500 elementary school students in the northern quadrant of the county. The new school will be constructed on a twenty-five-acre site located at the corner of Harding Road and Spruce Avenue in the Deercroft area. The school is to be ready for student occupancy by September 1, 2021. The school system staff is currently developing the educational specifications that will be the basis for the architect designing the new building.

    The school system is desirous of contracting for architectural services to design the facility. If your firm is interested in being considered for such a commission, I would like to invite you to send me data relative to the experience and qualifications of your staff. Any other information that would enable our staff to evaluate your firm adequately should be included. Please send your material to the Architectural Selection Committee, School Facilities Department, at the school system address. All submitted material and photographs will be returned to you after the selection process.

All information submitted will be reviewed by an architectural selection committee composed of school personnel. Following this review, three architectural firms will be selected from the pool of applicants for interview. The school board will interview these firms and then select one firm for the commission.

If you have any questions regarding this letter or any other phase of the selection procedure, please call me. I look forward to working with you.

Sincerely,
E. Russell Hooper, Superintendent

Appendix D

Letter to Request Presentation to School Board

Washington County Schools
100 Elm Street
Washington City, VA 22031-2045

July 1, 2019

William Jones, AIA
Jones and Jones Architects, Inc.
303 Elm Street
Washington City, VA 22031

Dear Mr. Jones,

Your firm has been selected to present a formal oral presentation to the Architectural Selection Committee and the School Board for designing a new elementary school.

Your presentation will take place on Wednesday, July 20, 2019, at 10:30AM in the Board Room of the school administration building on 100 Elm Street. Your presentation will be limited to twenty minutes, and facilities to present slides and overhead transparencies will be available.

The presentation shall include but not be limited to:

1. Your management approach to meeting the design requirements of the project
2. The personnel to be assigned to the project during the design phase and construction phase
3. The engineering consultants to be used in the design of the project

4. Your firm's approach and commitment to have the project ready for bidding on schedule and within the assigned budget
5. The experience and qualifications of your firm in similar projects

If you have any questions, please call me. We look forward to working with your firm.

   Sincerely,
   Anthony Phillips, Director of School Facilities

Appendix E

Standard Form of Agreement between Owner and Architect

AGREEMENT: made this *first* day of *July* in the year of Two Thousand and Nineteen BETWEEN the Owner: *Washington County Public Schools* and the Architect: *Jones and Jones, Architects, Inc.*
For the following Project: *New High School*
Maple Road and Hamilton Drive
Washington City, Virginia

The Owner and the Architect agree as set forth below:
1. The architect shall provide professional services for the Project in accordance with the Terms and conditions of this Agreement.
2. The Owner shall compensate the Architect, in accordance with the Terms and Conditions of this Agreement:
A. FOR BASIC SERVICES, as described in Item I. Basic compensation shall be computed as a PERCENTAGE OF CONSTRUCTION COST defined in Item IV.
The sum of *$2,778,765.00* percent (5 1/2%)
Based on a fixed limit construction cost of *Fifty Million, five hundred and twenty-three thousand and no/100 Dollars ($50,523,000.00)*

TERMS AND CONDITIONS OF AGREEMENT BETWEEN OWNER AND ARCHITECT
I. BASIC SERVICES
1. The architect's Basic Services consist of the six phases described below and include normal civil, structural, mechanical, and electrical engineering services. The Owner's General Design Requirements shall be considered a part of this contract. See Item XI, Other Conditions or Services.

2. Prior to beginning the Schematic Design Phase, the Architect shall provide a progress schedule based on the Owner's overall project schedule.

A. Schematic Design Phase
1. The Architect, working with the Owner, school staff, and community, shall develop the program based on the general scope of work contained in the Educational Specifications and furnished to the Architect by the Owner.
2. Based on the mutually agreed upon program, the Architect shall prepare Schematic Design Studies consisting of drawings and other documents illustrating the scale and relationship of Project Components for approval by the Owner. These plans will be presented to the school staff and community as required prior to proceeding with Design Development Drawings.
3. The Architect shall submit to the Owner a Statement of Probable Construction Cost based on current area, volume, or other unit costs.
4. The Architect shall provide to the Owner four sets of the Schematic Design Package for review and comments.
5. The Schematic Design Package shall be presented to the School Board for their approval.

B. Design Development Phase
1. The Architect shall prepare from the approved Schematic Design Studies, for approval by the Owner, the Design Development Documents consisting of drawings and other documents to fix and describe the size and character of the entire Project as to civil, structural, mechanical, and electrical systems, materials, and such other essentials as may be appropriate.
2. The Architect and consultants shall be required to make extensive field surveys as necessary to determine all conditions, which will affect new work, including but not limited to areas above ceilings, electrical panel spare capacity, etc.
3. The Architect shall submit to the Owner a further Statement of Probable Construction Cost.
4. The Architect shall provide to the Owner four sets of the Design Development Package for review and comments.
5. The Architect shall submit the Preliminary Design Plans to the Virginia State Department of Education for approval after the Design Development is approved by the Owner.

C. Construction Documents Phase
1. The Architect shall prepare from the approved Design Development Documents, for approval by the Owner, drawings and specifications setting forth in

detail the requirements for the construction of the entire project. The Architect and consultants shall use the Owner-provided educational and technical specifications, which, if modified, will require the Owner's approval.

2. The Architect shall provide the Owner Construction Document review sets at the 30% completion, 60% completion, and 100% completion stages with updated cost estimates.

3. The Architect shall provide to the Owner four review sets at the end of each Construction Document Phase.

4. The Owner will file the required documents for the Building Permit. It shall be the sole responsibility of the Architect to expedite and secure all required approvals of Plans and Specifications including but not limited to Department of Environmental Management, Department of Health, Department of Fire and Rescue, Water Authority, Virginia Department of Transportation, Virginia Department of Education, etc. The Architect shall provide weekly plan review status reports in writing to the Owner.

D. Bidding or Negotiation Phase

1. The Architect, following the Owners approval of the Construction Documents and of the latest Statement of Probable Construction Cost, shall assist the Owner in obtaining bids or negotiated proposals, and in awarding and preparing construction contracts.

E. Construction Phase—Administration of the Construction Contract

1. The Construction Phase will commence with the award of the Construction Contract and will terminate when the final Certificate of Payment is issued by the Contractor.

2. The Architect shall provide administration of the Construction contracts as set forth in the Owner-prepared General Conditions of the Contract for construction.

3. The Architect shall advise and consult with the Owner. The Architect shall have authority to act on behalf of the Owner to the extent provided in the General Conditions unless otherwise modified in writing.

4. The Architect shall at all times have access to the Work wherever it is in preparation or progress.

5. The Architect and consultants will attend construction progress meetings every week or more often if necessary, take minutes of the meetings, and provide written project status reports. On the basis of onsite observations, the architect shall endeavor to guard the Owner against defects and deficiencies in the work of the Contractor. The Architect may be required to meet at the site in emergency situations. The Architect shall not be responsible for construction means, methods, techniques, sequences, or procedures, or for

safety precautions and programs in connection with the work, and shall not be responsible for the Contractor's failure to carry out the work in accordance with the Contract Documents.

6. The Architect shall review the Contractor's Applications for payment and shall issue Certificates of payment based on project progress.

7. The Architect is the interpreter of the requirements of the Contract Documents and the impartial judge of the performance thereunder by both the Owner and Contractor. The Architect shall assist the Owner in making decisions on all claims of the Owner or Contractor relating to the execution and progress of the work and on all other matters or questions related thereto.

8. The Architect shall have authority to reject Work that does not conform to the Contract Documents. Whenever, in the Architect's reasonable opinion, it is necessary or advisable to ensure the proper implementation of the intent of the Contract Documents, the Architect will have authority to require special inspection or testing of any Work in accordance with the provisions of the Contract Documents whether or not such Work be then fabricated, installed, or completed.

9. The Architect shall expeditiously review and approve shop drawings, samples, and other submissions of the Contractor only for conformance with the design concept of the Project and for compliance with information given in the Contract Documents. The Architect shall coordinate with the Owner prior to approving any items that are in variance with the approved Contract Documents.

10. The Architect shall prepare Proposed Modifications and Change Orders.

11. The Architect shall not be responsible for the acts or omissions of the Contractor, or any Subcontractors, or any of the Contractor's or Subcontractor's agents or employees, or any other person performing any of the Work.

F. Project Closeout

1. The Architect shall conduct inspections to determine the dates of Substantial Completion and final completion, prepare the punch list, receive and review written guarantees and related documents assembled by the contractor, and issue a final Certificate for Payment.

2. The Architect shall prepare a set of reproducible record drawings showing significant changes in the work made during the construction process based on marked-up prints, drawings, and other data furnished by the Contractor to the Architect. The reproducible record drawings shall also include all addenda items and Change Orders issued during the construction process. The reproducible record drawings shall be Mylar.

3. The Architect shall provide extensive assistance in the utilization of any equipment or system such as initial start-up or testing, adjusting and

balancing, review and approval of operation and maintenance manuals, training personnel for operation and maintenance, and consultation during operation.

II. THE OWNER'S RESPONSIBILITY

A. The Owner shall provide full information, including a general scope of work regarding requirements for the project.

B. The owner shall designate a representative authorized to act in behalf of the school board in respect to the Project.

C. The Owner shall furnish a certified land survey of the site.

D. The Owner shall pay for the services of a soils engineer or other consultant when such services are deemed necessary by the Architect.

E. The Owner shall furnish structural, mechanical, chemical, and other laboratory tests, inspections and reports as required by law or the Contract Documents.

F. If the Owner becomes aware of any fault or defect in the Project or non-conformance with the Contract Documents, prompt written notice will be given to the Architect.

G. The Owner shall furnish information required as expeditiously as necessary for the orderly progress of the Work.

III. CONSTRUCTION COST

A. Construction cost shall be used as the basis for determining the Architect's compensation for Basic Services.

B. Construction Cost does not include the compensation of the Architect and consultants, cost of land, or any other cost.

C. Detailed Cost Estimates prepared by the Architect represent the best judgment as a design professional familiar with the construction industry.

D. A fixed limit on Construction Cost is established as a condition of this contract. The Owner and Architect together will determine what materials, equipment, component systems, and types of construction are to be included in the Contract Documents.

IV. PAYMENT TO THE ARCHITECT

A. Payments on account of the Architect's Basic Services shall be made as follows:

1. Payments for Basic Services shall be made monthly in proportion to services performed so that the compensation at the completion of each Phase shall equal the following percentages of the total Basic Compensation:

Schematic design phase: 15% Design development phase: 35% Construction documents: 75% Bidding or negotiation phase: 77% Construction phase: 100%

2. No deductions shall be made from the Architect's compensation on account of penalty, liquidated damages, or other sums withheld from payments to contractors.

V. TERMINATION OF AGREEMENT
A. This agreement may be terminated by either party upon seven day's written notice should the other party fail substantially to perform in accordance with its terms through no fault of the party initiating the termination.
B. In the event of termination due to the fault of parties other than the Architect, the Architect shall be paid compensation for services performed to termination date, including reimbursable expenses then due.

VI. OWNERSHIP OF DOCUMENTS
A. Drawings and Specifications as instruments of service are and shall remain the property of the Architect whether the Project for which they are made is executed or not. The Owner shall be permitted to use the Drawings and specifications for other projects on its property, for additions to this project and/or for completion of this Project by others.

This Agreement executed the day and year first written above. This Agreement is executed in three counterparts each of which is deemed as original.

OWNER   ARCHITECT

_____ Chair _____
_____ Clerk _____

(seal)   (seal)

Appendix F

Sample Agreement between Owner and Contractor

Agreement made as of the sixth day of March in the year Two Thousand and Nineteen.
Between the Owner: Washington County Public Schools
Washington City, Virginia
And the Contractor: Tidewater Construction Company
Virginia Beach, Virginia
The Project: New High School
Maple Road and Hamilton Avenue
Washington City, Virginia
The Architect: Jones and Jones, Architects, LLC The Owner and the Contractor agree as set forth below:

Article 1—The Contract Documents
The Contract Documents consist of the Agreement, the Conditions of the Contract (General Supplementary and other Conditions), the Architectural Drawings, the Technical Specifications, all Addenda issued prior to and all Modifications issued after execution of this Agreement. These form the Contract and all are as fully a part of the Contract as if attached to this Agreement or repeated herein. An enumeration of the Contract Documents appears in Article 7.

Article 2—The Work
The Contractor shall perform all the Work required by the Contract Documents for the New High School.

Article 3—Time of Commencement and Substantial Completion
The work to be performed under this Contract shall be commenced and, subject to authorized adjustments, Substantial Completion shall be achieved not later than Twenty-four (24) months from the date of this contract.

Article 4—Contract Sum

The Owner shall pay the Contractor in current funds for the performance of the work, subject to additions and deductions by Change Order as provided in the contract Documents, the contract Sum of $50,568,000.

The Contract Sum is determined as follows:

Article 5—Progress Payments

Based upon Applications for Payment submitted to the Architect by the Contractor and Certificates for Payment issued by the Architect, the Owner shall make progress payments on account of the contract Sum to the contractor as provided in the contract Documents for the period ending the fifth day of the month as follows: beginning with August 5, 2019.

Not later than _____ days following the end of the period covered by the Application for Payment percent (_____ %) of the portion of the Contract Sum properly allocable to labor, materials, and equipment incorporated in the Work and _____ percent (_____ %) of the portion of the Contract Sum properly allocable to materials and equipment suitably stored at the site or at some other location agreed upon in writing, for the period covered by the Application for Payment, less the aggregate of previous payments made by the Owner; and upon Substantial Completion of the entire work, a sum sufficient to increase the total payments to _____ percent (_____ %) of the contract Sum, less such amounts as the Architect shall determine for all incomplete work and unsettled claims as provided in the Contract Documents.

Article 6—Final Payment

Final payment, consisting of the entire unpaid balance of the contract Sum, shall be paid by the Owner to the contractor when the work has been completed, the contract fully performed, and a final Certificate for Payment has been issued by the Architect.

Article 7—Miscellaneous Provisions

7.1   Terms used in this Agreement, which are defined in the Conditions of the Contract, shall have the meanings designated in those conditions.

7.2   The Contract Documents, which constitute the entire agreement between the Owner and the Contractor, as listed in Article 1 and, except for Modifications issued after execution of this Agreement, are enumerated as follows:

This agreement entered into as of the day and year first written above

_____   _____

Owner   Contractor

Date: Date:

Appendix G

Position Description for Construction Supervisor

POSITION TITLE: Construction Supervisor
EFFECTIVE DATE: July 1, 2019
REPORTS TO: Director of Construction
QUALIFICATIONS:

A degree in engineering/engineering-related field preferred, or comparable experience in design and construction and five years' experience involving planning, design, and supervision of construction activities.

STATE REQUIREMENTS/QUALIFICATIONS: None

BASIC FUNCTION:
Performance of construction management activities in the planning, design, construction of educational facilities.

DIMENSIONS:
Budget responsibilities: None
Employees supervised: None

DUTIES AND RESPONSIBILITIES:
• This position encompasses coordination of activities and resolution of problems among contractor-supervisory personnel, architect/engineers, School Board staff, and governmental officials concerning technical matters related to building foundations, structures, mechanical systems, electrical and communications systems, grading, paving, and drainage.

Also involves resolving problems concerning scheduling and coordinating diverse construction activities.

- This position requires comprehensive knowledge of standards and procedures for planning, design, scheduling, and quality control of school building programs.
- Represents the owner on construction project sites by administering contracts between the School Board and general contractors, separate contractors, and architect/engineers.
- Consults with representatives of governmental agencies, School Board staff architects, contractors, and other interested officials to resolve problems concerning interpretation of contract documents.
- Establishes coordination and procedural policies for project accomplishment.
- Conducts preconstruction conferences and weekly job-site meetings.
- Resolves ongoing construction site problems.
- Establishes and maintains a continuous quality control program to assure that facilities are constructed to acceptable standards.
- Directs improvement in standards of work.
- Approves quality of completed work.
- Determines adequacy of and recommends approval of payment requests.
- Assesses work progress and scheduling and recommends actions for improvement.
- Prepares progress reports and maintains project records.
- Reviews and approves shop drawings, product data, and samples.
- Observes testing procedures, reviews test and inspection reports and expenditures for corrective action.
- Determines the need for contract changes, makes recommendations for accomplishment of changes, and processes change orders.
- Directs installation and inspection of owner furnished equipment and material.
- Directs the work of separate contractors.
- Conducts final inspections with contractors and architects/engineers.
- Coordinates project acceptance, building occupation, and start-up educational activities with staff and governmental agencies.
- Coordinates the orientation of maintenance and operational personnel on school plant operation.
- Supervises contractor activity during the guarantee period.
- Reviews and verifies project closeout documents, as-built drawings, operation manuals, and project releases.
- Assists in the development of contract specifications and contract documents.
- Reviews architect/engineer submissions for preliminary, intermediate, and final design stages and makes recommendations for design changes.
- Assists in the coordination of design review by appropriate governmental agencies.

- Coordinates new facilities requirements with the staff.
- Prepares cost estimates.
- Provides architect/engineer with design parameters, including minimum standards and building systems (type, size, model, quality, etc.).
- Prepares design and construction schedules.
- Makes recommendations on construction procedures and contracting methods.

Appendix H

Form to Evaluate the Planning Process

PRINCE WILLIAM COUNTY EDUCATIONAL SPECIFICATIONS PLANNING PROJECT

Directions: You participated in the planning of the new school for the Prince William School Division and the school administration would like your perceptions of the possible success of the planning process. Would you please respond to the items below? All Information will remain secret until after analysis and then destroyed. Thank you.

1. What is your sex? Male _____ Female _____
2. What is your age? _____
3. Do you have a child currently enrolled in the Prince William County School System? Yes _____ No _____
4. How many committee planning sessions were you able to attend? _____
5. Do you feel these planning efforts were worthwhile? Yes _____ No _____
6. Do you believe the recommendations of the committee will have significant impact on the final decisions concerning the new secondary facilities? Yes _____ No _____ Don't Know _____
7. Were you basically satisfied with the assistance you received from the VPI&SU Consultants? Yes _____ No _____ Don't Know _____
8. Were there additional services the consultants could have provided? Yes _____ No _____

If you answered yes, please state what services could have been provided.

9. Do you feel the community was adequately represented on the planning committee? Yes _____ No _____

If not, what segment should have been included? _____

10. Was there sufficient time for the committee to prepare an accurate and complete report? Yes _____ No _____
11. If you were involved in a similar planning process, what improvements or changes would you recommend?

_____

_____

12. Do you believe the school will reflect exactly the recommendations of the advisory committee? Yes _____ No _____
13. Do you think the completed secondary facilities will be different from existing secondary schools? Yes _____ No _____

Please add any comments:

_____

_____

14. Were there any constraints that you believe prevented the advisory committee from having a more significant input into the educational specifications document? Yes _____ No _____

If yes, what were those constraints?

_____

_____

15. Did your work and involvement on the advisory committee help to clarify or change your opinion about the goals or objectives of the Prince William County School Division?

Yes _____ No _____

References

CHAPTER 1: ORGANIZATION AND POLICY PLANNING

BEST (Building Educational Success Together). (2005). *Comprehensive planning ensures the most efficient and cost effective use of taxpayer dollars, May.* Retrieved July 24, 2008. www.21csf.org/csfhome/publications/modelpolicies/PlanningSectionMay2005.pdf.

Kowalski, T. J. (2002). *Planning and managing school facilities, 2nd ed.* Westport, CT: Bergin and Garvey.

Lunenberg, F. C. (2012). *Educational administration: Concepts and practice, 6th ed.* Belmont, CA: Wadsworth, Inc.

CHAPTER 2: PLANNING CONSIDERATIONS

Cary, K. D. (2011). *School district Master Planning: A practical guide to demographic and facilities planning.* Lanham, MD: Rowman & Littlefield.

Guthrie, J. W., Hart, C., Hack, W. G., and Candoli, I. C. (2008). *Modern school business administration: A planning approach.* Lanham, MD: Pearson.

Kaufman, R. (2006). *Change, choice, and consequences: A guide to Mega Thinking and Planning.* Amherst, MA: HRD Press, Inc.

Kaufman, R., Herman, J., and Watters, K. (2002). *Educational planning: Strategic, tactical, and operational.* New York: Scarecrow Press, Inc.

Lewis, J. (1983). *Long-range and short-range planning for educational administrators.* Boston: Allyn & Bacon, Inc.

Rollins, R. (2012). *Facility planning and development.* Hagerstown, MD: Washington County Public Schools.

Withum, F. (2006). *Educational facility planning: A systems model.* Pittsburgh, PA: Unpublished doctoral dissertation, Duquesne University, December. Retrieved May 5, 2008. www.lib.umi.comfdxweb.

CHAPTER 3: PLANNING IN PUBLIC SCHOOLS

Dewar, J. A. (2002). *Assumption-based planning: A tool for reducing avoidable surprises.* Cambridge: Cambridge University Press.

Garcia-Diaz, A., and MacGregor Smith, J. (2008). *Facilities planning and design.* Upper Saddle River, NJ: Pearson Prentice-Hall.

Tompkins, J. A., White, J. A., Bozer, Y. A., and Tanchoco, J. M. A. (2002). *Facilities planning, 3rd ed.* New York: John Wiley and Sons, Inc.

CHAPTER 4: LONG-RANGE PLANNING: EDUCATIONAL PROGRAM DEVELOPMENT

Clark, J. E. (2007). *Facilities planning.* New York: Prentice-Hall.

Hill, F. C. (2005). *Educational facility Master Planning: A 10 point checklist for educational excellence.* Washington, DC: National Clearinghouse for Educational Facilities. edfacilities.org.

Ohio School Facilities Commission. (2008). *Planning your school building project: Putting the pieces together.* Columbus, OH: The Commission.

Tanner, C. K., and Lackey, J. (2005). *Planning and programming for a Capital Project.* Athens, GA: University of Georgia School Design and Planning Laboratory.

CHAPTER 5: LONG-RANGE PLANNING: STUDENT ENROLLMENT PROJECTIONS

Cary, K. D. (2011). *School district Master Planning: A practical guide to demographic and facility planning.* Lanham, MD: Rowman & Littlefield.

Cooper, M. (2003). GIS in school facility planning. *School Planning and Management, 42*(2), 56–60. Retrieved October 24, 2008. www.peterli.com/archives/spm/420shtm.

Earthman, G. I. (May 2006). Using a Student Yield Index in planning for student growth. *School Business Affairs, 72*(5).

Gilmore, W. (1974). *ENSIM: Land use analysis based enrollment simulation. Research Report II, Santa Clara County Schools.* San Jose, CA: Office of the Superintendent of Schools.

MacConnell, J. D. (1957). *Planning school buildings.* Englewood Cliffs, NJ: Prentice-Hall.

Schellenberg, S. J., and Stephens, C. (1987, April). *Enrollment projection: Variations on a theme.* Paper presented at the annual meeting of the American Educational Research Association, Washington, DC.

Slagle, M. (2000). *GIS in community-based school planning: A tool to enhance decision-making, cooperation, and democratization in the planning process.* ED

452 686. Retrieved October 24, 2008. www.eric.ed.gov:80/ERICDocs/data/eric docs2sql/content_storage_01/0000019b/80/17/02/cf.pdf.

Tanner, C. K., and Lackey, J. (2005). *Educational facilities planning, leadership, and management.* Boston, MA: Allyn & Bacon, Pearson Education.

CHAPTER 6: LONG-RANGE PLANNING: EVALUATION OF EXISTING FACILITIES

CEFPI. (2004). *Creating connections: The CEFPI guide for educational planning.* Scottsdale, AZ: CEFPI.

Earthman, G. I. (1990). *Administering the planning process for educational facilities.* Jericho, NY: Wilkerson Press.

Earthman, G. I., and Lemasters, L. K. (2004). *School maintenance and renovation: Policies, practices & economies.* Lanham, MD: Pro > Active Publications.

CHAPTER 7: LONG-RANGE PLANNING: FINANCIAL PLANNING

Alexander, D., and Lewis, L. (2014). *Condition of America's Public School Facilities, 2012–2013* (NCES 2014-022). U.S. Department of Education, Washington, DC. Retrieved June 6, 2018. http://nces.ed.gov.pubsearch.

Alexander, K., and Alexander, M. D. (2012). *American public school law, 8th Ed.* St. Paul, MN: West Publishing Company.

American Recovery and Reinvestment Act of 2009 (P.L. 115-5).

American Society of Civil Engineers. (2017). *Infrastructure Report Card.* Washington, DC: Author.

Appalachian Regional Development Act of 1965 (P.L. 89-4).

Appendix A. (Winter 1997). School facilities. *The Future of Children, 7*(3).

Camp, W. (1983). *Public school bonding corporations financing public elementary and secondary facilities.* Unpublished dissertation, Virginia Polytechnic Institute and State University.

Chan, T. C., and Richardson, M. D. (2005). *Ins and outs of school facility management.* Lanham, MD: Scarecrow Education.

Council of Infrastructure Financing Authorities (CIFA). (1998). *State revolving fund: A decade of successful SRF performance, 1987–1997.* Washington, DC: CIFA, January.

Ducker, R. D. (1994). Using impact fees for public schools: The Orange County experiment. *School Law Bulletin, 25*(2), 1–14.

Education for All Handicapped Children Act of 1976 (P.L. 94-142).

Education Writers Association (EWA). (1989). *Wolves at the schoolhouse door: An investigation of the condition of public school buildings.* Washington, DC: EWA.

Emergency Relief Act of 1974 (P.L. 93-288).

Emergency Relief Act of 1983 (100-707).

Federal Surplus Property Act of 1941 (P.L. 94-519).

Higher Education Facilities Act of 1992 (92-318).

Holt, C. R. (2002). *School bond success: A strategy for building America's schools, 2nd ed.* Lanham, MD: Scarecrow Press.

Housing and Community Development Act of 1968 (P.L. 90-448).

Impact Aid Act of 1941 (P.L. 81-874).

Improving America's Schools Act of 1994 (P.L. 103-382).

Individuals with Disabilities Education Act of 1990 (P.L. 101-476).

National Education Association. (2000). *Modernizing our schools: What will it cost?* Washington, DC: National Education Association.

Partners to Rebuild America's Schools Act of 1997 (S. 456).

Regional Vocational High School Act of 1963 (P.L. 87-9).

Rehabilitation Act of 1973 (P.L. 93-112). Sections 502 and 504.

School District of Philadelphia. (1973). *Capital improvement program, 1973–1978.* Philadelphia, PA: School District of Philadelphia.

Standard & Poor's. (1998). *State credit enhancement programs, Tax-Backed Debt.* New York: Standard & Poor's Municipal Finance Criteria.

Taxpayers Relief Act of 1997 (P.L. 105-34).

CHAPTER 8: DEVELOPMENT OF THE CAPITAL IMPROVEMENT PROGRAM

Chan, T. C., and Richardson, M. D. (2005). *Ins and outs of school facility management.* Lanham, MD: Scarecrow Education.

Earthman, G. I., and Lemasters, L. K. (2004). *School maintenance and renovation: Administrator policies, practices, and economies.* Lanham, MD: Pro > Active Publications.

Montgomery County Public Schools. (2008). *Facilities master plan: 1999–2004.* Rockville, MD: School Facilities Department.

Oates, A., and Burch, A. L. (2002). *A model schedule for a capital improvement program.* ED 472 179. Retrieved September 22, 2008. www.eric.ed.gov/content-delivery.

Tanner, C. K., and Lackey, J. (2005). *Educational facilities planning: Leadership, architects and management.* Boston, MA: Allyn & Bacon, Pearson Education.

CHAPTER 9: DEVELOPING EDUCATIONAL SPECIFICATIONS

Earthman, G. I. (1976). *The process of developing educational specifications.* Blacksburg, VA: College of Education, Virginia Polytechnic Institute and State University.

Hill, F. C. (2005). *Educational facility Master Planning: A 10 point checklist for educational excellence.* Washington, DC: NCEF, schoolfacilities.com.

Ohio School Facility Commission. (2008). *Planning your school building project: Putting the pieces together.* Columbus, OH: The Commission.

Rollins, R. (2012). *Facility planning and development.* Hagerstown, MD: Washington County Public Schools.

CHAPTER 10: SITE SELECTION AND ACQUISITION

Coopers, M. (2003, February). GIS in school facility planning. *School Planning and Management, 42*(2), 56–60.

Council of Educational Facility Planners International (CEFPI). (2004). *Creating connections: The CEFPI guide for educational planning.* Scottsdale, AZ: CEFPI.

Earthman, G. I. (1976). The politics of site selection. *CEFPI Journal, 14*(5).

Grabe, K. (1975). *Economic advantages in site selection.* Paper presented at the 52nd Annual Conference of Council of Educational Facility Planners, International, Houston, TX.

International City/County Management Association (ICCMA). (2008). *Local government and schools: A community-oriented approach.* Washington, DC: ICCMA.

Neilson, C., and Zimmerman, S. (2011). *The effect of school construction on test scores, school enrollment, and home prices.* Bonn, Germany: Institute for the Study of Labor, IZA DP 6106.

School District of Philadelphia. (1973). *Capital improvement program, 1973–1978.* Philadelphia, PA: School Facilities Department.

CHAPTER 11: EMPLOYING THE ARCHITECT

Brubaker, C. W. (1998). *Planning and designing schools.* New York: McGraw-Hill Publishers, 1–201.

Rollins, R. (2012). *Facility planning and development.* Hagerstown, MD: Washington County Public Schools.

Tanner, C. K., and Lackey, J. (2005). *Planning and programming for a capital project.* Athens, GA: University of Georgia, School Design and Planning Laboratory.

Vickery, R. L. (1998). *Finding the right architect.* Charlottesville, VA: Thomas Jefferson Center for Educational Design, University of Virginia.

CHAPTER 12: MONITORING THE DESIGN PHASE

Earthman, G. I. (1990). *Administering the planning process for educational facilities.* Jericho, NY: Wilkerson Press.

References

Earthman, G. I. (1994). *School renovation handbook: Investing in education.* Lancaster, PA: Technomic Publishers, Inc.
Tanner, C. K., and Lackey, J. (2005). *Planning and programming for a capital project.* Athens, GA: University of Georgia School Design and Planning Laboratory.

CHAPTER 14: ALTERNATIVE CONTRACTING PLANS AND COMMISSIONING OF SCHOOLS

Means, R. S. (1996). *Cost planning and estimating for facilities and maintenance.* Kingston, MA: Construction Consultants. P 457.

CHAPTER 16: ORIENTATION AND EVALUATION

Council of Educational Facility Planners International (CEFPI). (2004). *Creating connections: The CEFPI guide for educational planning.* Scottsdale, AZ: CEFPI.

CHAPTER 17: PLANNING FOR TECHNOLOGY

Association of School Business Officials, International (ASBOI). (2001). *Technology solutions for schools.* Reston, VA: ASBOI.
Council of Educational Facility Planners International (CEFPI). (2004). *Creating connections: The CEFPI guide for educational planning.* Scottsdale, AZ: CEFPI.

CHAPTER 18: CRITICAL ISSUES IN SCHOOL FACILITY PLANNING: A LOOK TO THE FUTURE

AASA. (1992). *Schoolhouse in the red.* Arlington, VA: AASA, 1–40.
American Association of School Administrators (AASA). (1983). *The maintenance gap: Deferred repair and renovation in the nation's elementary and secondary schools.* Arlington, VA: AASA, Council of Great City Schools, National School Boards Association, 1–15.
Associated Press. (1998, December 11). Nation's schools not on track to meeting Goals 2000 panel reports. *Roanoke Times,* A9.
Bullock, C. C. (2007). *The relationship between school building conditions and student achievement at the middle school level in the Commonwealth of Virginia.* Blacksburg, VA: Unpublished doctoral dissertation, Virginia Polytechnic Institute and State University.
Cash, C. S. (1993). *Building condition and student achievement and behavior.* Unpublished doctoral dissertation, Virginia Polytechnic Institute and State University.

Crook, J. F. (2006). *A study of school building conditions and student achievement in the high schools of Virginia.* Blacksburg, VA: Unpublished doctoral dissertation. Virginia Polytechnic Institute and State University.

DeJong, W. (2008). *Top ten trends in school facility planning.* Retrieved August 13, 2008. www.schoolfacilities.com/coremodules/controldisplay.aspx?contentD=2902.

Earthman, G. I. (2004). *The prioritization of 31 criteria for adequate schools.* ACLU, Baltimore, MD: ACLU, 1–66.

Earthman, G. I., Cash, C.S., and Van Berkum, D. (1996). Student achievement and behavior and school building condition. *Journal of School Business Management, 8*(3), 26–37.

Educational Writers Association (EWA). (1989). *Wolves at the schoolhouse door.* Washington, DC: EWA.

Edwards, M. (1992). *Building conditions, parental involvement and student achievement in the DC public school system.* Unpublished master's thesis, Georgetown University, Washington, DC.

Fueslier, C. (2008). *A study of the relationship between selected school building components and student achievement in Pennsylvania middle schools.* Pittsburgh, PA: Unpublished doctoral dissertation, Duquesne University.

Goals 2000: Educate Americans Act of 1994.

Hines, E. W. (1996). *Building condition and student achievement and behavior.* Unpublished doctoral dissertation. Blacksburg, VA: Virginia Polytechnic Institute and State University.

Holt, C. R. (2002). *School bond success: A strategy for building America's schools.* Lanham, MD: Scarecrow Press.

Improving America's Schools Act of 1994 (P.L. 103-382).

Lanham III, J. W. (1999). *Relating building and classroom conditions to student achievement in Virginia's elementary schools.* Unpublished doctoral dissertation. Blacksburg, VA: Virginia Polytechnic Institute and State University.

McGuffey, C. W. (1982). Facilities. In *Improving educational standards and productivity,* ed. H. Walberg, chap. 10, 237–88. Berkeley, CA: McCutchan Publishing Corp.

National Education Association. (2000). *Modernizing our schools: What will it cost?* Washington, DC: National Educational Association.

Northwest Educational Technology Consortium. (2002). *Online essentials.* Accessed October 18, 2008. http://northwesteducationaltechnologyconsortium.org/.

O'Sullivan, S. (2006). *A study of the relationship between building conditions and student achievement in Pennsylvania's high school.* Unpublished doctoral dissertation. Blacksburg, VA: Virginia Polytechnic Institute and State University.

Partnership to Rebuild America's Schools Act of 1997 (S. 456).

Pauley v. Bailey. (1982). Circuit Court of Kanawah County, West Virginia, No. 75-1268, May 11.

Phillips, R. M. (1997). *Educational facility age and the academic achievement and attendance of upper elementary school students.* Athens, GA: Unpublished doctoral dissertation, University of Georgia.

Roosevelt Elementary School District No. 66 v. Bishop. (1994). 179 Arizona 233; 877 P. 2d 806.

Stevenson, K. (2007). *Educational trends shaping school planning and design 2007.* Retrieved August 10, 2008. www.edfacilities.org/pubs/trends2007.pdf.

Thornton, J. C. (2006). *The relationship between school building condition and minority and poverty students.* Unpublished doctoral dissertation. Blacksburg, VA: Virginia Polytechnic Institute and State University.

Tofler, A. (1980). *Third wave.* New York: William Morrow.

Uline, C., and Tschannen-Moran, M. (2006). The walls speak: The interplay of quality of facilities, school climate, and student achievement. *Journal of Educational Administration, 46*(1), 55–73.

U.S. General Accounting Office (GAO). (1995). *School facilities: Condition of America's schools.* Washington, DC: GAO/HEHS, B-259307.

———. (1996). *School facilities: America's schools report differing conditions.* Washington, DC: GAO/HEHS, B-260872.

Young, E. (2003). *Do K–12 school facilities affect educational outcomes?* Tennessee Advisory Commission on Intergovernmental Relations. Retrieved October 20, 2008. www.state.tn.us/tacir/PDF_FILES/Education.

CHAPTER 19: GREEN SCHOOLS

Heschong Mahone Group. (1999, August 20). *Daylighting in schools: An investigation into the relationship between daylighting and human performance.* Fair Oaks, CA: Pacific Gas and Electric Company.

National Research Council. (2007). *Green schools: Attributes for health and learning.* Washington, DC: National Academies Press.

U.S. Green Building Council. (2000). Leadership in Energy and Environmental Design (LEED).

Washington, DC: USGBC. Retrieved October 12, 2008. www.usgbc.org.

CHAPTER 20: PLANNING SCHOOLS FOR SAFETY

Carter, S., and Carter, S. (2001). Planning safer schools. *American School and University, 73*(912), 170–186.

Prager, G. (2003). *Designing safe schools,* (pp. 40–43). http://www.asumag.com.

Scanlon, P., and Pillar, R. (2000). Common sense design for safe schools: School Planning and Management. *Proquest Educational Journals, 39*(5), 60.

School Board Minutes. (2009, June 7). Christiansburg, VA: Montgomery County School Board, p. 7.

Trosper, S. (2017). *Safe school building characteristics in Virginia's elementary schools: Architect and principals perspective.* Unpublished doctoral dissertation. Blacksburg, VA: Virginia Polytechnic Institute and State University.

Walton, R. (2010). *Physical design for safe schools.* Unpublished doctoral dissertation. Blacksburg, VA: Virginia Polytechnic Institute and State University.

CHAPTER 21: PROBLEM-BASED LEARNING

Earthman, G. I. (2004). *Prioritization of 31 criteria for an adequate school.* Baltimore, MD: Maryland ACLU.

Earthman, G. I. (2015). *A report on research on school building conditions and student educational outcomes and responses to complaints of Francophone parents and Conseil Francophone.* British Columbia Supreme Court, No. S103975, Vancouver Registry.

Philadelphia Public Schools. (1970). *Capital Improvement Plan—1970.* Philadelphia, PA: The School District.

Roberts, L. W. (2013, July 11). Supreme Court of British Columbia, Document #12992685, No. S103975 Vancouver Registry.

About the Author

Dr. Glen I. Earthman has forty years of experience in the field of education and thirty years of specialized experience in the educational facilities planning arena. He has taught extensively about educational facilities for more than thirty years at Virginia Tech and has provided consultation to more than fifty school districts regarding the planning of educational facilities. He has authored six books on the subject of educational facilities, several book chapters, and published extensively in professional journals on this subject as well. He served as the first director of the National Clearinghouse for Educational Facilities. He continues a schedule of teaching and research in the field of school facilities specializing in the relationship between school building conditions and student and teacher health and performance.

CPSIA information can be obtained
at www.ICGtesting.com
Printed in the USA
LVHW042238200820
663773LV00001B/141